The *Sams Teach Yourself in 24 Hours* Series

Sams Teach Yourself in 24 Hours books provide quick and e
proven step-by-step approach that works for you. In just 24
or less, you will tackle every task you need to get the result
experienced authors present the most accurate informatior
answers—fast!

The Tool Palette

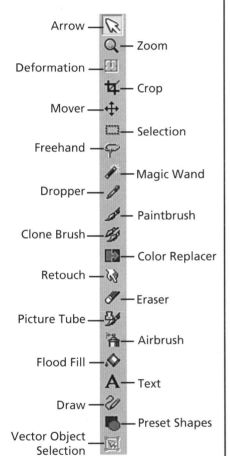

- Arrow
- Zoom
- Deformation
- Crop
- Mover
- Selection
- Freehand
- Magic Wand
- Dropper
- Paintbrush
- Clone Brush
- Color Replacer
- Retouch
- Eraser
- Picture Tube
- Airbrush
- Flood Fill
- Text
- Draw
- Preset Shapes
- Vector Object Selection

The Layer Palette

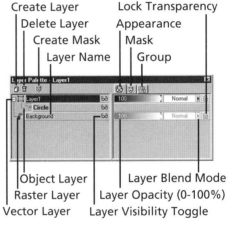

- Create Layer
- Delete Layer
- Create Mask
- Layer Name
- Lock Transparency
- Appearance
- Mask
- Group
- Object Layer
- Raster Layer
- Vector Layer
- Layer Blend Mode
- Layer Opacity (0-100%)
- Layer Visibility Toggle

The Toolbar

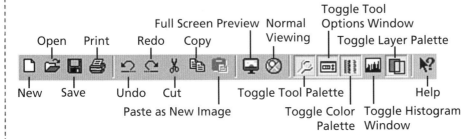

- New
- Open
- Save
- Print
- Undo
- Redo
- Cut
- Copy
- Paste as New Image
- Full Screen Preview
- Normal Viewing
- Toggle Tool Palette
- Toggle Tool Options Window
- Toggle Layer Palette
- Toggle Color Palette
- Toggle Histogram Window
- Help

SAMS

Teach Yourself **Paint Shop Pro 6** ™

in 24 **Hours**

Paint Shop Pro 6 Shortcuts

COMMAND	KEYBOARD SHORTCUT
File Menu	
New	Ctrl+N
Open	Ctrl+O
Browse	Ctrl+B
Save	Ctrl+S
Save As	F12
Save Copy As	Ctrl+F12
Delete	Ctrl+Del
Print	Ctrl+P
Edit Menu	
Undo	Ctrl+Z
Redo	Ctrl+Alt+Z
Command History	Shift+Ctrl+Z
Cut	Ctrl+X
Copy	Ctrl+C
Copy Merged	Shift+Ctrl+C
Paste	
As New Image	Ctrl+V
As New Layer	Ctrl+L
As New Selection	Ctrl+E
As Transparent Selection	Shift+Ctrl+E
Into Selection	Shift+Ctrl+L
As New Vector Selection	Ctrl+G
Clear	Del
View Menu	
Full Screen Edit	Shift+A
Full Screen Preview	Shift+Ctrl+A
Normal Viewing	Ctrl+Alt+N
Image Information	Shift+I
Grid	Ctrl+Alt+G
Image Menu	
Flip	Ctrl+I
Mirror	Ctrl+M
Rotate	Ctrl+R
Crop to Selection	Shift+R
Resize	Shift+S
Colors Menu	
Brightness/Contrast	Shift+B
Gamma Correction	Shift+G
Highlight/Midtone/Shadow	Shift+M
Hue/Saturation/Lightness	Shift+H
Red/Green/Blue	Shift+U
Colorize	Shift+L
Equalize	Shift+E
Stretch	Shift+T
Posterize	Shift+Z
Edit Palette	Shift+P
Load Palette	Shift+O
Set Palette Transparency	Shift+Ctrl+V
Decrease Color Depth	
2 Colors (1 bit)	Shift+Ctrl+1
16 Colors (4 bit)	Shift+Ctrl+2
256 Colors (8 bit)	Shift+Ctrl+3
32K Colors (24 bit)	Shift+Ctrl+4
64K Colors (24 bit)	Shift+Ctrl+5
X Colors (4/8 bit)	Shift+Ctrl+6
Increase Color Depth	
16 Colors (4 bit)	Shift+Ctrl+8
256 Colors (8 bit)	Shift+Ctrl+9
16 Million Colors (24 bit)	Shift+Ctrl+0

COMMAND	KEYBOARD SHORTCUT
Layers Menu	
Select Current Layer	Ctrl+(layer #)
Selections Menu	
Select All	Ctrl+A
Select None	Ctrl+D
From Mask	Shift+Ctrl+S
Invert	Shift+Ctrl+I
Feather	Ctrl+H
Transparent Color	Ctrl+T
Hide Marquee	Shift+Ctrl+M
Promote to Layer	Shift+Ctrl+P
Float	Ctrl+F
Defloat	Shift+Ctrl+F
Masks Menu	
Hide All	Shift+Y
Invert	Shift+K
Edit	Ctrl+K
View Mask	Ctrl+Alt+V
Capture Menu	
Start	Shift+C
Window Menu	
New Window	Shift+W
Duplicate	Shift+D
Fit to Image	Ctrl+W

BROWSER MENUS

COMMAND	KEYBOARD SHORTCUT
File Menu	
Browse New Folder	Ctrl+B
Update Thumbnails	F5
View Menu	
Refresh Tree	Ctrl+F5
Find Menu	
File Name	Alt+F3
Repeat Find	F3
ImageFile Menu	
Copy To	Ctrl+Y
Delete	Ctrl+Del
Move To	Ctrl+M
Rename	Ctrl+R
Information	Shift+I
Open	Enter

OTHER

COMMAND	KEYBOARD SHORTCUT
Center Floating Tool Palettes	Shift+Ctrl+T
Hide/Restore All Floating Palettes	Tab
Hide/Restore Toolbar	T
Hide/Restore Histogram	H
Hide/Restore Layer Palette	L
Hide/Restore Tool Palette	P
Hide/Restore Tool Options Window	O
Step Through Tools	Spacebar

Foreword

Ordinary people creating extraordinary graphics. That's what Jasc Software is all about. We're committed to making easy-to-use tools—like Paint Shop Pro 6—for Web developers, business people, and home users who want a powerful, affordable way to enhance digital photos and create Web graphics.

That's also why we're excited about this book, *Sams Teach Yourself Paint Shop Pro 6 in 24 Hours*. No matter what your level of experience, this step-by-step resource is specially designed to help you get the most from working with Paint Shop Pro. In a few short sessions, you'll be able to capture photos, enhance images, print and share photos, and even create great Web graphics.

We're confident *Sams Teach Yourself Paint Shop Pro 6 in 24 Hours* will open up a whole new world of creative possibilities. And Paint Shop Pro 6 provides all the tools you need to create amazing graphics that let you put your best foot forward.

So let's begin. Get ready to imagine…and create!

Kris Tufto

Chief Executive Officer

Jasc Software, Inc.

T. Michael Clark

SAMS
Teach Yourself

Paint Shop Pro™ 6

in 24 Hours

SAMS

A Division of Macmillan USA
201 West 103rd St., Indianapolis, Indiana, 46290 USA

Sams Teach Yourself Paint Shop Pro™ 6 in 24 Hours

Copyright ® 2000 by Sams Publishing

International Standard Book Number: 0-672-31720-6

Library of Congress Catalog Card Number: 99-066997

Printed in the United States of America

First Printing: November 1999

01 00 99   4 3 2 1

Trademarks

Warning and Disclaimer

ACQUISITIONS EDITOR
Randi Roger

DEVELOPMENT EDITOR
Jon Steever

MANAGING EDITOR
Charlotte Clapp

SENIOR EDITOR
Karen A. Walsh

COPY EDITOR
Gene Redding

INDEXER
Mary Gammons

PROOFREADER
Cynthia Fields

TECHNICAL EDITOR
Pamela Rice Hahn

TEAM COORDINATOR
Amy Patton

INTERIOR DESIGN
Gary Adair

COVER DESIGN
Aren Howell

COPY WRITER
Eric Borgert

PRODUCTION
Barndon Allen
Dan Harris
Staci Somers

Contents at a Glance

Contents

About the Author

An artist from the time he could hold a crayon, **T. Michael Clark** has always been fascinated by the visual arts. Although he later fell in love with the world of computers and the Internet, which led to his graduation from college as a programmer/analyst, Michael seemed destined to rediscover his love of art through the enormous potential of digital graphics software. His natural teaching talent, combined with his interest in art, computers, and communication, led to a new career as a technical writer and garnered a devoted readership. Michael's numerous best-selling books on computer imaging and design programs have been translated into over a dozen languages. Recent titles include *Sams Teach Yourself Photoshop 5 in 21 Days*, *Photoshop 5 Filters f/x and Design* from Coriolis, and *Sams Teach Yourself Paint Shop Pro 5 in 24 Hours*. Along with his clear, concise teaching style, Michael is known for his commitment to his readers, and he spends many hours each week replying to email, participating on Usenet, and serving as an associate member and moderator at i/us, the site for visual professionals. Michael, who also teaches Web design and computer graphics courses at the college level, immensely enjoys his work as a full-time author. The best part of his job, says Michael, is getting to play with cutting-edge graphics and design software and then writing about it in such a way as to make it more accessible to others. His Web site `www.grafx-design.com` offers hundreds of pages of free tutorials on Photoshop, Paint Shop Pro, CorelDRAW, and specialized Web graphics topics.

Dedication

This book is dedicated, as always, to my lovely wife, Pamela.

Acknowledgments

First, a very special thanks goes to three amazing women at Macmillan Computer Publishing: Jennifer Eberhardt, Beth Millett, and Karen Whitehouse. I can't thank you guys enough for believing in the original project as much as I did and for pushing so hard to have it realized.

Another special thank you goes to my agent, Margot Maley, for her help and wisdom.

I'd like to thank the team, both in-house and external, that helped make this book possible. A project of this size could not be completed without tons of talented people. Some of these people are

John Pierce
Mark Taber
Randi Roger
Karen Walsh
Amy Patton
Gene Redding
Jon Steever
Pamela Rice Hahn

There are many more whose names I don't even know, but whom I want to thank anyway.

John Kane, for giving me my first break and for being there when it all began.

For keeping my system running during this project, the incredible staffs both at Technor Informatique, Inc.:

Joe, Alex, and Eazy

and at CompuSmart (formerly Crazy Irving's):

Dave Tucci, Nigel, Steve Paul, Peter, Aldo, Michelle, Nancy and, last but not least, Claire. Thanks guys.

The software companies:

First of all, I'd like to thank the great people at Jasc Software for creating such a cool program, for being involved with the project, and for being as excited about it as the rest of us.

The team at Auto F/X.

Michael, Todd, Skip, and the others (a unique bunch) at Alien Skin.

Alexandre Clappier from RAYflect.

Dwight Jurling from Ulead.

Lloyd Burchill from Flaming Pear.

My models:

Marianne Dodelet and my niece Zöe Alexandra.

Last but certainly not least, you the reader, and the people who visit my Web site regularly. I depend on many of you and the wonderful ideas and questions you send me via email for many of the ideas that go into my books and online tutorials.

Tell Us What You Think!

As the reader of this book, *you* are our most important critic and commentator. We value your opinion and want to know what we're doing right, what we could do better, what areas you'd like to see us publish in, and any other words of wisdom you're willing to pass our way.

You can fax, email, or write me directly to let me know what you did or didn't like about this book—as well as what we can do to make our books stronger.

Please note that I cannot help you with technical problems related to the topic of this book, and that due to the high volume of mail I receive, I might not be able to reply to every message.

When you write, please be sure to include this book's title and author as well as your name and phone or fax number. I will carefully review your comments and share them with the author and editors who worked on the book.

Fax: (317) 581-4770
Email: office_sams@mcp.com
Mail: Mark Taber
         Associate Publisher
         Sams Publishing
         201 West 103rd Street
         Indianapolis, IN 46290 USA

Introduction

Years ago (many more than I care to think about), I got my first microcomputer. At that time, I was still drawing and painting using traditional media such as pencil, pen & ink, watercolor, and so forth. That very first evening, as I sought to learn as much as I could about the strange beast staring back at me from atop the coffee table, I realized that there was much potential for these machines to help artists create images.

Today my dreams have been realized. For the price of an entry-level desktop computer and Paint Shop Pro, virtually anyone can create amazing images.

Processes as simple as creating navigational and decorative graphics for Web pages or as complex as photo manipulation and restoration are now within the grasp of the average computer user.

Of course, some users will require a little help to get them up to speed. After all, as the hardware and software become more powerful, they also become more complex to use. That's where this book comes in.

Between the covers of this book, I intend to help you gain the knowledge you need to get going as quickly as possible. I will do so by presenting you with two dozen one-hour–long (give or take a few minutes) lessons. Each lesson will cover a specific topic that will not only help you accomplish a certain task using Paint Shop Pro but also help you build your expertise and comfort level when it comes to creating and working with digital graphics.

I've always been of the opinion that learning should be fun and that it should involve lots of hands-on experience. With that in mind, I like to write my books and my online tutorials in such a way as to make the lessons fun and inviting. I try not to assume anything on behalf of the reader. Whether I'm discussing a topic as complex as antialiasing or as simple as creating a button for a Web page, I'll include step-by-step descriptions and as many illustrations as I feel necessary for anyone to be able to get a handle on the concept.

I really like to teach, and it is my sincerest hope that you find this book to be as easy to follow as I intend, and that you find it as much fun to read as it was to write.

 If you need help installing the software, please refer to Appendix A, "Installing Paint Shop Pro." After you have the software properly installed, you'll be ready to take full advantage of this book.

From time to time during the lengthy process of writing, illustrating, and editing a book, errors get through. Although I hope that we managed to catch all of them, I'd like to take this opportunity to remind you that you can always visit my Web site (http://www.grafx-design.com) or email me at tmc@grafx-design.com with any questions, comments, or problems you have regarding this book. You can also visit the Web site of the publisher at http://www.mcp.com/product_support/ and enter this book's ISBN—0672317206—in the text field and click Search.

PART I

Getting Started in Paint Shop Pro

Hour

HOUR 1

Paint Shop Pro Basics, Tools, and Preferences

Welcome to Paint Shop Pro! This hour covers the following topics and tools:

- An introduction to Paint Shop Pro
- An overview of the Paint Shop Pro interface
- An overview of new 6.0 features
- Paint Shop Pro tools
- Paint Shop Pro preferences

Introduction to Paint Shop Pro

Even as a digital artist and author on the subject of image manipulation programs, I never cease to be amazed when a new version of one of my favorite programs hits the store shelves. Just when I think the software couldn't possibly get any better, the engineers and programmers still come up with ideas and features that make me say "WOW!"

That truly was the first comment out of my mouth when I ran the first beta copy of Paint Shop Pro 5, and it is still true for version 6. I can't believe the new features that have been packed into this already amazing piece of software.

With the success of Paint Shop Pro, and with the ever-growing popularity of the World Wide Web (and the need, therefore, for users to create their own Web-ready images), there is an increasing number of new users. Along with the increase in new users comes a need for material aimed at helping them get the most from the increasingly complex (yet still remarkably easy-to-use) Paint Shop Pro.

Now that version 6 has appeared, I believe that there is an even bigger need for more help and that a good Paint Shop Pro book is a must. The copy you're holding in your hands is the result of that belief.

Version 6 of Paint Shop Pro truly moves this already fine product to a much higher level. With this version come many new features and options that represent new concepts. To use this latest version effectively, you—the reader and digital artist—must learn to use these new higher-level features.

Why do you and others like you use Paint Shop Pro? I believe that there are several reasons. Paint Shop Pro, even with its new list of high-end features, is relatively easy to use and carries a modest price tag. Many competing products can easily cost 8 to 10 times more.

Another attractive feature of Paint Shop Pro is its speed. Some users say that opening Paint Shop Pro and making a correction to an image is faster than working in some other imaging programs. Personally, I like some of the features in Paint Shop Pro that you just don't find in other software (one of my favorites is the Hot Wax filter).

As you read this book and become more familiar with Paint Shop Pro, I'm sure you'll find reasons of your own that make your experience with this fun-to-use, powerful paint program a great one.

Overview of New Features

Version 6 of Paint Shop Pro is amazing in its depth. Some of the new features were previously available only on programs costing hundreds of dollars more. Other new features are not available at any price, except in Paint Shop Pro.

The following paragraphs outline some of these new features; I go into more detail on how to access and use these features in later hours.

- **Direct Support for Digital Cameras**   Paint Shop Pro 6 offers direct support for over 120 models of digital cameras. Normally, you would access digital cameras through the TWAIN interface, which you can still do, but you can now access many digital cameras' interfaces directly from a menu choice in Paint Shop Pro.

  Direct support enables Paint Shop Pro to take care of some of the interface details, such as which port the camera is plugged into. With the camera plugged in and turned on, you can access any images stored in the camera and manipulate them in Paint Shop Pro.

- **Support for Graphic Tablets**   With Paint Shop Pro 6, you now have enhanced support for pressure-sensitive graphic tablets such as Wacom's Art Pad.

  Pressure-sensitive tablets enable you to draw and paint using a stylus, or pen, on a tablet. The tablet plugs into a serial port, or USB port, on your computer and gives you a more natural way to draw and paint your images.

  With versions prior to 5, the pen acted much as a mouse, and the pressure-sensitive options were not available. Version 5 introduced tablet support and gave the user more control over how the pen interacted with Paint Shop Pro.

  With version 6, however, you have even more control and you can set the pen's options for each tool within the Tool Options window.

- **Vector Layers**   The Layer palette has been upgraded to enable the use of vector layers. Already a powerful tool, layers are now capable of containing editable shapes and text.

 Layers are analogous to sheets of tracing paper. You can have part of your image on one layer and another part on another layer. One difference between Paint Shop Pro layers and the tracing paper, though, is that in Paint Shop Pro you can make all the layers visible. You also can blend the information on different layers in many ways.

Vector objects are objects that can still be manipulated after they have been created. Unlike normal bitmapped objects, vector objects can be updated at any time. Paint Shop Pro now allows you to create fully editable text and shapes. This includes creating text that flows along a path. I'll cover vector objects in depth in Hour 13, "Working with Flexible Vector Tools."

You can use layers to create incredible collages and montages, create easily editable Web buttons, apply different textures to images with ease, blend images in ways you never thought possible, and much more.

I demonstrate layers and layering techniques in Hour 10, "Working Progressively with Layers." Also, I use layers throughout this book so that you can see how valuable this new feature really is.

- **Effects and Deformations**   Version 6 contains many new and exciting effects and deformations, many of which I'll demonstrate throughout the remainder of the book. Some of the more exciting, in my opinion, are Chrome, Inner and Outer Bevels, and Ripple. For a complete list, simply choose Image, Deformations or Image, Effects.

- **Multicolor Gradients**   Multicolor gradients are exactly that—gradients with more than two colors. In versions prior to 6 you could have a gradient that went only from the foreground color to the background color. Well, no more! You can now use all the colors of the rainbow to create your gradients. Just as exciting is the fact that you can now edit and save the gradients you create.

  Using multicolored gradients enables you to create all sorts of great effects with relative ease. Things such as metallic effects are only several mouse clicks away.

  I'll demonstrate multicolor gradients in Hour 8, "Using Color Effectively," and again in Hour 15, "Applying Filters."

- **Dialog With Zoom Preview**   When previewing effects within the dialog box in which you're applying them, you can zoom in and out to see how the effect looks on your image.

- **Multi-Image Printing**   This feature enables you to select more than one image from a list of currently open images and print them to a single page. I'll go into more detail about this topic toward the end of Hour 2, "Opening, Saving, and Printing Files."

- **Painting Operations** The Paintbrush, Eraser, and Clone Brush tools now include the option of a "Build Up Brush." This enables you to build up paint as you add to an image. You can start with a fairly transparent brush and let the effect build as you paint back and forth over your image. This can help create effects and is great for image correction and enhancement.

- **More Accessible Preferences and Options** Many of the options for different tools have been moved to make them more accessible. These changes enable you to work more productively. For example, the pen and tablet settings have been moved from the Preferences dialog box to the Tool Options window (click the Cursor and Tablet Options tab in the Tool Options window with the Paint Brush tool selected). Another addition is a right-mouse click–selectable Recent Colors option on the Color palette.

- **New Picture Tube Format** The Picture Tube file format has changed. Not to fear, though—you can convert all of your existing version 5 picture tubes using the Tube Conversion program included with Paint Shop Pro 6. Picture tubes will be covered in more detail in Hour 14, "Using and Creating Picture Tubes."

- **Digital Watermarking** Digital watermarking is a relatively new technology that enables a digital artist to embed an invisible signature within an image. This feature, which may require a subscription to the service, is a good way for an artist to keep track of and identify his digital artwork.

- **Picture Frames** You can now create a frame around your images with a click of the mouse. Paint Shop Pro includes many different frames for you to choose from.

- **GIF and JPEG Export Wizards** These new wizards walk you through the process of creating Web-ready GIFs and JPEGs.

- **Browser Enhancements** Enhancements that have been made to the image browser include better thumbnail quality and ToolTips that display basic image information when the mouse is held over the thumbnail.

- **Adjustment Layers** Adjustment layers enable you to apply image correction without changing the actual image. For example, you can adjust the color balance of an image using an adjustment layer. Because the change has been applied to the adjustment layer and not the actual image, you can easily change or reverse the correction.

- **Preference for Last File Type Used in Save As Dialog Box** A much-requested interface enhancement, this option remembers the file type you used during the last Save As operation and defaults to that file type.

- **Floating Palette Roll-Ups**   This feature enables you to have the palettes "roll up" out of the way when they're not in use.

- **Layer Palette**   The Layer palette has been updated and now includes buttons for Create Layer, Delete Layer, and Create Mask. Also, there are three new tabs that enable you to control the view. You can see the layers, their masks (if present), and any layer groups you've created.

- **Action History**   The Undo History feature from version 5 has been updated and renamed Action History.

- **Postscript Import Support**   Enables you to import vector drawings from programs such as Adobe Illustrator and CorelDRAW.

Using Online Help

As with many other Windows programs, Paint Shop Pro offers extensive online help. You can access the online help feature from the menu bar. Choose Help, Help Topics to open the Paint Shop Pro Help panel (see Figure 1.1).

FIGURE 1.1

The Paint Shop Pro Help panel.

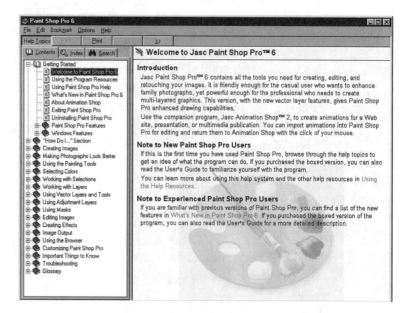

Paint Shop Pro 6 uses the new WinHelp 2000, which combines the tabbed Help window and the Help Topics window from previous versions into one single Help window.

Taken altogether, the Help files are a great resource that you should spend some time exploring.

Overview of the Paint Shop Pro Interface

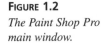

To run Paint Shop Pro for the first time, click the Windows 95/98/NT Start button and then choose Programs, Paint Shop Pro 6, Paint Shop Pro 6 to open the main Paint Shop Pro window (see Figure 1.2). You also can double-click the PSP icon to start the program.

FIGURE 1.2

The Paint Shop Pro main window.

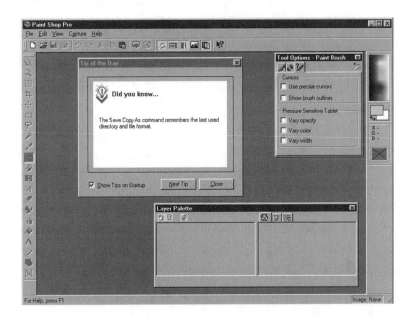

If you're a first time user, you'll notice how clean the interface is. If, on the other hand, you've used previous versions of Paint Shop Pro, you'll notice a few additions to the interface. If you've used or seen other graphics programs, you might also find yourself saying "Wow!" The Paint Shop Pro interface is clean and easy to use; it's even customizable.

When you run Paint Shop Pro initially, and at the beginning of each subsequent use (unless you turn off the feature), you'll see a Tip of the Day dialog box (see Figure 1.2).

Although you can turn off this feature, it's a useful way to pick up tips from the Paint Shop Pro team. To turn off the tips, remove the check mark from the Show Tips on Startup check box. To restore this feature, simply run the Tip of the Day from the Help menu and place a check mark in the Show Tips on Startup option.

The title bar, the menu bar, and the toolbar appear along the top of the main window.

The title bar is similar to any other Windows 95/98/NT program's title bar in that it contains a control icon and the standard Windows window control icons. These icons enable you to minimize, maximize, and restore the program's main window, as well as close the program.

The menu bar should be somewhat familiar. It contains a list of options that, when clicked, display a pull-down menu of further options. The toolbar contains icons that are basically shortcuts to some of the common menu choices. The toolbar is separated into various palettes, as follows:

- The first palette contains icons for creating a new file, opening an existing file, saving a file, and printing a file. These options are the same as those found under the File menu choice.

- The second palette contains icons that enable you to quickly use five of the Edit menu commands: Undo, Redo, Cut, Copy, and Paste.

- The third palette contains two icons that enable you to control the display mode. You can display your image either in full-screen preview or in Normal viewing mode.

- The fourth palette contains five icons that enable you to toggle on and off five different palettes or windows. The palettes/windows you can toggle are the Tool palette, the Tool Options window, the Color palette, the Histogram window, and the Layer palette.

- The context-sensitive Help icon is in a palette by itself. Clicking this icon, followed by clicking another object in the Paint Shop Pro window, will give you some details about the object you've clicked.

- Along the left side of the screen is the Tool palette. It contains all of the tools you need to create and manipulate your images. I explain each tool in more detail later in this hour.

- Down the right side, you'll see the Color palette. The Color palette enables you to set the foreground and background colors (see the second half of this chapter for a demonstration).

- Floating in the upper-right corner of the main window you'll see the Tool Options window and the Layer palette.

  The Tool Options window enables you to set the various options for a particular tool (see the second half of this hour for a demonstration).

  The Layer palette enables you to work with layers, a powerful feature introduced in Paint Shop Pro 5. I briefly cover the Layer palette later in this hour and demonstrate in depth how layers work in Hour 10.

Along the bottom of the main window is the status bar. It displays constantly updated information about the current image file and gives you information about the different tools available. When you move the cursor over a tool, the status bar displays a short description of the tool's function. With the cursor over the current image, you'll see the cursor's x and y coordinates. This information is extremely helpful under certain circumstances, as you'll see later. You also see the current image's size in pixels, its color depth, and its size in kilobytes.

The Toolbar

The toolbar (see Figure 1.3) holds some of the most frequently accessed menu choices.

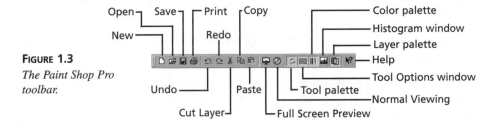

FIGURE 1.3
The Paint Shop Pro toolbar.

Having these popular menu choices available as icons means that often-used menu choices are one click away. For example, the first icon in the toolbar enables you to open a new image. Clicking the New icon (it looks like a small sheet of paper with one corner folded over) saves you from choosing File, New. The other icons represent Open (File, Open); Save (File, Save); and Print (File, Print).

These four icons represent the four most common File menu choices.

The next five icons on the toolbar represent the most common Edit menu choices: Undo (Edit, Undo); Redo (Edit, Redo); Cut, or Cut Layer, (Edit, Cut); Copy (Edit, Copy); and Paste As New Image (Edit, Paste, As New Image).

Sequentially, the next two icons on the toolbar are the Full Screen Preview and the Normal Viewing icons. Clicking the Full Screen Preview icon displays the active image against a black full-screen background. You can choose this option from the toolbar or from the View menu. To return to normal viewing, click anywhere on the Full Screen Preview screen.

The Normal Viewing icon returns an enlarged or reduced image to normal (1:1) magnification.

The next portion of the toolbar holds five icons that toggle the various palettes on and off. From the left, you have the following icons:

- **The Tool Palette icon**   This icon toggles the Tool palette on and off. It is on by default. Note that this tool resembles the Zoom tool but is actually a small wrench.
- **The Tool Options Window icon**   This icon toggles the Tool Options window and is on by default.
- **The Color Palette icon**   You can toggle the Color palette on and off by clicking this icon. The palette is on by default.
- **The Histogram Window icon**   This icon toggles the Histogram window, which is off by default.
- **The Layer Palette icon**   The Layer Palette icon toggles the Layer palette, which is on by default.

Being able to toggle palettes on and off is very helpful, especially if you run Paint Shop Pro on a lower-resolution screen or in a smaller window.

If you generally don't need immediate access to a certain palette, you can toggle it off. If you suddenly find that you're in need of something within that palette, though, you can simply toggle it back on.

On the far right is one last icon—the Help icon. Selecting the Help icon won't bring up online help, as you might expect. Rather, selecting this icon adds a question mark to the regular mouse cursor. That's when the magic starts. When you move this new cursor over virtually any part of the Paint Shop Pro window and click the mouse, you bring up the Help window, with the help text set to whatever you clicked. For example, if you click the Help icon and then click the Color palette, the Help menu opens with help specific to the Color palette. This feature is called *context-sensitive* help.

Point-and-click help is great if you suddenly need help but can't remember the name of the tool or palette.

The Toolbox

The toolbox, or Tool palette, quite naturally contains the Paint Shop Pro tools (see Figure 1.4).

You have tools to make selections, draw and paint, create lines and shapes, and more. As you pause the mouse over any tool in the toolbox, Paint Shop Pro displays a small tag telling you what the tool is.

FIGURE 1.4

Paint Shop Pro's Tool palette.

Arrow
Zoom
Deformation
Crop
Mover
Selection
Freehand
Magic Wand
Dropper
Paint Brushes
Clone Brush
Color Replacer
Retouch
Eraser
Picture Tube
Airbrush
Flood Fill
Text
Draw
Preset Shapes
Vector Object Selection

Even better than just seeing the tool's name, though, you also find a description of what the tool does. This brief information appears in the lower left of the status bar. To see how this feature works, hold the mouse over one of the tool buttons and look for the tool description on the bottom-left side of the Paint Shop Pro window.

The following sections describe the tools that are available in Paint Shop Pro.

The Arrow Tool

The Arrow tool enables you to quickly bring an image to the front. This technique is helpful when you have several images open at one time. Simply select this tool and click the image you want to bring to the front.

The Arrow tool does double duty. It also enables you to scroll around images that are too big to be completely displayed in the window. To scroll around an image, simply click and drag with the Arrow tool (the cursor icon becomes a hand icon during this procedure) to move the image around within its window.

The Zoom Tool

The Zoom tool enables you to zoom in on an image for close-up, detailed work, and it also enables you to zoom out to see the entire image at once. Left-clicking the current image zooms in; right-clicking the current image zooms out. (Hold the Zoom tool and click the image area that you want centered while increasing or decreasing the zoom factor.)

The Deformation Tool

The Deformation tool enables you to rotate, resize, skew, or distort the current layer. (This tool is inactive on the Background layer.) With a multilayered image, you can use this tool to quickly rotate, resize, skew, or distort the contents on any layer other than the Background.

When you select the Deformation tool, a bounding box surrounds the object(s) on the current layer. This bounding box has several control handles: one at each corner; one in the middle of each side, the top, and the bottom; and one in the center. The control handles enable you to "deform" the object surrounded by the bounding box. For example, you can resize and rotate the object(s). I describe this process in more depth in Hour 5, "Working with Deformations."

The Crop Tool

The Crop tool enables you to quickly crop an image. To do so, select the Crop tool and simply click and drag to outline the area you want to crop.

If you're not satisfied with the sizing or placement of the cropped area, don't worry. You can easily resize the cropping area by clicking and dragging the edges of the area, and you can click and drag the cropped area until it fits exactly over the portion of the image you want to crop. Once the cropping area is suitably placed and sized, double-click anywhere within the image to finalize the cropping.

If you've taken a step that you're not happy with, you can always undo it by choosing Edit, Undo. In fact, you can undo several steps. Knowing that nothing's really permanent frees you to put a little playfulness into your explorations. Much can be learned by clicking away with some abandon. However, the best way to experiment is to work on backup copies. If you have only one copy of an image and you *do* make some irreversible change, you're out of luck. However, if you work on a backup copy, nothing you do in Paint Shop Pro can damage the original.

The Mover Tool

The Mover tool performs a little magic. It moves whatever you place the cursor over, no matter which layer is currently active. That is, the Mover tool knows which layer an object is on. If you have a green square on layer 1 and a red circle on layer 2, you can move either by simply selecting the Mover tool and clicking and dragging the object you want to move.

For this tool to perform its magic, though, each object must be on its own layer, because the Mover tool can't differentiate between objects on the same layer. It will move the entire layer that's associated with the object you click and drag. Still, this tool is very useful for placing multiple objects over several layers.

The Selection Tool

The Selection tool enables you to make selections. You can select rectangular, square, elliptical, and circular areas of an image for easier manipulation. Before you can cut, copy, and paste portions of an image, you must select that portion. Selections also enable you to work on the selected area of an image without affecting the rest of the image.

To select a portion of the current image, simply click the Selection tool. Hold the Selection tool cursor over the active image and click and drag to define an area of the image. You can set the various selection shapes in the Tool Options window, which I describe later in this chapter, in the section on palettes.

The Freehand Tool

The Freehand tool enables you to draw freehand selections anywhere on the current image.

You can make three types of selections with the Freehand tool. You can simply draw a freehand selection, you can draw a point-to-point (or *polygonal*) selection, and you can draw a Smart Edge selection.

- The *Freehand* option enables you to draw selections of any shape. All you need to do is click and drag the mouse to define the area you want to select.
- The *Point-to-Point* option enables you to make polygonal selections. All you need to do is click at each corner of the polygon as you move the mouse. When you're done, simply double-click to finish the polygonal selection.
- The *Smart Edge* option attempts to define your selection based on brightness and contrast between adjacent pixels. You use this option to draw loosely around an area, and the Smart Edge feature will try to draw the best selection around the area.

The Magic Wand Tool

The Magic Wand tool enables you to select an area of your image based on its color. You simply select this tool and click within an area. All pixels of the same color and adjacent to the pixel under the cursor are selected, as if by magic. You can set rules and a tolerance level that will help this tool perform its magic. These options can be set in the Tool Options window.

The Dropper Tool

The Dropper tool enables you to pick up a color from the current image and apply it to the foreground and background.

To set the foreground color, simply select the Dropper tool and click over a color in the current image. To set the background color, do the same but right-click instead.

The Paint Brushes

The Paint Brushes tool enables you to paint on your images. You can use the Tool Options window to select different brushes and to set the opacity, hardness, size, and shape of the brushes. From the Tool Options window, you can also select a texture that enables you to imitate painting over various surfaces.

The Clone Brush

The Clone Brush tool enables you to copy portions of an image over another area of the same image or any other open image. This tool can selectively remove or edit parts of an image. For example, you can remove electrical lines from an otherwise pristine scenic photograph.

The Color Replacer

The Color Replacer tool enables you to selectively change one particular color to another throughout the entire image. The process for swapping color seems mysterious, but it is fairly simple.

To swap an existing color with a new color throughout an image, set the foreground to the old color and set the background to the new color. To do so, use the Dropper tool or click the foreground/background color swatches to display the Color dialog box.

With the colors set, select the Color Replacer tool, and double-right-click anywhere in the image to swap any instance of the foreground color with the current background color.

You can swap any pixel of the existing background color in the image with the current foreground color by double-left-clicking anywhere in the image.

I describe this process again with some examples you can work through in Hour 3, "Creating Your First Image."

The Retouch Tool

With the Retouch tool, you can selectively retouch areas of your images. The Retouch tool uses the same brush tips as the other painting and drawing tools, but the controls enable you to lighten, darken, soften, change the saturation, and more. Select this tool to make minor retouches to a photograph.

The Eraser Tool

The Eraser tool enables you to erase portions of your image. You can erase to the current background color or, on higher layers, to transparent. The Eraser tool uses the same brush tips as the drawing and painting tools.

The Picture Tube

The Picture Tube tool, added in version 5, enables you to use tubes to paint on an image. Tubes are built from images arranged in a grid. These images, which usually share a common theme, display at random as you paint with the Tube brush.

This concept is easier to explain through example, and I cover tubes in more depth on Hour 14.

The Airbrush

The Airbrush tool simulates an airbrush. Changing the Opacity and Density settings changes the amount of digital paint that is sprayed onto your image.

The Flood Fill Tool

The Flood Fill tool fills an image or a selected area of your image with either the current foreground color or the current background color. Left-clicking fills with the foreground color, and right-clicking fills with the background color.

You can also choose to fill with a pattern or with a gradient. You can use any image as a pattern for the fill.

New in version 6, gradients can be multicolored, and you can choose from several patterns. You can use gradients to give depth to an image, build complex masks, and create special effects. Examples appear throughout the book.

The Text Tool

The Text tool creates and enters text onto your images. The text can be in any font. The Text tool is quite easy to use. Simply select it and click somewhere within your image to bring up the Text Tool dialog box. You can select the font, the size, and several other options. This dialog box is also where you enter the text you want to appear in your image. You have many opportunities to use the Text tool as you work through this book.

The Draw Tool

The Draw tool enables you to draw lines on your images. You can set the width, choose whether or not the line will be antialiased, and select from Single Line, Bezier Curve, Freehand Line, and Point-to-Point Line. You can also decide if the lines should be drawn as vectors and if the path created by the line should be closed.

Antialiasing is a process that softens the hard edges in digital graphics. The process uses mathematics and involves applying varying shades of colors between the contrasting edges. This process produces a smoother, softer-looking image. You'll see how antialiasing affects different images throughout the rest of the book.

Bézier curves are named after the mathematician who developed the algorithm, or set of computer steps, that enables graphic artists to draw and manipulate smooth curves on the computer.

The Point-to-Point Line tool is similar to the Bezier Curve tool. The Bezier Curve tool allows you to make only two changes, though, and the Point-to-Point Line tool allows you to make unlimited changes.

The Preset Shapes Tool

The Preset Shapes tool enables you to draw stroked (outlined) or filled shapes such as rectangles, squares, ellipses, and circles. In version 6, the shapes created with the Preset Shapes tool can be either bitmap or vector in nature.

The Vector Object Selection Tool

Last but certainly not least, the Vector Object Selection tool enables you to select and modify vector shapes that you created previously with the Text, Draw, or Preset Shapes tool. This assumes, of course, that you created these objects as vectors rather than bitmaps.

Although the preceding descriptions of the tools are brief, as you work through the following hours you'll get plenty of hands-on experience with them.

1

The Menus

The various menu choices are available from the main menu bar. Several of the choices will be familiar to you as a Windows user. The File, Edit, Window, and Help choices are similar to those choices in most Windows programs. However, they may include some new, unfamiliar choices.

Also, many main menu choices in Paint Shop Pro may be unfamiliar. You may not recognize choices such as Image, Layers, Selections, and Masks if you are new to digital imaging. These menu choices will rapidly become second nature, though, as you work your way through this book.

The following sections briefly outline the menu choices. You'll get some hands-on experience with the various choices as you work through the book.

The File Menu

The File menu enables you to open, close, create, save, import, export, browse, revert, print, and batch convert image files. As you work through the rest of the book, you'll become quite proficient at using the File menu options.

> The Revert choice under the File menu enables you to revert the file to the state it was in when you first opened it. This is analogous to closing the file, choosing not to apply the changes, and then re-opening the file. Be aware that Revert cannot be undone and will discard ALL of the changes you have made since you first opened the file.

One other choice under the File menu is Preferences, which I explain later in this hour.

The Edit Menu

The Edit menu enables you to undo the most recent change, redo the last Undo, and access the Action History (multiple undo). The Cut, Copy, Copy Merged, Paste, Clear, Update Back to Animation Shop, and Empty Edits options also are available on the Edit menu.

Most of these choices should be familiar to you if you've used other Windows-based programs. A couple that might be unfamiliar are the Clear and Empty choices:

- Clear deletes anything in a selected area of your image. The selected area will delete to transparent if on a higher layer and will delete to the current background color if on the background layer. Although similar to cutting, the Clear option does not copy the selected area to the Clipboard. You have an opportunity to use the Clear option later in the book.

- Empty enables you to free up some computer memory. You can choose to empty either the Clipboard or the Undo history. If you have many files open and find that the system is running out of memory, you can get a little back by applying this feature.

The View Menu

The View menu gives you access to different viewing modes. You can view the image and the workspace in Full Screen Edit mode. This mode is toggled, meaning that you choose it from the View menu to select it and choose it again to deselect it. The Full Screen Edit mode opens the Paint Shop Pro window to completely cover any other open windows. In addition, this mode hides the menu bar, which you can still access by pressing and releasing the Alt key.

The next view is Full Screen Preview mode. In this mode, all that you see on the screen is your image. To return to Normal viewing mode, press the Esc key or click anywhere on the screen.

You can use other menu choices in the View menu drop-down box to zoom in and zoom out, access information about the current image, and enter creator information.

Finally, you can use the View menu to access the grids, the rulers, and the Toolbars dialog box. I'll demonstrate the grids and rulers in several exercises throughout the book.

The Image Menu

The Image menu enables you to change and manipulate your images by flipping, mirroring, and rotating them. From this menu, you can also choose the various plug-in filters. Paint Shop Pro comes with several filters that enable you to create different effects.

You also can purchase many third-party filter programs. After installing the extra filters, you can access them through the Image, Plug-in Filters menu choice. I demonstrate how to install and set up filters in Hour 15.

The Colors Menu

The Colors menu is where you can access all of the color options pertaining to your images. You can adjust the color, colorize, change the brightness and contrast, select a palette, set a color for transparency, and set the number of colors in your image.

1

As you work through the rest of this book, you use the choices under the Colors menu quite often—often enough that many of the choices and their options will become second nature.

The Layers Menu

From the Layers menu you can add, duplicate, delete, reorder, and change the properties of the various layers that make up your image.

I demonstrate and cover layers in detail in Hour 10. Many of the exercises throughout the book give you plenty of opportunity to use and become accustomed to layers.

The Selections Menu

The Selections menu enables you to manipulate selections. For example, you can create selections, modify the current selection, save and load selections, and create masks from your selections.

I demonstrate selections throughout the book, especially in Hour 4, "Creating and Working with Selections."

The Masks Menu

The Masks menu gives you access to the masking functions. You can create, edit, save, and load masks. I cover masks in detail on Hour 11, "Utilizing Masks for Precision."

The Capture Menu

You can use the Capture menu to make screen captures of your images (such as for use on the Web). Under the Capture menu, you can set up preferences for the key combinations that will run the Screen Capture function, whether it'll capture the whole screen or just a portion of it, whether the cursor will be included in the capture, and so on.

The Window Menu

The options on the Window menu should be familiar to you if you've used Microsoft Windows for any length of time. This menu is pretty much standard across all Windows programs. The choices under this menu enable you to set the way that windows are displayed within Paint Shop Pro.

The Help Menu

The Help menu enables you to use online help, which was discussed earlier in this chapter. You can search for keywords and get context-sensitive help from the Help menu choices.

Using the Palettes

Palettes are common in graphics programs. They operate like visual menus and let you set options for various tools. Paint Shop Pro has three palettes, along with a couple of windows, a toolbar, and a status bar, that you can use to set options and choose tools and color settings. The palettes are as follows:

- The Color palette
- The Layer palette
- The Tool palette

You can turn the palettes on and off via the View, Toolbars command. Choose View, Toolbars to open the Toolbars dialog box (see Figure 1.5).

FIGURE 1.5

The Toolbars dialog box.

To turn off a palette, simply remove the check mark next to its entry in the dialog box. To restore a palette, place a check mark next to its entry.

The three palettes (Color, Layer, and Tool) and the Tool Options window enable you to use the various settings and options associated with the palette.

The Color Palette

The Color palette (see Figure 1.6) enables you to set the foreground and background colors for the drawing and painting tools.

FIGURE 1.6

The Color palette.

You can set a color by moving the mouse over the main swatch in the Color palette. Clicking the left mouse button sets the foreground color, and clicking the right mouse button sets the background color.

You can open the Color dialog box (see Figure 1.7) by clicking on either the foreground or background color swatch.

FIGURE 1.7
The Color dialog box.

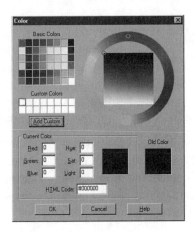

The Tool Options Window

The Tool Options window (see Figure 1.8) enables you to set the options associated with a particular tool.

FIGURE 1.8
The Tool Options window, showing the Tool Controls tab for the cursors and the pressure sensitive tablet.

Figure 1.9 shows the options you can set for the Paint Brushes tool Brush Tip.

FIGURE 1.9
The Tool Options window, showing the Brush Tip options for the Paint Brushes tool.

The Layer Palette

The Layer palette (see Figure 1.10) enables you to set the options and blending modes for the layers that make up your images.

FIGURE **1.10**

The Layer palette.

You also can create and delete layers from within the Layer palette through the two small icons at the top left of the palette. The first enables you to create a new layer, and the second enables you to delete a layer.

You can create or delete layers by clicking one of these two icons. You also can drag and drop layers onto either icon. Dragging and dropping a layer onto the New Layer icon duplicates the layer, and dragging and dropping a layer onto the small trash can icon deletes the layer.

The Tool Palette

The Tool palette contains the various tools that you can use to paint, draw, make selections, and so on. The tools in this palette were discussed previously in this hour.

Setting Preferences

Like many of today's advanced programs, Paint Shop Pro enables you to set various preferences. To set Paint Shop Pro's preferences, choose File, Preferences. Another pull-down menu opens, with the choices you see in Figure 1.11.

FIGURE **1.11**

The Preferences submenu.

Each of the menu choices in this pull-down menu opens a dialog box in which you can set preferences to make using Paint Shop Pro easier for you.

General Program Preferences

You can tab through the Paint Shop Pro Preferences dialog box to set up levels of Undo (keeping in mind that higher levels take more memory), the size and color of the rulers, how cursors are displayed (precise or tool shape), and more. See Figure 1.12.

FIGURE 1.12

The Paint Shop Pro Preferences dialog box.

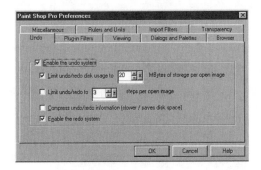

CMYK Conversion Preferences

The CMYK Conversion Preferences dialog box enables you to tell Paint Shop Pro how to handle conversions between CMYK (a standard file mode for high-end printing) and RGB files (the standard mode for onscreen computer images). See Figure 1.13.

FIGURE 1.13

The CMYK Conversion Preferences dialog box.

Unless you plan to send your images to a prepress shop (something you might want to do to print 5,000 full-color brochures), you really don't need to bother with this setting.

File Format Preferences

The File Format Preferences dialog box (see Figure 1.14) enables you to set the file format preferences for the FITS/Import, PCD, PostScript, raw data (RAW), and Windows Meta-File (WMF) file formats. Most of these file types normally are not used, with one exception: New to version 6, you can now import PostScript files. PostScript files are vector-based and are usually created by drawing programs, such as Adobe Illustrator and CorelDRAW.

FIGURE 1.14

*The File Format
Preferences dialog
box.*

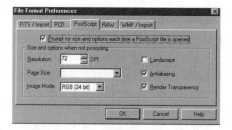

File Format Associations

The File Format Associations dialog box (see Figure 1.15) enables you to set and unset
the file formats to associate with Paint Shop Pro. Any file whose format is associated
with Paint Shop Pro opens in Paint Shop Pro when you double-click on its icon.

FIGURE 1.15

*The File Format
Associations dialog
box.*

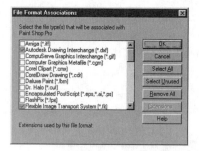

This feature is handy if, for example, you want always to edit JPG or GIF files with
Paint Shop Pro. With their respective file formats set in the File Format Associations dialog box, you can open JPG and GIF files in Paint Shop Pro by double-clicking their
icons in Windows Explorer.

Customize Toolbar Preferences

The Customize Toolbar dialog box (see Figure 1.16) enables you to select which tools
are displayed on—and thus made available through—the toolbar.

FIGURE 1.16

*The Customize Toolbar
dialog box.*

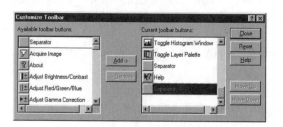

For example, you could add a button to acquire images with your scanner. This option would save you from having to go through the various menu choices to select the acquire option.

After you become more comfortable with Paint Shop Pro, you should take the time to see which buttons are available. Setting up a couple of buttons for often-used features can be a real timesaver.

Color Management Preferences

If you own Windows 98 or NT 5, you can take advantage of the built-in color management of these operating systems.

Monitor Gamma Adjustments

The Monitor Gamma Adjustment dialog box (see Figure 1.17) enables you to set the Gamma (the overall color cast and brightness/contrast) of your monitor.

FIGURE 1.17

The Monitor Gamma Adjustment dialog box.

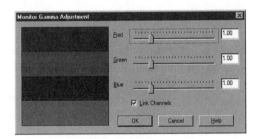

To brighten the display, move the sliders to the right. To darken it, move them to the left. If your monitor gives a color cast (that is, the neutral gray seems to contain a little red, green, or blue), you can adjust each color separately. To do so, unlink the channels and move the sliders separately until the color cast disappears.

If you're not sure how your display is set, you should ignore the settings in this dialog box and leave the defaults. You can't harm your monitor by playing with these settings, but they are best left alone if you think your monitor is functioning correctly.

Summary

You have çovered a lot of ground already. You explored the Paint Shop Pro interface (maybe for the first time) and learned how to find your way around. You also glanced at the new features available in version 6.0. You should spend a little extra time exploring the interface and familiarizing yourself with the different tools and menus.

Workshop

The Workshop contains a question and answer section to help answer the most commonly asked questions and quiz questions to help you solidify your understanding of the material covered.

Q&A

Q Why are some menu choices also offered as icons?

A It's probably because different people like to work in different ways. For example, I prefer to keep my hand on the mouse and rarely use the shortcut keys. I actually work more quickly this way, whereas others may work more efficiently with the keyboard shortcuts.

Q Can I change the way the interface looks? For example, can I change the icons?

A Yes, you can change which tool icons are used, and you can select from several different icons to enhance Paint Shop Pro for the way that you work.

Q Where can I set the options for any given tool?

A You can usually set a tool's options in the Controls palette. You can open the Controls palette by clicking the Control Palette icon on the toolbar or by choosing View, Toolbars and placing a check mark next to the Control Palette check box.

Q How do I determine which version of Paint Shop Pro I'm using?

A Choose Help, About Paint Shop Pro. The version number is displayed in the splash screen.

Quiz

1. If you wanted to pick up a color from an image and copy that color to another image, which tool would you use?

2. Is it possible to change one color in an image to another color? How?

3. Is it possible to work on an image without the clutter of all of the tools and palettes getting in the way? How?

4. How do you turn off the Tip of the Day dialog box?

Answers

1. You should use the Dropper tool.

2. Yes. You can do so with the Color Replacer tool.

3. Yes. You can toggle the screen between Full Screen Edit mode and Normal mode. You can also selectively turn on and off the various palettes and toolbars.

4. To turn off the Tip of the Day, remove the check mark from the Show Tips on Startup check box.

Hour 2

Opening, Saving, and Printing Files

This hour introduces the following actions in Paint Shop Pro:

- Opening files
- Saving files
- Importing and exporting files
- The basics of printing files
- Multi-image printing

Opening a File

To get an image into Paint Shop Pro, you can create a new image (File, New), open an existing image (File, Open), or import an image from a digital camera or scanner (File, Import).

Opening a New File

To open a new file, choose File, New. Doing so opens the New Image dialog box (see Figure 2.1).

FIGURE 2.1

The New Image dialog box.

Within the New Image dialog box, you can set the width, height, and resolution of the new image. You also can set the background color and the image type (the number of colors used). You'll be accessing this dialog box many, many times as you work through the rest of this book.

Generally, I give you the dimensions, resolution, background color, and image type. Later, as you create your own images, you can decide on the settings that are appropriate for each one.

Opening an Existing File

You can open an existing file by choosing File, Open. This action opens the standard Windows Open dialog box (see Figure 2.2).

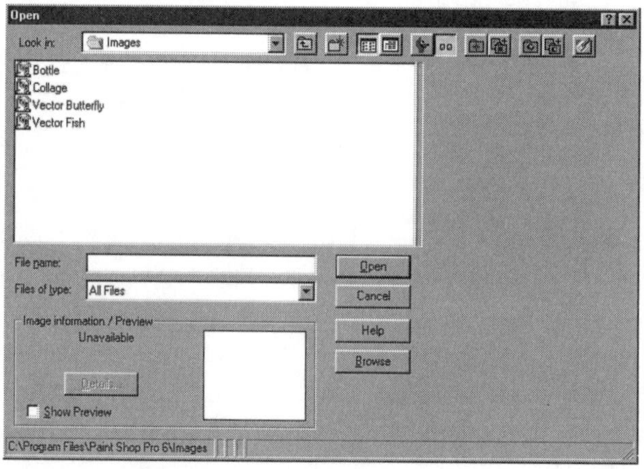

FIGURE 2.2

The Open dialog box.

You may notice some extra buttons that appear in the Open dialog box in Figure 2.2. These appear because the author runs Image Fox, a program from ACDSYS. This program provides thumbnail views of files. You can download a demo version from www.acdsys.com.

2

The first time you run Paint Shop Pro after installing it, you're offered the opportunity to choose files that will be associated with the program. Any file that you associate can be opened by double-clicking its icon.

Starting with Paint Shop Pro 6, you can open EPS (Enhanced PostScript) files. These files are generally images created with drawing programs such as Adobe Illustrator or CorelDRAW. Many logos, for example, are created with this type of software. Until now you would have had to save an illustration created in a drawing program in a bitmap format before opening it in Paint Shop Pro. This wasn't a problem if you owned the program that the file was created with. However, if you wanted to work on an existing illustration and you didn't own the drawing program, you were out of luck. Now, though, you can open the file easily and set some of the options, such as antialiasing, as well.

Browsing for an Existing File

You can browse through folders to find the file or enter a file's name. You also can see previews of the files if they're recognized by Paint Shop Pro.

You can use Paint Shop Pro's file browser (see Figure 2.3) to browse through folders visually.

FIGURE 2.3

The Browse dialog box.

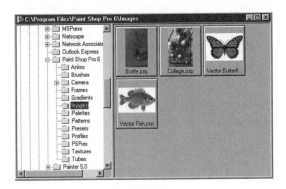

The file browser enables you to see at a glance all the images in a folder. A small button, or *thumbnail*, represents each image in the currently selected folder.

To open an image after identifying it from its thumbnail, simply double-click the thumbnail. After you open an image, you can manipulate it in many different ways. You learn about the amazing things that you can do with new and existing images as you progress through this book.

Importing Files

You can import images into Paint Shop Pro from any digitizing hardware, such as a scanner or a digital camera.

Paint Shop Pro offers an interface to your TWAIN hardware. When you buy a scanner or a digital camera, you must install it. Part of the installation process involves installing the drivers and the device's software.

Figure 2.4 shows Paint Shop Pro importing a photo by running Hewlett-Packard's DeskScan II 2.7.

FIGURE 2.4

Paint Shop Pro running the TWAIN scanner driver for a Hewlett-Packard 4c desktop scanner.

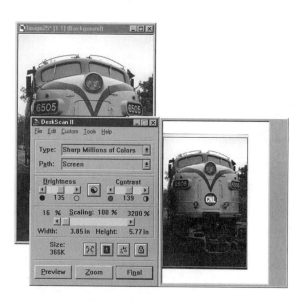

If you have a TWAIN scanner or digital camera, the interface you see will depend on the software included with your hardware.

Although the process of importing an image is a little more complicated than simply opening a file, this step is much like accessing an image from your hard drive.

Saving Files

After you acquire your image, correct it, or manipulate it to your satisfaction, you need to save it to your hard drive.

Starting with version 5 and continuing with the present version, Paint Shop Pro has its own file format. If you created new layers or used any of the vector tools during the processing of your image, you should use Paint Shop Pro's native format, .psp, to save the file. This format preserves the layers and their associated blending modes and the vector object information. Saving under any other format, with the exception of the .psd file format (Photoshop's native format), discards any separate layer information and *flattens* the image into one layer.

Flattening the image is not a bad thing and is actually necessary for formats such as JPG and GIF. If you've done extensive work with layers or with vector objects (such as vector text), though, you may want to save at least two copies of your image. One copy should be in .psp format and the other can be in some other format—GIF or JPG for a Web-based file, for example. Another factor to consider is saving the image as you work. You might want to create a temporary working directory and save incremental backups of your work. Even with the advanced state of today's technology, computers crash. They most often do so right after you've put in several hours of uninterrupted work and just before you finally decide that you should save the changes you've labored over.

You can save every 5 to 10 minutes or so and use names such as Image001, Image002, and so on. When you are finished, you can save the final image (most likely as a .psp file) and delete the Image files from your temporary folder.

Besides the Save option, you can use Save As or Save a Copy. These two options are essentially the same, except that Save a Copy doesn't affect the current image in any way.

For example, using Save As to save your image to the GIF format flattens the image and reduces the color palette to only 256 colors or fewer. Using Save a Copy saves a copy of the image with the layers flattened and the color palette reduced but leaves the current image in its unaltered state.

Exporting Files

In addition to saving your images, you can export them. Exporting your images requires the use of export filters. Paint Shop Pro comes with one built-in export filter. In fact, exporting is how you create tubes (at least in part). I demonstrate how to create tubes in Hour 14, "Using and Creating Picture Tubes."

Exporting a file is similar to saving a file. The main difference is that exporting a file enables you to use certain export filters or plug-ins. Export filters
or plug-ins allow third-party programmers to extend the built-in capabilities
of a program such as Paint Shop Pro.

In addition to the built-in export filters, many third-party filters are available. For example, you can get filters that hide a copyright number in your image to help you keep track
of your digital artwork. One of my favorite export filters, though, is SmartSaver from
Ulead (see Figure 2.5).

SmartSaver saves images in JPG, GIF, and PNG and is a Web-based image export filter.
If you have to save Web-ready images on a regular basis, I highly recommend this filter.
In addition to being a timesaver, SmartSaver offers real-time color resolution changes
and transparency blends for GIF files. It offers 100 levels of JPG compression and more.
You can get a free demo version of this wonderful plug-in from Ulead at
`http://www.ulead.com`.

Printing Basics

After all the work you put into your masterpiece, you may want to print it. Paint Shop Pro makes printing relatively easy. The first thing you should do is choose File, Page Setup. Doing so will bring up the Page Setup dialog box (see Figure 2.6).

FIGURE 2.6

The Page Setup dialog box.

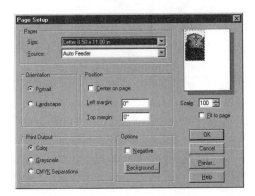

Within this dialog box, you can set the size and source of the paper. For most printers, the default settings, Letter 8.50×11.0 inches and Auto Feeder, should be fine.

You can also set the Orientation option to either Portrait (vertical) or Landscape (horizontal). You can choose to center the image on the page or not and set the left and top margins. Using the Scale option, you can set the size of the image.

You can also specify the Print Output setting. If you own a color inkjet, you can select the Color option, or you can select Greyscale if you own a black-and-white printer (for example, a laser printer). You can even print a CMYK separation.

To preview the job before sending it to the printer, select File, Print Preview to open the Print Preview screen (see Figure 2.7).

This screen gives you an idea of what your printed image will look like. It is a good idea to preview your image if only to make sure the margins are set where they should be.

If you're satisfied with the preview, you can click the Print button. This step opens the dialog box specific to your printer and prints the image. It's as simple as that!

FIGURE 2.7
*You can preview an
image before you print.*

Multi-Image Printing

New to version 6 is the ability to print multiple images on one page. The images must be currently open in Paint Shop Pro for this new tool to do its magic.

With the images you would like to print open in Paint Shop Pro, choose File, Print Multiple Images. Doing so will open a new window, showing you the current open images and a blank canvas.

To add the images you want to print, simply drag and drop them onto the canvas (see Figure 2.8).

You can drag and drop the images from the left onto the canvas. You also can resize the images.

You can save and open layouts that you've created. This can be a real timesaver if you often create layouts with the same number of images placed in the same way.

This new feature can save you money as well as time if you find yourself printing photo-quality images on expensive photo paper.

FIGURE 2.8

The multi-image printing window.

Summary

In this hour, you've learned how to open, save, import, export, and print your images. You might want to practice opening some images (you can find a few nice images on the Paint Shop Pro CD-ROM) and saving them as different file types. You might even open a file and print it to see how images look on your printer.

In the next hour, I show you how to create your first image. I discuss some of the concepts you should know about before starting an image, and I take you on a brief tour of the various tools that are available in Paint Shop Pro.

Workshop

The Workshop contains a question and answer section to help answer the most commonly asked questions and quiz questions to help you solidify your understanding of the material covered.

Q&A

Q How do I know what my image will look like when it's printed?

A You can preview your printed image by choosing File, Print Preview.

Q What types of files can Paint Shop Pro open and save?

A Paint Shop Pro directly supports 47 different file types, including the most popular image types. A few of these are BMP, JPG, GIF, TIF, and PSD (Photoshop files). Starting with version 6, Paint Shop Pro can also open Enhanced PostScript (EPS) files.

Q Why would I want to export a file?

A Exporting files enables you to use export filters or plug-ins that extend the capabilities of Paint Shop Pro.

Q What is the purpose of the .psp file extension?

A Having multiple layers in a file, a new feature in version 5 and above, and the .psp file type (native Paint Shop Pro file) enables you to preserve the layering information. I discuss layers in Hour 10, "Working Progressively with Layers."

Quiz

1. How do you save a Paint Shop Pro file for use on the Web?

2. Is it important to preview your image before printing it?

3. Is it possible to view a folder of files visually; if so, how?

4. Are there any built-in export filters in Paint Shop Pro?

Answers

1. You need to save the file as a GIF or a JPG. You can do so via the Save As or Save a Copy choice under the File menu.

2. It takes only a moment to preview your image before printing it. It might be a good idea to do so until you're familiar with the printing process.

3. You can view all of the image files in a folder that are compatible with Paint Shop Pro by choosing File, Browse.

4. Yes, Paint Shop Pro comes with the Tube Export filter. This filter enables you to create tubes (see Hour 14). Starting with version 6, there are also the GIF and JPEG export filters.

HOUR 3

Creating Your First Image

This hour introduces the following topics regarding images:

- Issues to consider before constructing your first image
- Creating your first image
- Editing your first image
- Fixing mistakes in an image

Issues to Consider Before Constructing an Image

It's often quite tempting to just jump right in and start painting and drawing when creating a new image. However, stopping for a moment and thinking about the image before you actually begin can end up saving you time.

Some things to consider are the overall size of the image (including its dimensions), the number of colors needed (which can affect the resulting file size), and the file size, especially if the image is intended for the Web.

Choosing an Image Size

Whether the image is intended for the Web, general onscreen viewing, or print media, the dimensions are among the first things to consider.

If your image is intended for onscreen presentation, you'll usually want it to fit within the limits of a computer screen.

More and more people use 800×600 settings for their computer monitors. Some are even using much higher resolutions. Nevertheless, many people still run their screens at 640×480. If you know your audience well or are designing for a particular screen resolution, you're all set. If not, choose the resolution of your own screen or smaller.

With that decision out of the way, it's time to decide on the resolution in terms of dots per inch (dpi) or pixels per inch (ppi). If you're designing for onscreen or Web use, set the resolution to 72dpi, which is the norm for most computer screens. The differences you'll encounter won't be significant and, for onscreen use, the most important aspects to consider are width and height.

If you'll be printing your image or having it printed, the dpi you choose becomes a more important issue. If your final output is destined for print, you'll want to use a much higher resolution than that for onscreen presentations.

Most of today's printers are capable of 300×300, 600×600, or higher resolution, and sending a 72dpi image to one of those printers will result in either a much smaller image than you wanted or final print quality that's just not acceptable.

Be aware, though, that images with a higher resolution will be much larger. An image at 72dpi that's 4"×6" (which is about the standard size for prints you get back from most one-hour photo stores) is about 385KB uncompressed, whereas the same image at 300dpi takes up a whopping 6MB of hard drive space.

Keep in mind, too, that resizing an image down results in better quality than resizing an image up. If you take a small image and make it larger, you'll be disappointed with the results. If you take a larger image and make it smaller, though, the results, although not perfect, will be much better.

Choosing an Image Type

Another issue to consider is the *image type*, or number of colors (color resolution). If you're scanning an image into Paint Shop Pro, you should normally use the highest setting available—especially for real-world images such as photographs. You should use a lower color setting when scanning in black-and-white art, though. If you're opening and working on an existing image, plan to stay with the existing color resolution.

Normally, your scanning software will adjust the number of colors based on the type of image it's scanning. You can still use a higher number of colors, especially if you'll be applying effects to the image.

When you are finished working on the image, you can lower the number of colors if necessary. This change decreases the final file size and may even be necessary if you are saving to a file type such as GIF.

When you're starting a new image, you are faced with the most options as far as color resolution is concerned. This is when you have to decide on the image type. The image type you choose depends on the image you are creating and its intended purpose (such as the final output method).

Generally, you should start out with high color resolution, especially if you intend to use any of the special effects in Paint Shop Pro. Most of the effects are grayed out or otherwise not available when you work on lower color resolution images.

You can always change the image type after you complete the image. In fact, this step is necessary if you're working on an image with thousands or millions of colors that needs to be converted to a GIF file for the Web.

I recommend keeping a copy of the original image in the higher color resolution in case you need to make changes later. This approach means that you won't have to change the color resolution over and over, which ultimately causes an image's quality to degrade.

The choice for image type or number of colors is set when you open a new image. Figure 3.1 shows the New Image dialog box.

FIGURE 3.1

The New Image dialog box.

This dialog box pops up when you choose File, New. You can set the width, height, and resolution. You also can set the background color and the image type. For image type, you can choose from the following options:

- 2 Colors (1 Bit)
- 16 Colors (4 Bit)
- Grayscale (8 Bit)
- 256 Colors (8 Bit)
- 16.7 Million Colors (24 Bit)

You can also reset the color resolution by choosing either Colors, Decrease Color Depth or Colors, Increase Color Depth. The Decrease Color Depth menu gives you more control than you get from the New File dialog box and the Increase Color Depth menu choice. From the Decrease Color Depth menu, you can also choose 32,000 colors, 64,000 colors, or an arbitrary number of colors for any image.

Normally, I start an image with 16.7 million colors so that I can effectively apply all the tools at my disposal. The image can always be downgraded to a lower color resolution when I'm done. That said, let's open a new image and explore a few of the tools at hand.

Creating a Simple Image

The best way to learn is to roll up your sleeves and get right to it. The following exercise introduces the Paint Shop Pro tools used for drawing, painting, and creating lines and shapes.

Using the Preset Shapes Tool

To get started, open a new image at 500×500 pixels with the resolution set to 72ppi, the background color set to White, and the image type set to 16.7 Million Colors. Then follow these steps:

1. Set the foreground color to one of your favorite colors by moving the mouse over the Color palette and clicking the color.
2. Select the Preset Shapes tool from the Tool palette.
3. In the Tool Options window, set the shape to Rectangle, the style to Stroked (known as Outline in earlier versions of Paint Shop Pro), and the Stroke Width to 2. Leave the Antialias option checked, but remove the check mark from the Create as Vector option (I'll discuss vector shapes in Hour 13, "Working with Flexible Vector Tools").

4. Click and drag the mouse within the image window. As you drag the mouse, a rectangle forms, grows, and changes shape. When you release the mouse, a perfect rectangle will be drawn where the outline was.

Try another!

1. Reset the foreground color by choosing a color from the color swatch in the Color palette.

2. In the Tool Options window, change the style to Filled and draw another rectangle. This one will be filled with the foreground color instead of just outlined in it.

3. Choose another color and, in the Tool Options window, set the shape to Circle.

4. Click and drag the mouse in the image window again. This time you'll be drawing a circle. You may notice that, unlike the rectangular shape, the circle is drawn from the center out. This piece of information will come in handy when you want to draw more complex shapes by combining various lower-level shapes.

Avoiding Aliased Images

If you haven't placed a check mark in the Antialias check box of the Tool Options window, and if your circle is large enough and it contrasts enough in color with the background, you may notice that it's a bit jagged (see Figure 3.2).

FIGURE 3.2
An aliased circle.

This jaggedness is called *aliasing,* and it's the result of taking an analog shape such as a circle and digitizing it. A shape such as a circle is *analog* by nature in that it has an infinite number of points that make up its circumference.

When you draw a circle on a computer screen, it must be represented by pixels. All of these pixels together make up a grid of 640×480 pixels, 800×600 pixels, 1,024×768 pixels, and so on. Because the circle is being drawn on a grid, it is digitized. That is, only a certain number of points are available, and each point on the circumference of the circle that is being drawn must be represented by one of the pixels that make up the grid on your computer screen.

What all this really means to you, the digital artist, is that many of your shapes and lines will be aliased. This of course means that your images will have jagged edges. Or does it? Actually, it does and it doesn't. How can that be, you ask? Simple! You can use a process known as *antialiasing* to give jagged edges the appearance of being smooth.

Antialiasing uses mathematics and shades of colors that range between the colors along the edge to fool your eye into believing that the edge is smooth.

Figure 3.3 shows another filled circle drawn in Paint Shop Pro. This time, when I drew the circle, I placed a check mark in the Antialias check box in the Tool Options window.

FIGURE 3.3
An antialiased circle.

To show you the difference, I zoomed in on both Figure 3.2 (the aliased circle) and Figure 3.3 (the antialiased circle). Seeing the two images side by side (see Figure 3.4) will give you a better idea of what aliasing and antialiasing are all about.

The image containing the aliased circle is obviously made up solely of black and white pixels, whereas the image containing the antialiased circle shows pixels of varying shades of gray along the circle's edge. It's those pixels that give the second circle its appearance of smoothness.

In version 6 of Paint Shop Pro, most of the tools have antialiasing capabilities. I go into more detail on drawing shapes in Hour 6, "Drawing Tools and Techniques."

FIGURE 3.4

Aliased and antialiased circles side by side.

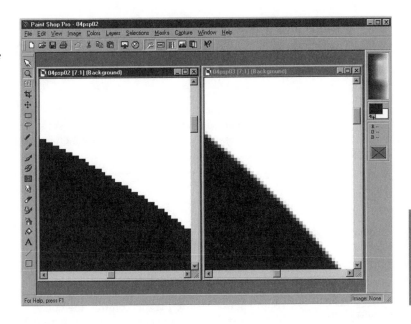

Using Brush Tips

Close the image you've been doodling on and open a new image with the same settings as before. (You can save the first one if it is the beginning of a masterpiece you want to get back to later.) Then follow these steps:

1. Select the Paint Brushes tool. In the Tool Options window, click the Brush Tip tab to bring up the Brush Tip palette (see Figure 3.5).

FIGURE 3.5

The Brush Tip palette.

2. Use the controls in the Brush Tip palette to set the various options for the Paint Brush tool. You can set the size, the opacity, the hardness, the density, and the step of the brush. In addition, you can select a brush from the pull-down menu. To access that menu, click the brush icon at the upper-right of the tabbed palette.

   You can choose from a variety of brushes. I talk more about brushes in Hour 7, "Painting Tools and Techniques."

3. After you are finished selecting a brush and playing with the settings, draw on the new image to get the feel of the various brushes and their settings. Change the color, the brush type, and the opacity to see what happens.

One nice option here is the brush preview in the upper-left corner of the Brush Tip tabbed palette. This small window shows you what the brush looks like and gives you a good idea of the effect you'll get when you use any given brush.

4. Try lowering the opacity. If you lower the opacity enough, you'll be able to see previous lines you've made through the new lines you're drawing. This powerful feature enables you to mimic real-world drawing tools.

A new option in the Tool Options window of version 6 is the addition of a control button next to the spin controls (the spin controls are the small arrows that enable you to change a numeric setting by clicking either the up arrow or the down arrow). The new control buttons can be recognized by the small icon with a small underlined, black, downward-pointing arrow. Clicking one of these, where available, will open a small sliding control. The sliding control, although not as accurate as the spin control, is much quicker to use when precision is not as important.

Figure 3.6 shows how I mimicked an orange highlighter marker drawn over some black text.

FIGURE 3.6
Orange highlighter over black text.

To create this quick highlighter fakery, I simply added black text to a new image and then drew over the text with an orange brush. I set the brush to Normal with the shape set to Round, and I set the size to 104 (just enough to cover the height of the text).

I set the Opacity to 52 (I played around with this setting a couple of times and used Edit, Undo until I got just the opacity effect I wanted). I set the Hardness to 0 (I wanted a very soft edge so that it would blend into the white background, as an older marker might do). I left the Density set to 100 and the Step set to 25. All of these settings combined to give the effect I wanted, that of a marker highlighting some text.

Try playing around with the brushes and their settings to see how they work. Don't worry if some of the options seem confusing for now. I cover them in depth in Hour 7.

Editing a Simple Image

Paint Shop Pro also enables you to edit existing images. You can use the drawing and painting tools as well as the Text, Line, and Shape tools to change an image.

Two other tools that enable you to edit an existing image are the Color Replacer tool and the Retouch tool. The Retouch tool acts much the same as the Paint Brush tool and, in fact, you can set the options for this tool as if it were a brush.

The difference is that you can use the Retouch tool to apply various retouching effects such as Lighten, Darken, Soften, Emboss, and more. I cover these options in more depth in Hour 17, "Retouching Your Images."

The Color Replacer tool, although powerful, can be somewhat confusing. I think, though, that if you follow along with the next example, the workings of this tool will become clear.

To see how the Color Replacer tool works, open a new 500×500 image with a white background and the image type set to 16.7 million colors. Then follow these steps:

1. Set the foreground color to black. Make sure that it's black; it must have the value 0 for each of the colors Red, Green, and Blue. You can see these numbers scroll as you move over the color swatch in the Color palette.

2. You should be able to move the mouse far enough to the left of the color swatch to get the color to perfect black. If you can't quite get it, just complete the following two steps:

    a. Click the foreground color swatch to bring up the Color dialog box (see Figure 3.7).

    b. With the Color dialog box open, you can easily enter the RGB values. After you enter zeros for each entry, click OK and the foreground color will be perfectly black.

FIGURE 3.7
The Color dialog box.

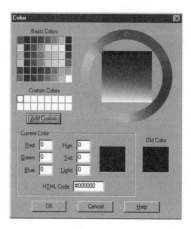

Within the Color dialog box, you will see a swatch in the upper-left corner. This swatch contains some common colors, including pure red, yellow, green, cyan, blue, magenta, black, and white. Clicking one of these small squares is a great way to quickly select one of these commonly used colors.

3. Draw two circles that don't touch. You can place them in opposite corners as I've done in Figure 3.8.

FIGURE 3.8
Two circles filled with black.

4. Change the foreground color to a really dark blue. You don't have to be too fussy, just make sure that the color is almost black. The values for the color I'm using are R: 4, G: 4, and B: 8.

5. With the new foreground color set, draw a Filled rectangle so that it partly covers each circle, as shown in Figure 3.9.

FIGURE 3.9

Two circles filled with black and a nearly black rectangle.

6. Select the Color Replacer tool.

7. Click the Color Replacer Options tab (the second tab) in the Tool Options window and set Tolerance to 0.

8. Set the background color to a nice bright yellow. You don't need to be fussy; just select a color that's different from the two circles and the rectangle. You can set the background color by right-clicking a color in the main color swatch in the Color palette.

9. With the new background color set and the foreground color still set to the color you chose for the rectangle, double right-click anywhere in the image.

   The rectangle should turn yellow. What happened? It turned yellow because that's the current background color. The Color Replacer tool replaced all the pixels in the image containing the current foreground color with pixels using the current background color.

10. You can reverse the process by double-clicking. Try it. Double left-clicking replaces pixels containing the current background color with pixels using the current foreground color.

11. With the image back to its original state, bump Tolerance up to around 50.

    Double right-clicking replaces the color of all three objects with the current background color.

The Tolerance setting controls how close a color needs to be to the color being changed before it gets replaced with the new color. Almost like magic, right? And now you know how it works.

I encourage you to play with this awesome tool until you feel comfortable with it.

Fixing Errors

To help you keep your creativity alive, Paint Shop Pro has an Undo feature (a multiple Undo feature, actually). If you make a change (or several changes) to an image and find that you don't like the change or that it isn't quite what you expected, you can undo it.

To undo the most recent change, choose Edit, Undo. This backs up to just before the most recent change you made. To see Undo in action, open a new file and draw a shape. Then follow these steps:

1. Select another tool such as the Line tool or the Paint Brush tool and draw over the shape you created.
2. Choose Edit, Undo, and the line or the mark you made will disappear.
3. Choose Edit, Undo again, and the shape disappears, too.
4. Oops! What if you intended to keep the first shape? No problem! Choose Edit, Redo to make the shape reappear.

There's even an Undo History. If you choose Edit, Command History, you'll get the Command History dialog box (see Figure 3.10).

FIGURE 3.10

The Command History dialog box.

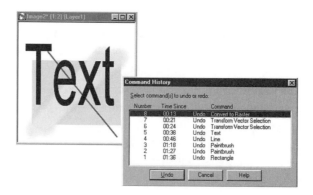

In Figure 3.10 the Command History dialog box contains a list of the most recent changes I made to the image, which is also visible in the figure. To restore the image to an earlier state, simply click the corresponding point in the Command History dialog box and select Undo.

Unfortunately, the history is linear, so you can't pick and choose which Undos you want. Anything else that is highlighted in the list is also undone. This feature is a great way to return to a specific point in your work, though.

Summary

In this hour, you've learned a little about how to create an image, draw shapes, and use the Paint Brush tools. You've also learned how to edit an image and how to change any color in the image to another color. Also, you've seen how to undo an error and redo the Undo, and you've taken a quick look at the Undo History feature.

The next hour explains how to create, edit, save, and load selections.

Workshop

The Workshop contains a Q&A section to help answer the most commonly asked questions and quiz questions to help you solidify your understanding of the material covered.

Q&A

Q How do I set the size of a brush?

A You can change a brush's size and some of its other characteristics in the Tool Options window.

Q How can I draw an outline of a shape such as a circle or a square?

A You can set the Preset Shapes tool to draw either Filled or Stroked (outlined), or Stroked & Filled shapes. These options can be set in the Tool Options window.

Q I drew a shape in a color other than the color I really wanted. What can I do?

A Choose Edit, Undo and redraw the shape after changing the color.

Q Can I undo a couple of steps?

A Yes, you can undo as many steps as you've made. The default is 20MB of disk space, but you can change this setting in the Preferences dialog box or choose a number of undos. To set the number higher (you'll need more memory for this, though) or lower, open the Preferences dialog box (choose File, Preferences, General Program Preferences) and click the Undo tab. You can also use the Command History option to reset the image to a previous state.

Quiz

1. What guidelines do you use to pick your image size?
2. What is the easiest way to avoid aliased images?
3. Why should you open new images at 16.7 million colors?
4. Is it possible to change one color to another throughout an image?

Answers

1. The size of the image really depends on what the image will be used for. For Web images, file size is a little more important than the actual dimensions. I like to make an image large enough to be readily evident.
2. Make sure that the Antialias option is checked on all the tools that you use to create an image.
3. Many tools and options require all available colors to work properly. You can always change the number of colors after you've completed the image.
4. Yes, you can change one color for another with the Color Replacer tool.

PART II
Editing Your Images

Hour

HOUR 4

Creating and Working with Selections

This hour introduces the following issues regarding working with selections:

- Using the selection tools
- Editing selections
- Loading and saving selections
- Learning about Alpha channels

A *selection* masks off an area of an image so that you can make changes to that area without affecting the rest of the image. You can fill selections, run effects on them, and more. You can save selections and load them later. You also can copy and paste selections within an image or from one image to another, and you can add to and subtract from selections.

Using the Selection Tools

Selections are essential for creating and manipulating digital images, and Paint Shop Pro provides a number of tools for making selections. From the Tool palette, you can select one of three selection tools:

- The Selection tool
- The Freehand tool
- The Magic Wand tool

Each of these tools is discussed in the following sections.

The Selection Tool

The Selection tool enables you to make selections using different shapes. After choosing the Selection tool, you can set the desired shape in the Tool Options window. You can choose from a rectangle, a square, an ellipse, and a circle. Using the Selection tool is similar to using the Preset Shapes tool.

To try out the Selection tool, open a new 500×500 image at 72dpi with the background set to white and then follow these steps:

1. Select the Selection tool.

2. In the Tool Options window, set the shape to Rectangle. For the moment, ignore the Feather value and the Antialias check box.

3. Place the mouse cursor in the upper-left corner of the image and click and drag toward the lower-right corner of the image.

   As you drag the mouse, you'll see an outline of a rectangle. When you release the mouse, however, the rectangle becomes a marquee (see Figure 4.1). Some people refer to this marquee as "marching ants" because of the movement.

FIGURE 4.1

A rectangular selection.

5. To clear the selection, either choose Selections, Select None or click anywhere outside the marquee area.

Try making a couple of selections, using the other shapes. If you forget to remove one selection before making another, the first selection disappears. Later in this hour you see how you can keep any current selection and either add to it or subtract from it. You also learn how to modify the selection.

The Freehand Tool

The second selection tool is the Freehand tool. You can use the Freehand tool to draw freehand selections. Doing so enables you to isolate irregular-shaped areas of an image. To see how this tool works, clear any other selections you still have active by choosing Selections, Select None. Select the Freehand tool and click and drag with it around the image as if you were drawing a doodle.

As you draw, you'll see a line being drawn by the tool. When you release the mouse button, the line turns into a marquee, and a straight line joins the starting and ending points (see Figure 4.2).

FIGURE 4.2

A Freehand tool selection.

4

The Freehand tool has several settings available from the Tool Options window, as well. You can draw freehand as you did in the previous example. You can also make point to point or Smart Edge selections.

Point to point enables you to draw polygonal selections. To do so, select the Freehand tool and set the Selection Type option to Point to Point in the Tool Options window.

Move the mouse cursor into the image and click. Move the mouse again and click once more. As you continue to move and click, you'll see lines being drawn between the points you click. To finish the selection, simply double-click. What you should end up with is a polygonal selection (see Figure 4.3).

FIGURE 4.3

A polygonal selection.

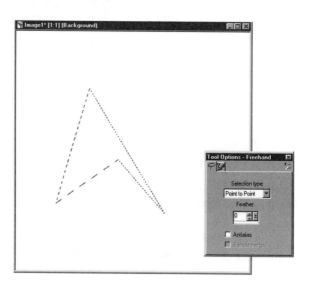

The third option for the Freehand tool is the Smart Edge. With the Smart Edge option, Paint Shop Pro can help you make difficult selections along the edges of contrasting areas. To see how this option works, clear any current selections you have by choosing Selections, Select None. Then follow these steps:

1. Select the Preset Shapes tool and set the Style to Filled in the Tool Options window. Draw a circle in the upper-left corner of the image. Change the shape to a rectangle and draw a rectangle below and to the right of the circle (see Figure 4.4).

   If you're not sure how to complete these steps, refer to Hour 3, "Creating Your First Image."

2. With the shapes drawn, select the Freehand tool and set the Selection Type option to Smart Edge in the Tool Options window.

3. Move the mouse cursor to a point along the bottom-left of the circle.

4. Click and drag the mouse toward the rectangle. As you drag, you'll see a bounding box (see Figure 4.5). When you get to the point where you're just overlapping the rectangle, as shown in Figure 4.5, release the mouse button.

FIGURE 4.4

A circle and a rectangle drawn with the Preset Shapes tool.

FIGURE 4.5

A bounding box highlights the edge that the Smart Edge is selecting.

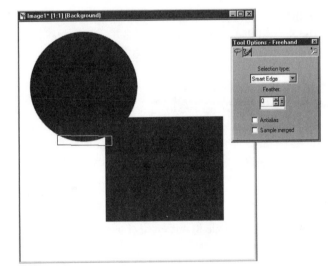

5. Click the mouse again without moving it and then move the mouse to the lower-left corner of the rectangle.

6. Double-click the mouse; you should end up with a selection like the one in Figure 4.6.

FIGURE 4.6

*A completed selection
along the lower left of
the circle and the rec-
tangle drawn with the
Smart Edge Freehand
tool.*

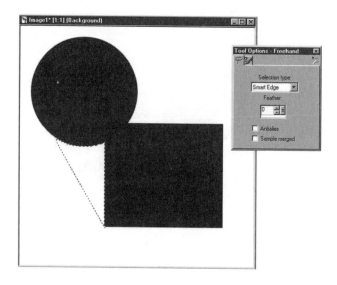

Although this powerful tool is a bit difficult to work with at first, it is worth learning about. The Smart Edge option of the Freehand tool enables you to make selections around areas that might otherwise be impossible.

The Magic Wand Tool

You can use the Magic Wand tool to select areas of an image based on the RGB value, hue, or brightness. You can set the Tolerance level to select more or fewer pixels, based on the relative values. The Magic Wand tool is quite easy to use. You simply select it, set the options, and click on a portion of the image that you want selected.

To try this tool, open a new 500×500 image at 72dpi with the background set to white and then follow these steps:

1. Draw a filled rectangle in one color (I used a pale blue) and a filled circle in a very different color (I used red). Make the shapes overlap, as shown in Figure 4.7.

2. Select the Magic Wand tool.

3. In the Tool Options window, set the Match Mode option to RGB and the Tolerance option to 15.

4. Click the circle. The circle should be outlined by a selection marquee. The marquee means that the circle has been selected. Nothing else has been selected, though, only the circle.

FIGURE 4.7

A circle and a rectangle drawn with the Shapes tool.

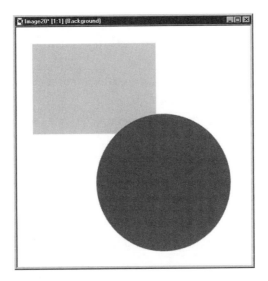

Only the circle is selected because it is red, the rectangle is blue, and the background is white. If the overlapping rectangle were a shade of red that closely matched the red of the circle and the Tolerance was high enough, the rectangle would be selected also.

The Magic Wand tool doesn't care about the shapes of the areas it's selecting; it bases its selections on the Match Mode and Tolerance settings.

> You may have noticed a Sample Merged check box in the Controls palette for some of the selection tools. When checked, this option allows selections to be made throughout all the layers of an image. I describe layers in depth in Hour 10, "Working Progressively with Layers."

You can also make and adjust selections using the Selections menu. From the Selections menu you can choose:

- Select All (Ctrl+A), which selects the entire image.
- Select None (Ctrl+D), which deselects the current selection.
- From Mask (Shift+Ctrl+S), which makes a selection based on the current mask (masks are covered in Hour 11, "Utilizing Masks for Precision").
- Invert (Shift+Ctrl+I), which inverts the selection. If you still have the circle selected from the previous section and you choose Selections, Invert, everything but the circle is selected. If you choose Selections, Invert again, the circle is reselected. Try it!

- Matting, which can remove fringes that sometimes appear around a selected area.
- Modify, which can modify a selection (I cover this in more depth in the next section).
- Hide Marquee (Shift+Ctrl+M), which hides the marquee while leaving the selection active.
- Convert to Seamless Pattern, which creates seamless tiles for repeating patterns and backgrounds.
- Promote to Layer (Shift+Ctrl+P), which turns a selection into a new layer.
- Load from Disk, which loads a saved selection from your disk drive.
- Load from Alpha Channel, which loads a selection that you saved as a channel.
- Save to Disk, which saves a selection to your hard drive.
- Save to Alpha Channel, which saves a selection in an Alpha channel.
- Float (Ctrl+F), which floats the selection and enables you to move it around the image while leaving the area below untouched. In other words, you create a duplicate of the selected area, which you can freely move around within the image.
- Defloat (Shift+Ctrl+F), which drops the selected area. When you defloat a selection, you can still move the selected area around, but it will be the actual area that moves and not a duplicate of the area. Of course, you can float the selection again.

I explore some of these options in the next section and use most of these tools extensively throughout the remainder of the book.

Editing Selections

Making a selection is not necessarily the end of your work. You can add to the selection, subtract from the selection, expand and contract the selection, and more.

Adding to a Selection

After making an initial selection, you can add to it. To see how this option works, open a new 500×500, 72dpi image with the background set to white. Then follow these steps:

1. Choose the Selection tool and, in the Tool Options window, set the Selection Type to Rectangle.
2. Draw a rectangular selection in the upper-left corner of the image.
3. Place the mouse in the lower-right corner of your selection (not too near the corner, though) and, while holding down the Shift key, draw another rectangular selection.

   You should now have an area selected that resembles two overlapping rectangles (see Figure 4.8). Interesting.

FIGURE 4.8

Adding to a selection.

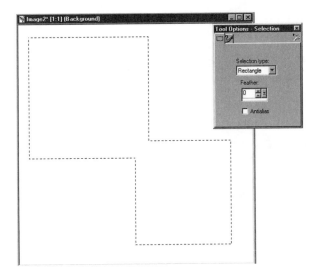

4. Try that again, but this time change the Selection Type to Circle and start somewhere near where the two rectangles overlap.

Hmmm…you should now have a fairly complex shape building up, consisting of a couple of rectangles and a circle (see Figure 4.9).

FIGURE 4.9

Adding more to a selection.

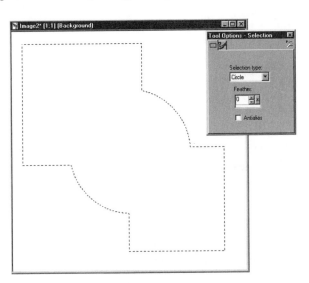

You may be getting the idea that you can actually create some fairly complex shapes using just the selection tools, and you are right. In addition to adding to a selection, you also can subtract from it, as discussed in the next section.

Subtracting From a Selection

To subtract from a selection, select a selection tool and, while holding down the Ctrl key, make a selection that overlaps the current selected area. To give it a try, follow these steps:

1. Select the Selection tool and, in the Tool Options window, set the Selection Type to Ellipse.

2. On the selection made in the previous section, move the mouse to the middle of the left side of the bottom rectangle.

3. Hold down the Ctrl key and draw an elliptical selection. When you release the mouse button, the ellipse will be cut from the selected area (see Figure 4.10).

FIGURE 4.10

Subtracting from a selection.

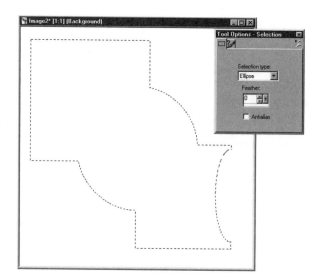

Wow! Can you see some of the possibilities? You can use any of the selection tools to add to and subtract from a selection. Using these tools together, you can make very sophisticated selections. These selections can be around existing portions of an image or, as you've just done, on new images.

To see how these techniques can be used, I subtracted a couple more shapes, filled the image with black, embossed it, and added a new layer in which I filled the selection with a wood texture. The result is shown in Figure 4.11.

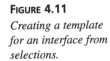

FIGURE 4.11

Creating a template for an interface from selections.

All of these techniques are covered throughout this book. In fact, by the end of this book, you'll be able to create interfaces like the one pictured in Figure 4.11.

4

Expanding and Contracting a Selection

Sometimes a selection is almost right, but not quite the way you want it. You may need to expand or contract the selection. To do so, choose Selections, Modify, Expand or Contract and then enter a value in the dialog box. This step expands or contracts the selection by the number of pixels you enter in the dialog box.

Growing a Selection

At other times, you may need to include a little more of an area that has similarly colored pixels. You can do so by choosing Selections, Modify, Grow Selection. This option is useful if you made a selection with the Magic Wand tool and, with the setting you chose for Tolerance, selected most of the area you needed. Instead of resetting Tolerance and trying again, Selections, Modify, Grow Selection is often enough to get those extra pixels.

Selecting Similar Areas

Growing a selection grabs adjoining pixels, but what if the area you want isn't contiguous to the area you've already selected? Simple. You can select areas in the image based on whether or not they are *similar* to the area already selected.

For example, say you have some black text on a white background, and you select the background area by clicking the background with the Magic Wand tool. Doing so selects the background area around the text, but it doesn't select the white area inside letters such as *O* and *P*.

No problem. Choose Selections, Modify, Select Similar. This selects the rest of the white areas (because the background that you selected is white), including those pesky areas inside of certain letters.

Loading and Saving Selections

What should you do if you've made a really complex selection and you'd like to save it? You should do just that. Save it!

With an area selected, you can save the selection in two ways. You can save the selection to disk, where it will remain until you need it later, or you can save it to an Alpha channel. *Alpha channels* are special areas that keep selections. These channels are saved along with the file and can be reloaded later.

To save a selection as a file, choose Selections, Save to Disk. A standard Windows Save dialog box enables you to name and save the selection.

To save a selection as an Alpha channel, choose Selections, Save to Alpha Channel. This option opens the Save To Alpha dialog box, in which you can choose the document with which to save the channel and see the available channels (see Figure 4.12).

Figure 4.12

Save To Alpha dialog box.

After you select the document and click OK, you can name the selection. This option is handy if you'll be saving multiple selections with a document. After you save a selection, you can reload it into the current image. The nice thing about saving a selection to disk is that you can also load the selection into other images, as well.

To load a selection that you saved as a file, choose Selections, Load From Disk. This step brings up a standard Windows Open dialog box, where you can browse for and open any selection you previously saved.

To load a selection that has been saved as an Alpha channel, choose Selections, Load From Alpha Channel. Doing so brings up the Load From Alpha dialog box, which enables you to choose the document and the channel you want to load (see Figure 4.13).

FIGURE 4.13

Load From Alpha dialog box.

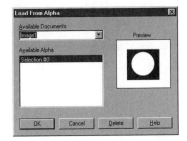

Note that the Load From Alpha dialog box shows a thumbnail preview of the selection, which comes in handy if you have saved several selections. Being able to choose the selection visually is a big plus if, like me, you're too lazy to name your selections as you save them.

Summary

Now that you've learned the basics of creating and editing selections, it's time to move on to Hour 5, "Working with Deformations."

Don't worry if you think that you haven't had much practice with selections. You'll be using selections throughout the remainder of the book, and you'll soon have made enough of them to be considered an expert.

Workshop

The Workshop contains a Q&A section to help answer the most commonly asked questions and quiz questions to help you solidify your understanding of the material covered.

Q&A

Q **I have black text on a white background. I want to make the background blue. When I use Selections, Modify, Select Similar and then apply the Paint Bucket color to the white background, the inside of the letters doesn't turn blue! Why not?**

A Even though the areas have been selected, the Paint Bucket tool might not fill in noncontiguous areas. To fill these extra areas, simply apply the Paint Bucket tool to them, as well.

Q **I sometimes find the marquee distracting. Can I hide it and still keep the selection active?**

A Yes, you can toggle the marquee on and off by choosing Selections, Hide Marquee or by pressing Shift+Ctrl+M. Hiding the marquee does not affect the selection.

Q **Can I save a selection with the image instead of as a separate image?**

A Yes. You can save a selection in an Alpha channel. The Alpha channel is saved along with the file if you save the image as a PSP, TIF, or PSD file.

Quiz

1. Name one way to make a selection from an image.

2. What does the Magic Wand tool do for you?

3. How can you add to a selection?

4. How can you subtract from a selection?

Answers

1. You can use the Selection tool to make a selection.

2. The Magic Wand tool enables you to make a selection based on the colors in an image.

3. You can add to a selection by holding down the Shift key while making subsequent selections.

4. You can subtract from a selection by holding down the Ctrl key while making subsequent selections.

HOUR 5

Working with Deformations

This hour introduces the following issues regarding working with deformations:

- Using the Deformation tool
- Resizing and rotating your images
- Adding perspective to images
- Using fades and fills

You can use menu choices to resize, rotate, add perspective to, and skew your images. Even better, though, you can apply these deformations to your images interactively. In this hour, you learn how to apply these effects simply by clicking and dragging the mouse.

Using the Deformation Tool

If you can believe it, all of these cool deformations can be applied with one single tool!
To see this tool in action, open a new 500×500, 72dpi image with a white background.
Then follow these steps:

1. In the Layer palette, click the Create Layer icon to add a new layer over the background layer. I know we haven't covered layers yet, but you don't really need to know how they work at this point.

2. In the Layer Properties dialog box, click OK.

3. Select the Text tool and click the image.

4. In the Text Entry dialog box, enter some text. The text you enter doesn't really matter; it could be your name, for example. Make sure that the size is large and that the Antialias and Floating check boxes are checked.

5. Click the Color button and choose a color from the Color dialog box. I'm using black so that the results will be easy to see in black and white. You can use any font and style you like (see Figure 5.1).

FIGURE 5.1

The Text Entry dialog box.

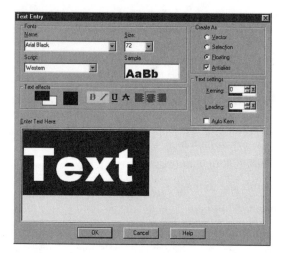

6. Click OK to place the text as a new floating selection over the new layer (see Figure 5.2).

FIGURE 5.2
Text as a floating selection over a new layer.

7. Select the Mover tool and use it to grab the text and move it to the center of the image.

8. Select the Deformation tool. When you do, you'll notice a change in your image. A bounding box is added, and this bounding box has several control handles (see Figure 5.3).

FIGURE 5.3
The Deformation tool's bounding box and control handles with the Layer palette shown.

5

9. As you move the mouse over the bounding box and the different control handles, the mouse pointer changes, too.

If you move the mouse inside the bounding box away from any of the control handles, the pointer changes to a cross with an arrowhead at each end. This pointer enables you to move the selection along with the bounding box. Try it. Move the text around the image.

As you move the pointer, the bounding box follows; when you release the mouse button, the text snaps back inside the bounding box.

10. Move the pointer over one of the corner or the side handles.

As you move over a side handle, the mouse pointer becomes a two-headed arrow with a small rectangle above it. As you move the pointer over a corner handle, the mouse becomes a four-headed arrow (different from the four-headed arrow described previously) with a small rectangle over it.

Each type of control handle enables you to resize the bounding box, and the selection contained within it, interactively:

- With the side handles, you can adjust the width and height separately.
- With the corner handles, you can adjust the width and height of the selection simultaneously.

Try it. Move the mouse pointer over the one of the handles and click and drag it. As you do, you'll see the bounding box change shape. When you release the mouse button, the text resizes so that it fits into the box again.

If the resizing moves the text from the center of the image, just grab the text (or the bounding box, actually) and move it back into position (see Figure 5.4).

FIGURE 5.4

Text enlarged with the Deformation tool.

Rotating Text

With the text resized, try rotating it. Simply grab the right side of the center control handle and give it a spin. When you move the pointer over the control handle box, the mouse becomes a crosshair in the box and two circular arrows appear.

When you get it into position, double-click the mouse and, when the dialog box pops up, choose Yes to apply the deformation. You should have something similar to Figure 5.5.

FIGURE 5.5

Text rotated with the Deformation tool.

Using the Perspective, Shear, and Distort Options

In this section, I use a practical application of the Deformation tool to demonstrate the Perspective, Shear, and Distort options. Follow these steps:

1. Open a new 500×500, 72dpi image with the background set to white.
2. Create a new layer by clicking the New Layer icon at the bottom of the Layer palette.
3. Set the foreground color to a mid-to-dark gray.
4. Select the Text tool and add some text as you did in the preceding example.
5. Choose Image, Flip to flip the text (see Figure 5.6).

5

FIGURE 5.6

Text flipped with Image, Flip.

6. Select the Deformation tool and move the text to the right a little.
7. Grab the middle control handle along the bottom of the bounding box and drag down to resize the text vertically (see Figure 5.7).

FIGURE 5.7

Text resized with the Deformation tool.

8. Hold down the Ctrl key and drag the bottom-left corner down and out so that the bottom of the text gets larger while the top remains the same (see Figure 5.8). This is how you can add perspective to an image. If the text seems to be running off the right side of the image, just drag the text toward the center with the mouse.

FIGURE 5.8

Perspective added with the Deformation tool.

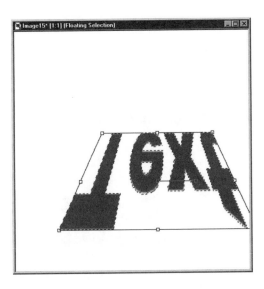

9. Add a little shear to the text by holding down the Shift key while you drag any of the corners. I've sheared both bottom corners to the right a little (see Figure 5.9).

FIGURE 5.9

Shear added with the Deformation tool.

5

10. With the deformations complete, double-click within the bounding box and click OK in the dialog box that appears. Choose Selections, Select None to deselect the text.

11. Select the Text tool and enter the same text with the same size and font settings that you used for the deformed text. Make sure that you choose a color other than white or the color you used for the deformed text.

12. Position the text directly over the deformed text, as shown in Figure 5.10.

FIGURE 5.10

Text with a perspective shadow.

Amazing! You've just created a much sought-after effect. You've created text with a perspective shadow.

Adding a Shadow Effect

If you're daring enough, you can finish up this hour by making the shadow seem a little more realistic. To do so, you'll have to employ a technique from Hour 3, "Creating Your First Image," and use a new technique as well. Follow these steps:

1. Access the Command History command and back up to the point just before you added the new text. You should be at the point where you just finished deforming the text.

2. Click the foreground color swatch and set the color to a medium gray.

3. If the current background color as seen in the background color swatch is not white, use the Dropper tool to set it to white. To do so, right-click on the background of the image. Alternately, you can click the background color swatch and select white from the Color dialog box.

4. Select the Flood Fill tool.

5. In the Tool Options window, click the Flood Fill tab (it's the first tab).

6. Set Fill Style to Linear Gradient, set Match Mode to None, and click the Flood Fill Options tab (it's the second tab).

7. In the Gradient rollup, choose Foreground-Background and set the angle to 180 degrees (see Figure 5.11).

FIGURE 5.11

The Tool Options window, showing the Gradient Fill options.

8. Click the small trashcan icon (it's the second icon from the left in the upper-left corner of the palette) in the Layer palette to remove the floating selection layer. This will make the gradient fill easier to apply. If you don't remove the floating layer, the antialiasing will prevent the gradient from filling properly, and there will be a black matting effect around the letters.

9. Click anywhere in the selected text to fill it with the gradient. The letters should get paler as they get closer to the bottom of the image.

10. Use the Text tool to add the same text as before.

11. Maneuver the text into place over the perspective shadow (see Figure 5.12).

FIGURE 5.12

Text with fading perspective shadow.

5

Wow! Now that is amazing! I consider this to be a fairly advanced technique, and here you've done it after only a few hours with the program.

Some other deformations are available under the Image, Deformations menu. I cover these later, though, in Hour 15 "Applying Filters."

Summary

Although this hour may have seemed long, it wasn't really. It's just that you covered quite a bit, even if it was with only one tool. You've just created a really cool image and some text. Not bad for an hour's work.

I'd say that you're ready to head on to the next hour, where you learn how to use the drawing tools.

Workshop

The Workshop contains a question and answer section to help answer the most commonly asked questions and quiz questions to help you solidify your understanding of the material covered.

Q&A

Q How do I know when I can apply a certain deformation, such as rotating the object?

A The mouse pointer changes as you move it over the various control handles. These changes signify when a deformation can be applied.

Q I enlarged an object using the Deformation tool and part of it is off the image window. How do I get it back?

A If the Deformation tool is still active, you can simply click and drag the object back to the center of the image. If you've applied the deformation, you can reactivate the Deformation tool and drag the object back into view.

Q How do I apply a deformation once I'm done?

A You can either click the Apply button in the Tool Options window or double-click the image and answer Yes in the dialog box that pops up.

Quiz

1. Explain how you enlarge a selection using the Deformation tool.

2. What is a bounding box? What can it help you do in relation to the Deformation tool?

3. How do you rotate an image with the Deformation tool?

4. How do you add perspective with the Deformation tool?

Answers

1. You can enlarge an object with the Deformation tool by dragging the middle control handles. The middle control handles are located at the center of the top, sides, and bottom of the bounding box.

2. The bounding box appears around an object when you activate the Deformation tool. It outlines the object that the deformations will affect.

3. You click and drag the handle near the middle of the bounding box. As you grab this control handle, the mouse pointer changes to a pair of semicircular curves with arrows at the ends.

4. You can add perspective by holding down the Ctrl key and clicking and dragging one of the corner control handles.

5

Hour 6

Drawing Tools and Techniques

Paint Shop Pro provides a number of drawing tools. For example, you can use the Draw tool to draw lines of varying thickness, and you can use the various Preset Shapes tools to draw different shapes, such as rectangles and circles.

New in version 6, the drawing tools have vector capabilities. I'll introduce these capabilities in this hour and cover them fully in Hour 13, "Working with Flexible Vector Tools."

This hour introduces the following issues regarding drawing tools and techniques:

- Using the drawing tool options
- Drawing shapes
- Drawing normal lines
- Drawing Bezier lines

The Drawing Tools and Their Options

Like other tools, the Draw and Preset Shapes tools have options that you can set to change their behavior. All line styles and shapes can be created as either vectors or bitmaps. In this hour I describe the bitmap behavior.

The Draw tool has four styles. You can draw Single lines that are straight and go from one point on your image to another; Bezier curves, which can be manipulated as vectors, even with the Create as Vector box unchecked; Freehand curves, which cannot be changed after you've drawn them (unless you create them as vectors); and Drawing lines, which are the most flexible and behave like Bezier curves on steroids. In this hour I'll cover Single lines and Freehand curves and touch on Bezier curves. Bezier curves and Drawing curves will be covered in more depth in Hour 13.

> Even if you're not totally new to digital graphics, you may not recognize terms such as Bezier and vector. Bezier refers to a type of curve that is drawn on your computer screen using a mathematical formula developed by a French mathematician named Bézier (hence the term Bezier curve). Vectors refer to lines and curves saved in computer memory as mathematical formulas rather than as bitmaps. A bitmap is simply an array (much like a spreadsheet, except that all of the cells are the same size) of pixels, each containing its own color information.

The Preset Shapes tool is near the very bottom of the Tool palette, and the Draw tool is directly above the Preset Shapes tool. The Preset Shapes Tool icon has a small blue rectangle and a red ellipse on it, and the Draw Tool icon has a curve and a small pencil on it.

Besides having four styles of line tools to choose from, you also can set the width of the lines and choose aliased or antialiased. You also have the option of setting the tracking for Freehand curves, which determines how closely a curve follows the mouse as you draw it. For all lines you can set the Cap, which determines how the end of the line will be drawn; the Miter, which determines how lines are joined; and the Miter Limit, which determines the length of miter joins.

With version 6, you also can choose whether lines will be Stroked (outlined), Filled, or both. These options can be set in the Tool Options window.

The Preset Shapes tool has a couple of options more than the Draw tool. You can choose from the following shapes:

- Rectangles
- Squares
- Rounded-rectangles
- Rounded-squares
- Ellipses
- Circles
- Triangles
- Pentagons
- Hexagons
- Octagons
- Two different star shapes
- Three different arrow shapes

The shape can be filled in the current foreground color or simply stroked (outlined). You can choose the thickness of the stroke, and you can choose to have the shapes aliased or antialiased. In addition, all shapes can be drawn as bitmaps or vectors.

The best way to see how these options work is to roll up your sleeves and do a little drawing, so let's get started.

Drawing Shapes

To get a feeling for the Preset Shapes tool, open a new 500×500 image with the resolution set to 72 pixels per inch, the background color set to white, and the image type set to 16.7 million colors. Then follow these steps:

1. Set the foreground color to anything but white and select the Preset Shapes tool.

2. If the Tool Options window is not visible, turn it on by clicking the Toggle Tool Options Window icon in the toolbar or by choosing View, Toolbars and placing a check mark next to the Tool Options Window option in the Toolbars dialog box.

   The Tool Options window (see Figure 6.1) is where you can set the options that are available for the Preset Shapes tool. This assumes that you've selected the Preset Shapes tool.

3. Set Shape to Circle, Style to Filled, ignore Line Width for the moment, and place a check mark in the Antialias check box. Be sure that the Create as Vector option is unchecked, for now.

6

FIGURE 6.1

The Tool Options window.

4. Click and drag the mouse anywhere in your image, and you'll notice a circular outline being drawn.
5. Move the mouse until you get a good-size circle and then release the mouse. When you release the mouse, a filled circle appears where the outline was (see Figure 6.2).

FIGURE 6.2

Drawing a circle.

You'll notice that the circular shape is drawn outward from the center. Knowing this trick makes it easy to place your circles. How? You can place your cursor anywhere on the image by viewing the current mouse coordinates. In the bottom-left corner of the main Paint Shop Pro window is a set of numbers. These numbers are the current x and y coordinates of the mouse pointer.

To see how these coordinates work, move the mouse pointer onto the image and then look at the numbers as you move the mouse around the image window. The numbers constantly change as you move the mouse. You can use these numbers as a guide for placing the mouse pointer anywhere on your image.

To see how this technique works, follow these steps to draw a bull's eye:

1. Choose Edit, Undo to undo the last circle that you drew.

2. Set the foreground color to black by moving the mouse pointer over the black area of the main color swatch and clicking or, if you have trouble setting the color this way, click the foreground color swatch to bring up the Color dialog box and set the color to black.

3. In the Color dialog box (see Figure 6.3), you can choose the color directly from the color grid if the color you want is there. You can also choose the color from the color wheel (and fine-tune it in with the square inside the wheel), or you can enter the exact RGB values for the color. The RGB values for black are 0, 0, 0.

FIGURE 6.3

The Color dialog box.

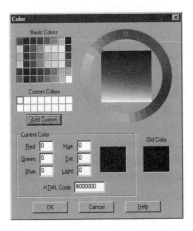

4. With the foreground color set to black, set the background color to red by clicking the background color swatch and choosing red from the Color dialog box. The reason to set the two colors is that you can easily switch between them by clicking the small two-headed arrow to the lower-left of the foreground and background color swatches. This technique makes it easy to use two colors without going back to the Color dialog box or guesstimating the colors with the main color swatch.

5. If you're not comfortable moving the mouse into position using the coordinates, you can turn on the grid. To do so, choose View, Grid. This action places a grid over the entire image (see Figure 6.4).

6. The default setting for the grid has a line every 10 pixels. You can change this setting to suit your needs for a particular image. To change the spacing of the grid, choose File, Preferences, General Program Preferences.

6

FIGURE 6.4

The image window with the grid visible.

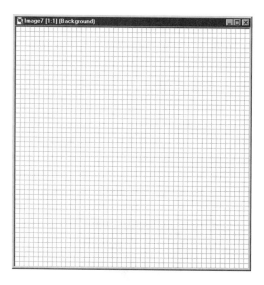

7. In the Paint Shop Pro Preferences dialog box, click the Rulers and Units tab to bring up the dialog box that enables you to set the grid preferences (see Figure 6.5).

FIGURE 6.5

The Paint Shop Pro Preferences dialog box.

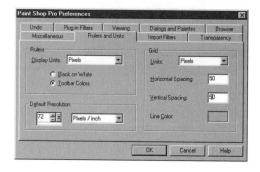

8. Change both the Horizontal and Vertical Spacing to 50 and click OK. This gives you a more workable setting for drawing the bull's eye.

9. If you've chosen to go with the coordinates method, place the mouse pointer at the coordinate 250,250 (the center of the image).

   If you're using the grid, move the mouse pointer into the center of the image where the gridlines cross.

10. Click and drag the mouse until you get a circle that's about 300 pixels in diameter. You can see the diameter of the circle in the lower-left corner of the main window as you drag the mouse.

Along with the current coordinates, you get additional information in this portion of the main window. This information is very helpful when drawing or painting.

The additional information depends on the particular tool you're using. For example, if you're using the Preset Shapes tool to draw a rectangle, you will see the coordinates of the upper-left corner and the lower-right corner as well as the width and height of the rectangle. If you're using the Draw tool to draw a line, you'll see the starting and ending coordinates as well as the angle of the line.

11. Swap the foreground and background colors by clicking the small two-headed arrow just below and to the left of the foreground and background color swatches.

12. Place the mouse back at the center of the image and draw another circle. Make this circle about 250 pixels in diameter. You should now have two concentric circles (see Figure 6.6).

FIGURE 6.6
Partially completed bull's eye.

13. Swap the foreground and background colors again and draw a third circle.

You can save a few mouse clicks when drawing your circles for the bull's eye. To do so, simply draw the circles in the background color by clicking and dragging with the right mouse button. This great shortcut works in other situations as well. Click and drag with the left (primary) mouse button to draw with the foreground color; do so with the right (secondary) mouse button to draw with the background color.

6

14. Continue swapping the foreground and background colors and drawing smaller and smaller circles until the image contains five concentric circles (see Figure 6.7).

Figure 6.7

The completed bull's eye, created with the Preset Shapes tool.

15. Save this image so that you can load it later. To save the image, choose File, Save. Give the image a name (`bullseye.psp` will do nicely) and choose a folder to store it in. I often save files in a temporary folder if I think I'll need them to complete a drawing at a later sitting.

You might want to open a new file at this point and explore the other shapes that you can create with the Preset Shapes tool. Try using different colors and drawing stroked (outlined) shapes as well as filled shapes. Use the grid to help you place various shapes, and try to draw something by combining the different shapes, colors, fills, and strokes (outlines).

Note how the rectangular and square shapes are drawn from a corner outward, unlike the circular and elliptical shapes, which are drawn from the center outward.

Drawing Lines

You can use the Draw tool to draw straight lines and curved lines. You can set the width of the line and whether the line is antialiased in the Tool Options window. As mentioned earlier, I'll cover vector lines in Hour 13.

The Single Line Tool

As an exercise, and to get some hands-on experience with the Draw tool, you can add an arrow to the bull's eye from the previous exercise.

Open the bull's eye file that you saved and then follow these steps:

1. Set the foreground color to a shade of blue or some color other than the black and red you used for the rings of the bull's eye.

2. Select the Draw tool and, in the Tool Options window, set the Line Type to Single Line and the Width to 12, and place a check mark in the Antialias check box. Make sure the Create as vector option is unchecked. For now, you can ignore the settings for Curve Tracking, Cap, Join, and Miter Limit. These options are accessible under the Draw Options (second) tab of the Tool Options window with the Draw tool selected.

3. Place the mouse pointer near the center of the bull's eye. Click and drag toward the upper-right corner of the image until the line goes past the outer circle of the bull's eye (see Figure 6.8).

FIGURE 6.8

Adding an arrow to the bull's eye with the Draw tool.

4. Set the Line tool's Width to 2 and draw a smaller line perpendicular to the first line and across the first line about a third of the way up from the center of the bull's eye (see Figure 6.9).

5. Draw two more lines that extend toward the center of the bull's eye, starting at the ends of the cross line (see Figure 6.10).

6

FIGURE **6.9**
*Creating an arrow-
head at the end of
the line.*

FIGURE **6.10**
*Completing the
arrowhead lines.*

6. You may want to zoom in to help with the placement of the lines. To do so, select the Zoom tool and click near the area that you're working on, in this case the center of the image. When you've zoomed in enough, reselect the Line tool and draw the lines.

7. To fill in the arrowhead, select the Flood Fill tool. In the Controls palette, set Fill Style to Solid Color, Match Mode to RGB, Tolerance to about 10, and Opacity to 100.

8. Click inside the areas of the arrowhead where the circles are showing through.

9. If the color leaks out to fill other parts of the drawing, choose Edit, Undo and set Tolerance to a lower value.

10. The fill doesn't fill in the areas completely because of the antialiased lines that make up both the circles and the arrowhead (see Figure 6.11).

FIGURE **6.11**

The nearly completed arrowhead, needing some touchups.

To fix this small problem, you can fill in the areas by hand. Select the Paint Brushes tool and, in the Tool Options window, select the Paint Brush tab.

11. Set Shape to Round, Size to 1 or 2, Opacity to 100, Hardness to 0, and Density to 100; ignore the Step setting for now.

12. Zoom in as much as you need to and fill in the areas that didn't get color from the Flood Fill tool.

Your final image should resemble Figure 6.12.

FIGURE **6.12**

The final bull's eye image, complete with arrow.

A while back, I created a banner to advertise a marketing group's Web site, starting with an image very similar to the bull's eye. With the addition of a little text and a couple of special effects, you can use this image as a banner for your Web site.

The Bezier Curve Line Tool

The Bezier Curve Line tool is a little harder to understand and control than the Single Line tool. However, the Bezier Curve tool is a powerful addition to Paint Shop Pro and enables you to draw smooth curves that you couldn't draw with the older versions (previous to version 5) of this product. Getting used to this tool will also give you a head start on understanding the vector tools later.

6

Again, the best way to learn how to use this tool is to jump right in and draw some curves. Follow these steps:

1. Open a new 500×500 image with the resolution set to 72 pixels per inch, the background color set to white, and the image type set to 16.7 million colors.

2. Select the Draw tool and, in the Tool Options window, set Line Type to Bezier Curve and Width to 10 and choose Stroked for the style. Place a check mark in the Antialias check box and make sure that the Create as vector and Close path options are unchecked. You can turn the grid on or off for this exercise.

   In Figure 6.13, I've placed several crosses with numbers to help you follow along as I show you how to draw your first Bezier curve.

FIGURE 6.13

Several crosses to help with your first Bezier curve.

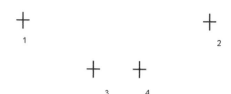

3. The Bezier curve Line tool requires a few mouse clicks (and a little magic) to draw your curve. Place your mouse pointer on your image at approximately the position of the first cross in Figure 6.13.

   Click and drag the mouse to a point that's about where I've placed the second cross in Figure 6.13 and release the mouse button.

4. Move the mouse pointer to about where I've drawn the third cross and click the mouse button. A control handle should appear. Ignore it for the moment, move the mouse a little to the right (near where I've placed the fourth cross), and click once more. Don't release the mouse yet. A second control handle should appear (see Figure 6.14).

The control handles, although a little difficult to see on the printed page and with my crosses in the way, should be readily visible as straight red lines with circular ends. It's control handles such as these that you'll use to manipulate vector objects in Hour 13.

FIGURE 6.14

Drawing a smooth Bezier curve with the Line tool.

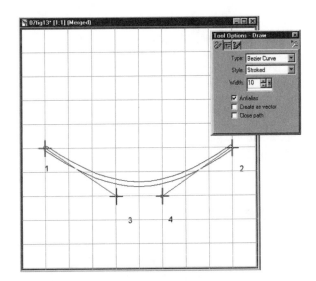

5. Now move the mouse around without releasing the button. You should see the curve bend and twist as you move the mouse around.

   After you release the mouse, the curve will be drawn in the width you specified in the Tool Options window (see Figure 6.15). Be sure to click near the third and fourth crosses so that your curve resembles the one in Figure 6.15.

FIGURE 6.15

A smooth Bezier curve drawn with the Line tool.

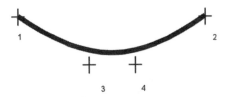

Points 1 and 2 are the endpoints of the curve, and points 3 and 4 are where the control handles will appear. You can use this method to create semicircular curves. In fact, you can manipulate the first control handle as well as the second. Give it a try!

To create S curves, click once in the third position and then click again above and to the right or left of the middle of the first two points.

6

You can draw lines in either the current foreground color or the current background color. To draw in the foreground color, click and drag with the primary mouse button. To draw in the current background color, use the right mouse button.

You should spend some time learning how this tool works. It is a powerful addition to Paint Shop Pro, and learning how to use it will give you an edge over other Paint Shop Pro artists. Figure 6.16 shows some curves drawn with the Bezier Line tool.

FIGURE 6.16

Some S-shape and semicircular curves drawn with the Bezier Curve tool.

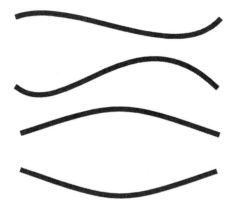

Summary

In this hour, you learned how to draw shapes, lines, and curves. You saw how to use the coordinates and other information displayed at the lower-left corner of the main window, and you learned how to use the grid feature and how to set its options.

You're about ready to move on to the next hour, where you'll learn how to use the painting tools.

Workshop

The Workshop contains a question and answer section to help answer the most commonly asked questions and quiz questions to help you solidify your understanding of the material covered.

Q&A

Q Is it possible to draw triangles with the Preset Shapes tool?

A Yes. Starting with version 6, there are many shapes now available with the Preset Shapes tool, including triangles.

Q Can I change the color of the lines that make up the grid?

A Yes. In the Paint Shop Pro Preferences dialog box (choose File, Preferences, General Program Preferences) under the Rulers and Units tab, you can set the line spacing and the color of the grid lines.

Q Is it possible to determine the angle of the line that I'm drawing with the Draw tool?

A Yes. At the lower-left corner of the screen, this information is available as you're using the drawing tools. Note that straight up is 0 degrees and that the angle increases as you go clockwise.

Q Can I use the Preset Shapes tool to create complex shapes other than rectangles, squares, ellipses, and circles?

A Yes, you can create complex shapes by drawing several simpler shapes on top of each other. By combining shapes and colors, you can draw almost anything.

Quiz

1. Which basic shapes are available with the Preset Shapes tool?
2. How do you draw a line or a shape in the current background color?
3. How many different types of curves can be drawn with the Bezier Curve tool?
4. How do you draw a line with the Draw tool?

Answers

1. The Preset Shapes tool provides these basic shape: ellipse, circle, and more.
2. Click and drag the mouse while holding down the secondary mouse button.
3. Two. You can draw semicircular and S-shape curves with the Bezier Line tool.
4. Click and drag from where you want the line to begin to where you want the line to end.

6

HOUR 7

Painting Tools and Techniques

This hour introduces the following issues regarding Paint Shop Pro's painting tools:

- Painting and drawing with the Paint Brush tool
- Using the Airbrush tool
- Using the Flood Fill tool
- Creating and editing multicolored gradients
- Working with the Clone Brush tool

Paint Shop Pro provides a number of painting tools: the Paint Brush, the Airbrush, the Flood Fill, and the Clone Brush tools. In this hour, you learn how to use these tools effectively.

Some readers may consider the Picture Tube a painting tool, and rightly so. However, the Picture Tube is complex enough to deserve its own hour. You learn all about the Picture Tube tool in Hour 14, "Using and Creating Picture Tubes."

Painting and Drawing with the Paint Brush Tool

The Paint Brush tool (the tenth tool from the top in the Tool palette; it looks like a small paint brush) enables you to draw and paint freehand lines with a variety of brushes and textures. After selecting the Paint Brush tool, you can set the various options in the Tool Options window (see Figure 7.1).

Using the Tool Controls

FIGURE 7.1

The Tool Options window, showing the controls for the Paint Brush tool.

From within the Tool Options window, under the Paint Brush tab (the leftmost tab), you can set the shape and the brush type (this option is accessible under a small icon containing a brush and a small black triangle placed in the upper-right corner of the Tool Options window). You can also set the size, opacity, hardness, density, and step. Clicking the Brush Types icon opens a pull-down menu from which you can select the brush type.

Under the Paint Brush Options tab (the second tab from the left), you can select a texture to be used with the brush.

To see how these settings work, open a new 500×500 image with the resolution set to 72 pixels per inch, the background color set to white, and the image type set to 16.7 million colors. Then follow these steps:

1. Select the Paint Brush tool.

2. Set the foreground color to a pale blue.

3. In the Tool Options window, set Shape to Round, the brush options to Normal, Size to 13, Opacity to 100, Hardness to 50, Density to 100, and Step to 25. Some of these settings are the defaults and may not need to be set.

4. Click and drag in the image to draw a line (see Figure 7.2).

FIGURE 7.2

Drawing a line with the Paint Brush tool.

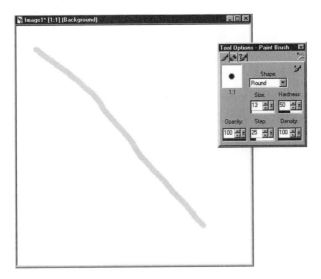

5. Increase the Size setting to 45 and decrease the Hardness setting to 20. If you have trouble getting these exact numbers by moving the slider, don't worry about it. Either get as close as you can or click in the small window to the right of the slider and enter the value.

6. Draw another line. Compared to the first line, the new line is larger and its edges are softer (see Figure 7.3).

FIGURE 7.3

Drawing a larger, softer line with the Paint Brush tool.

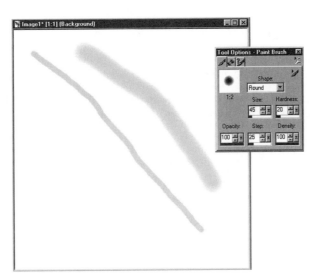

7

7. Set the foreground color to a bright yellow and change the brush option so that the brush is a pencil. To do so, click the Brush Types icon and choose Pencil from the drop-down menu.

8. Set Opacity to about 30 and then draw another line that passes over the first two.

The mark made by the pencil is different from the mark made by the brush. In addition, you can see the first two lines through the third line (see Figure 7.4).

FIGURE 7.4

Drawing a third line with the Paint Brush tool set to a pencil and with a lower opacity.

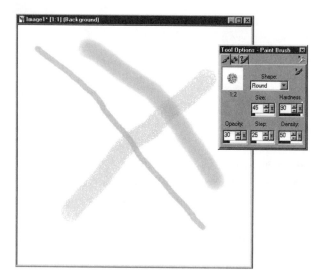

Try drawing some lines with the other options. Each is a different brush shape.

Try varying the opacity and the color that you're using. If you'd like to draw with the background color, you can do so by clicking and dragging with the right mouse button.

When you've drawn a few lines, you can try the Density control. Density controls how much paint the brush lays down. The higher the density, the more paint is laid down. To see how the Density setting controls the output, follow these steps:

1. Select the Paintbrush option; the Density setting should move to 100.

2. Drag the Density slider to about 50, and you'll notice that the brush preview starts to resemble the Pencil brush.

3. Draw a line at this setting and compare it to one of the lines you drew with the Pencil option. The lines are quite similar.

Changing the various settings gives you quite a bit of control over the Paint Brush tool.

The Step setting is a bit more mysterious than the other settings. It works in combination with a brush's diameter. The "step" is a percentage of the diameter of the brush. For example, with the brush Size set to 30 and the Step set to 30, the brush operates at 100 percent and draws a definite line (because 30 is 100 percent of 30).

With Size set to 30 and Step set to 60, the brush paints only 50 percent of the time (because 30 is 50 percent of 60; see Figure 7.5).

FIGURE 7.5

The left line shows the Step option at 100 percent (both Size and Step set to 30), and the right line shows the Step option at 50 percent (Size set to 30 and Step set to 60).

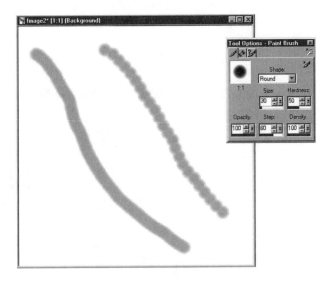

As you increase Step relative to the brush size, less paint is used.

Play around with the Size and Step settings until you're comfortable with them.

Custom Brush Tips

You've seen how the various controls work, and you've used several brush tips. You can also use custom brushes to create new effects.

Click the Brush Options icon and, from the pull-down menu, choose Custom. Use the Custom Brush dialog box to select a custom brush (see Figure 7.6).

Choose one of the brushes and click and drag within the image. The pattern you've chosen is used as a brush for the lines you're drawing.

7

FIGURE 7.6

*The Custom Brush
dialog box.*

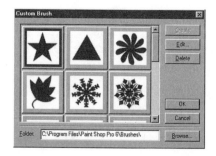

Figure 7.7 shows some paint strokes drawn with the leaf brush in various colors.

FIGURE 7.7

*The Custom Brush
tool, used to draw
some leaves in
different colors.*

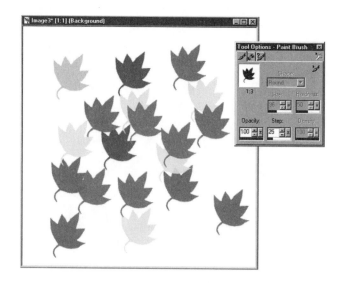

You may notice that some of the settings for the Paint Brush tool are grayed out in the Controls palette. These tools are not available for use with this particular brush.

Practice using some of the brushes. When you're done, you can set the Paint Brush tool back to Normal or to one of the other options.

Using Different Textures

Along with the different tips and other settings, you can choose from several textures.

You can choose a texture from the Tool Options window by clicking the Paint Brush Options tab (it's the second tab in the Tool Options window) and choosing from the pull-down menu. Choices include Sidewalk, Marble, Parchment, Fruit Peel, Construction Paper, Ocean, Lava, Mist, Fog, and many more.

To see how the textures work, click the Tool Controls tab and choose a texture. When you draw or paint, the texture appears under your brush strokes. In Figure 7.8, the Woodgrain texture has been applied with a very wide Normal brush.

FIGURE 7.8

Woodgrain texture applied with a wide brush set to Normal.

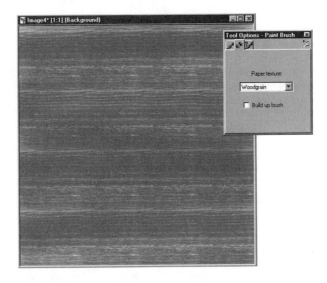

Using the Airbrush Tool

The Airbrush tool allows paint to build up if you stay in one place for a moment. Note that the paint buildup isn't a selectable option; rather, it is the behavior of the Airbrush tool. In other respects, the Airbrush tool acts much like the other Paint Brush tools. You can still change the various options and settings in the Tool Options window, and you can still use textures.

To see how the airbrush effect works, select the Airbrush tool (the sixth icon from the bottom in the Tool palette; it looks like a spray can) and draw a few lines, stopping every so often. When you stop, keep the mouse button down; you'll notice that the paint builds up. This effect is more noticeable with Opacity set fairly low. Even then, the brush will build up paint until it completely covers whatever is beneath it.

Other than that, the Airbrush tool acts much like the other Paint Brush tools. You can still change the various options and settings in the Tool Options window, and you can still use the textures.

7

Using the Flood Fill Tool

You can use the Flood Fill tool (the fifth icon from the bottom of the Tool palette; it looks like a tilted paint can) to fill areas of an image with either a color, a gradient, or a pattern.

Filling an Area with a Solid Color

To fill an area with a solid color, simply set the foreground or background color to the color you want to use and click within the area you want to fill. Clicking with the left mouse button fills with the foreground color, and clicking with the right mouse button fills with the background color.

Several factors determine how the Flood Fill tool fills an area. If you've made a selection and you click within the selected area, the Flood Fill tool fills that area. If you've made a selection and you click outside the selection, even if you've chosen to hide the selection marquee, the Flood Fill tool has no effect.

You can also click in an area that already contains a certain color. The Flood Fill tool will then fill the area that contains that color. It may also fill surrounding areas, depending on the settings that you've chosen. Changing the Tolerance option, for example, determines how much of an area is filled. Higher Tolerance allows more of an area to be filled, whereas a lower Tolerance setting constrains the fill to areas that are similar in color or exactly the same color as where you initially click. You can change the Tolerance setting in the Tool Options window under the Flood Fill (first) tab.

Match Mode also affects how an area is filled. Selecting RGB compares neighboring pixels' RGB values, selecting Hue compares neighboring pixels' hues, selecting Brightness compares neighboring pixels' brightness values, and selecting None fills the entire area, regardless of any settings. You can change the Match Mode setting in the Tool Options window under the Flood Fill (first) tab. Once a comparison has been made according to Match Mode, a pixel will be filled according to the Tolerance setting.

You can also choose the Flood Fill tool's Opacity. A higher value makes the fill more opaque, and a lower value makes the fill more transparent. The Sample Merged option has to do with layers; I cover that option in Hour 10, "Working Progressively with Layers."

Finally, you can set the options for each Fill style by clicking the Flood Fill Options (second) tab. Each Fill style has different options associated with it. For example, you can set the direction of a Linear Gradient fill.

Filling with a Gradient

In addition to filling an area with a solid color, you can fill it with a gradient. A *gradient* is a blend from one color to another or several colors blended together, as in a multi-colored gradient, which I discuss in the next section.

Figure 7.9 shows the gradient styles that are available in Paint Shop Pro.

FIGURE **7.9**

Paint Shop Pro has several gradient fill styles.

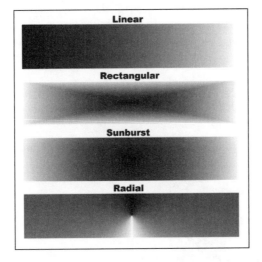

You can set the angle for the Linear gradient, and you can set the horizontal and vertical starting points for the Rectangular, Sunburst, and Radial gradients. To access these options, click the second tab in the Tool Options window after selecting one of the gradient styles.

I demonstrate some of the uses for gradients in later chapters. For now, you can experiment with this setting to see the effect it has on the gradient.

Creating and Editing Multicolored Gradients

Starting with version 6, Paint Shop Pro enables you to edit, create, save, and load multicolored gradients. This is a very powerful tool that can give you amazing effects with a couple of mouse clicks.

The button bar in Figure 7.10 was created using the built-in Metallic 2 gradient, which is a grayscale gradient that uses various shades of gray and white to achieve a metallic effect.

7

FIGURE 7.10

A metallic button bar created using a multi-colored Gradient fill.

To create the button bar, I filled a rectangular selection with the gradient set to Linear at an angle of 0 degrees. I then filled three more selections with the same gradient at an angle of 180 degrees. All that was left was to add some shadows, highlights (done using black and white lines drawn with the Draw tool), and the text. All of these techniques will be explored throughout the remainder of the book. The following steps illustrate how to create an image like the one shown in Figure 7.10:

1. Select the Flood Fill tool.

2. Set Fill Style to one of the gradients. Doing so will activate the second tab in the Tool Options window.

3. Click the tab to bring up the Gradient window (see Figure 7.11).

FIGURE 7.11

The Gradient window in the Tool Options window.

4. Choose one of the gradients that ship with Paint Shop Pro 6 by clicking the downward-facing arrow to the right of the Gradient space to activate the drop-down menu.

If you'd like to create your own gradient, follow these steps:

1. From the Gradient Editor dialog box (see Figure 7.12), you can create new gradients, rename or copy existing ones, and import/export gradients that you create.

   In the Type window, you'll notice a list of existing gradients. These are the gradient styles that ship with Paint Shop Pro. Any gradients that you create or import will also be in this list.

   Near the middle of the dialog box you'll see a representation of the current gradient. This area is where you'll edit existing gradients or create your own.

FIGURE 7.12

The Gradient Editor dialog box.

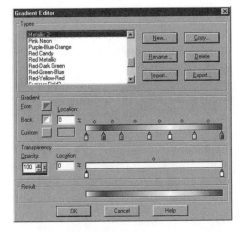

2. Click the New button.

3. In the New Gradient window, enter a name for your gradient. I entered "MyGradient." The editing area will fill with one color, and there will be only two sliders, one at each end.

4. Click the leftmost slider (see Figure 7.13—its small arrow will turn black) and click the color swatch to the left of the filled area to bring up the Color dialog box.

FIGURE 7.13

Select the leftmost slider to change one of the colors in your new gradient.

Leftmost slider

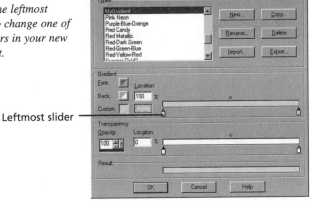

5. Select a light blue color.

6. Click the rightmost slider and then click the small color swatch again to bring up the Color dialog box.

7

7. Select a medium brown.

8. Click between the two sliders at the bottom of the filled area (see the marked area in Figure 7.14) and a new slider will appear.

FIGURE 7.14
Click to add a new slider and another color in your gradient.

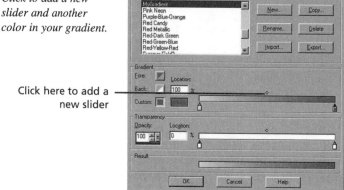

Click here to add a new slider

9. Click the color swatch and, this time, choose white for the color.

You've just created a multicolored gradient in the pattern that many artists use for chrome.

Here are some tips you can use to manipulate the appearance of your custom gradients:

- You can move the sliders around and add more, changing the color of each as you go. Also, you can move the small diamond slider at the top of the fill area to change the way that colors interact with each other in your gradient.

- To remove any of the sliders you added, simply click and drag them off the dialog box. Doing so will cause them to disappear.

- You can change the transparency of your gradient, as well. This is accomplished using the fill area at the bottom of the Gradient dialog box.

   The principles are the same as when you add sliders and colors to a gradient, except that you don't choose a color. Instead, you can set the amount of transparency at any point in the gradient.

   The sliders will change shades from white to gray and finally to black as you make an area more transparent. This is similar to how masks work, as you'll see in Hour 11, "Utilizing Masks for Precision."

- Take a look at some of the included gradients to see how they were created.

I encourage you to play with the various settings to see what cool gradients you can create.

10. When you're done creating your new gradient, click OK. The new gradient will be added to the list and ready for you to use.

To share your gradient with others, click Export. Doing so will bring up the Export dialog box, which will enable you to name and save the file. This file can then be sent to others for them to use in their own artwork.

If someone sends you a gradient file, you can add it to your collection by opening the Gradient dialog box and clicking the Import button.

As you'll soon discover, multicolored gradients are a very powerful addition to Paint Shop Pro's collection of tools.

Filling with a Pattern

Along with solid colors and gradients, you can also use the Flood Fill tool to fill an area with a pattern. To set the pattern, select the Flood Fill tool. In the Tool Options window, choose Pattern in the Fill Style pull-down menu and click the Flood Fill Options (second) tab (see Figure 7.15).

FIGURE 7.15

The Tool Options - Flood Fill Options window.

You can select any open image from the New Pattern Source pull-down menu. If some part of the current image is selected when you choose the pull-down menu, the selected area will be chosen as the pattern.

This option enables you to quickly fill an area or an entire image with a predefined pattern. If the area you're filling is larger than the pattern you've selected, the pattern will tile over the selected area.

Because the pattern fill repeats in the same manner as a Web page background, you can get a good idea of how your tiles will look. Simply create a new image that's larger than the pattern and use the Flood Fill tool to fill the image with the pattern.

7

Learning the Mysteries of the Clone Brush Tool

The Clone Brush (the eleventh tool from the bottom of the Tool palette; it resembles two paint brushes) is a mysterious and powerful tool. You can use the Clone Brush tool to paint over an area of an image with another area of the same image or an area from another open image or from one layer to another.

In Figure 7.16, I've started cloning the image in the foreground into the image in the background. The image in the background was opened as a new file with a white background. I then opened the file I wanted to clone and set the texture of the Clone Brush tool to Woodgrain.

FIGURE 7.16

Using the Clone Brush tool to "paint" one image onto another.

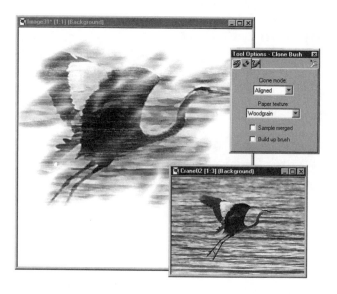

 The Clone Brush tool can only be used on 16 million color and grayscale images. If you need to apply this tool to a 256 (or less) color image, change the color depth (choose Colors, Increase Color Depth, 16 Million Colors), apply the tool and change the depth back (choose Colors, Decrease Color Depth—and choose the color depth you need).

I activated the Clone Brush tool by right-clicking the image at the position I wanted to clone.

All I needed to do to draw a clone of the bird was to draw in the new image by clicking and dragging. Because of the Texture feature, I got a nice artsy-looking clone of the bird in the new image.

The Clone Brush can also remove blemishes from portraits, remove telephone wires from photographs, and retouch images. I demonstrate this tool in more depth in Hour 17, "Retouching Your Images."

The options available for the Clone Brush tool, under the Clone Brush Options (second) tab in the Tool Options window, are Aligned and Non-aligned. You can also set a texture for the brush, sample merged layers, and use the Build-up Brush.

The Aligned option moves the source area relative to the original area even if you release the mouse and start to clone again. The Non-aligned option restarts the source area from the original area if you release the mouse and start again. If you're cloning a layered image, the Sample Merged option draws from all layers, and the Build-up Brush functions the same as was described in Hour 1, "Paint Shop Pro Basics, Tools, and Preferences."

Summary

In this hour, you've learned how to use Paint Shop Pro's many painting tools. I've just hinted at the real power of some of these tools. As you work through the rest of this book, you'll learn to apply this power.

In the next hour you learn how to use color effectively in the images you create with Paint Shop Pro.

Workshop

The Workshop contains a question and answer section to help answer the most commonly asked questions and quiz questions to help you solidify your understanding of the material covered.

Q&A

Q Can I use different textures within the same image?

A Yes, you can use as many textures as you want. All you need to do is change the Texture setting in the Tool Controls palette before you add a new effect.

Q How do I change the size of a Paint Brush tool?

A You can change the size of a Paint Brush tool, along with its other options, in the Tool Options window.

7

Q **When I make a selection for use with the Pattern option of the Flood Fill tool, do I need to use Edit, Copy to set the pattern?**

A No. All you need to do is select the image with the active selection from the pull-down menu in the Flood Fill Options dialog box.

Q **How do I paint with the current background color?**

A You can paint with the current background color by clicking and dragging with the secondary mouse button (normally the right).

Quiz

1. What is the difference between the Airbrush tool and the Paint Brush tool?

2. Can you use the Clone Brush tool to clone from one image to another? How?

3. What does the Density setting in the Paint Brush tool do?

4. What does the Opacity setting in the Paint Brush tool do?

5. What effect does the Tolerance setting have on how an area is filled with the Flood Fill tool?

Answers

1. The Airbrush tool lays down more paint if held in one spot for any length of time.

2. Yes. Open both images. Then right-click the image you want to clone from and paint in the image you want to clone to.

3. The Density setting in the Paint Brush tool determines how much paint is laid down with each stroke. Increasing and decreasing the density effectively adds and removes bristles from the brush.

4. The Opacity setting in the Paint Brush tool determines how much of the underlying image is visible through the application of the painting tool. A setting of 1 is almost transparent, whereas a setting of 100 is totally opaque.

5. The Tolerance setting determines whether a pixel will be filled based on its value relative to its neighbor. This setting goes hand in hand with the Match Mode setting.

HOUR **8**

Using Color Effectively

This hour introduces the following issues regarding the use of color:

- Using the Color tools
- Learning the color models used with Paint Shop Pro
- Adjusting shadows, highlights, and midtones
- Adjusting hue, saturation, and luminance

As you would expect, color is extremely important to digital art. Paint Shop Pro provides several ways of choosing and adjusting colors. In this hour, you learn how to choose and adjust colors effectively.

The Color Tools

Paint Shop Pro offers several ways to choose and adjust the colors you use to create and edit your images. You can choose from the colors that exist in an image, and you can choose new colors in a number of ways.

To choose colors from an existing image, you use the Dropper tool. To set new foreground and background colors, you use the Color palette.

Using the Dropper Tool

The Dropper tool (shaped like an eyedropper) is one of the easiest tools to use. To use the Dropper tool, simply select it and move it over an existing image. As you move the Dropper tool over the image, the color that the tool is over appears in the bottom of the Color palette.

Clicking the left (or primary) mouse button sets the current foreground color to the color under the Dropper tool; clicking the right (or secondary) mouse button sets the current background color to the color under the Dropper tool.

Using the Dropper tool is a great way to pick certain colors from an image for use in the same or another image.

Using the Color Palette

The Color palette (see Figure 8.1) is where you pick new foreground and background colors from scratch.

FIGURE 8.1
The Color palette.

The Color palette has three parts:

- First is the main color swatch. You can use this area of the Color palette to quickly choose a new foreground or background color. To choose a new color from the main color swatch, simply move the mouse pointer around the main swatch until the color you want appears in the new color swatch at the bottom of the Color palette.

  To set the foreground color to the color you see displayed in the new color swatch, left-click the mouse. To set the background color to the color you see displayed in the new color swatch, right-click the mouse. It's as simple as that. Unfortunately, getting exactly the right color in this manner is a little tricky. I'll show you a more exact method in a moment.

- The second part of the Color palette contains the current foreground and background color swatches. There is also a small two-headed arrow to the lower-left of

8

the twin swatches. Clicking the two-headed arrow swaps the current foreground and background colors. The arrows act as a toggle, meaning that each time you click the icon, the foreground and background colors will change places.

The twin swatches do more than just show you the current foreground and background colors, though. Clicking either one brings up the Color dialog box. I'll get back to this in a moment.

- Below the foreground and background color swatches is a small RGB readout. This readout displays the RGB (for red, green, and blue, the most common way of describing the colors used with computer displays) values for the color that the mouse pointer is over in the main color swatch. This color is displayed in the new color swatch.

The Paint Shop Pro Color Dialog Box

To bring up the Color dialog box and subsequently use it to choose a new color, simply click either the foreground or the background color swatch.

Either the Paint Shop Pro Color dialog box or the standard Windows Color dialog box appears, depending on your selection in the Paint Shop Pro Preferences dialog box. If you haven't specified a Color dialog box, Paint Shop Pro defaults to its own (see Figure 8.2).

FIGURE 8.2

The Paint Shop Pro Color dialog box.

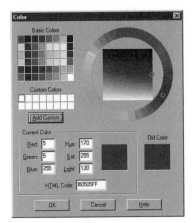

If you've chosen to work on an image with 256 or fewer colors or an image that is grayscale, you'll get a Color palette instead of a Color dialog box. Color palettes are limited to 256 colors or shades of gray.

The Paint Shop Pro dialog box, in my opinion, is the better choice here. It's much easier to zero in on a color using this Color dialog box than it is with the Windows Color dialog box. The Paint Shop Pro Color dialog box contains several areas:

- In the upper-right is the color wheel. You can choose an approximate color from the color wheel.

- Inside the color wheel is the Saturation/Lightness box. You use this area to fine-tune your color selection.

- At the upper-left is a set of basic colors that you can choose from. Below the basic colors is an area where you can store your own custom colors by clicking the Add Custom button.

- At the lower-right is a swatch that displays the current color.

- At the lower-left is a series of numbers. You'll find the RGB and HSL (Hue, Saturation, and Lightness) values, as well as the HTML number (or hexadecimal value) of the color you're choosing from the color wheel and the Saturation/Lightness box.

Besides seeing the values for any color in the RGB, HSL, and HTML number areas, you can set the values for a particular color manually.

The Windows Color Dialog Box

If you prefer to use the Windows Color dialog box, you can do so. To set the preferences to bring up the Windows Color dialog box, choose File, Preferences, General Program Preferences. In the Paint Shop Pro Preferences dialog box, click the Dialogs and Palettes tab (see Figure 8.3).

FIGURE 8.3

The Paint Shop Pro Preferences dialog box, showing the Dialogs and Palettes tab.

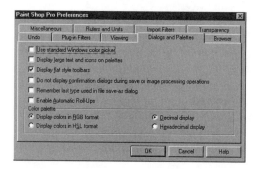

If you place a check mark in the Use Standard Windows Color Picker check box, the next time you click either the foreground or background color swatch, you'll get the Windows Color dialog box (see Figure 8.4) instead of the Paint Shop Pro Color dialog box.

FIGURE 8.4

The Windows Color dialog box.

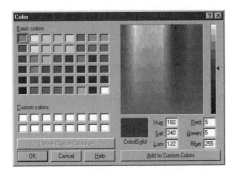

The main difference between the Windows Color dialog box and the Paint Shop Pro Color dialog box is how you go about choosing new colors.

With the Windows Color dialog box, you choose an approximate color from the main color swatch and then fine-tune it with the slider to the right of the color swatch. I find this method less exacting than using the Paint Shop Pro Color dialog box. Because the result is the same, though, the choice is up to you.

The Color Models Used with Paint Shop Pro

Because Paint Shop Pro is geared more toward onscreen imaging than high-end printing, the main color mode is RGB. Paint Shop Pro uses two other methods, as well. You can use CMYK, which is used in the printing industry, and HSL, which is another way of describing RGB colors. Each of these methods is discussed in the following sections.

The RGB Model

RGB (for Red, Green, and Blue) is a method of describing the colors that you see on your computer screen. Each of the three colors can have a value ranging from 0 to 255, for a total of 256 values.

If you multiply the three total values together (256×256×256), you get 16,777,216, or 16.7 million colors. Look familiar? It should. It is one of the image types you can choose when you open a new file. The 16.7 million colors that you can see on your screen are made up of combinations of red, green, and blue.

For example, the value 255, 0, 0 is bright red. This color is made up of 256 parts red, no green, and no blue. The color 0, 255, 0 is bright green because there is no red, 256 parts green, and no blue. What color do you think you'd get from 0, 0, 255? If you said bright blue, you are right.

If you combine 256 parts red with 256 parts green and no blue, you get a bright yellow. If you mixed no red, 256 parts green, and 256 parts blue, you get a bright pale blue or cyan.

Mixing 256 parts red with no green and 256 parts blue yields a bright purple or magenta.

Setting all the values to 255 gives you white, whereas setting them all to 0 gives you black. This brings up the interesting question: How do you get shades of gray?

Easy! Any time all of the values are equal, you'll get a shade of gray. Between 0, 0, 0 (black) and 255, 255, 255 (white) you have the possibility of 254 shades of gray. The grays range from very dark (almost black) 1, 1, 1 to very light (almost white) 254, 254, 254 and all the shades of gray you'll need.

A nice medium gray can be entered as 128, 128, 128—right in the middle between 0, 0, 0, and 255, 255, 255. You might want to open up the Color dialog box and enter some values for R, G, and B to see how the colors are affected.

The CMYK Model

The CMYK (for Cyan, Magenta, Yellow, and a percentage of blacK) model is used with printing inks. Cyan, magenta, and yellow inks are mixed to produce the various colors used to reproduce images on printers.

When cyan, magenta, and yellow inks are mixed, they produce black. However, it's very difficult to produce true black because of impurities in these inks. This is where the black ink comes in. By adding various amounts of black ink, you can get richer tones and deeper, darker blacks.

Normally, before printing an image in CMYK, you separate the image into different plates. Each plate contains one of the CMYK colors. When combined, the four plates reproduce your color images on high-end color printers.

Unless you'll be doing high-end printing of your digital images, you'll probably never have to use the CMYK model.

The HSL Model

The HSL model (for Hue, Saturation, and Lightness) is another way of looking at RGB colors. It is a more natural way of describing colors (at least in terms of humans versus computers) and is fairly easy to understand.

To set a color with this mode, you choose a color—or *Hue*—from 0 to 255. You then set the *Saturation*, or amount of color and, finally, you set the *Lightness*, or brightness of the color.

8

Hues start at 0 (red) and move through brown, yellow, green, light blue, dark blue, purple, and finally back to red.

If you look at the color wheel in the Paint Shop Pro Color dialog box, you'll notice that the top of the wheel is red, and it then moves counterclockwise through the progression.

Saturation sets how much color you see. A lower setting makes the color more gray, and a higher setting yields a brighter color.

The Lightness value determines how bright or dark a color is. A lower number means less light and, therefore, a darker color, whereas a higher number means more light and a brighter color.

You can try changing the HSL values in the Color dialog box to see how the values affect the different colors.

Adjusting Shadows, Highlights, and Midtones

You can use the Highlight, Midtone, and Shadow control to adjust the overall tonal range of an image or to correct an image's tones separately. You access this command from the Colors, Adjust, Highlight/Midtone/Shadow menu.

To see how the tones of an image are distributed, you can view the image's histogram. Click the Histogram Palette icon on the toolbar to bring up the Histogram palette (see Figure 8.5). (The Histogram Palette icon is the third-to-last icon on the standard toolbar at the top of the Paint Shop Pro window.)

FIGURE 8.5

The Histogram palette, showing an image's Red, Green, Blue, and Luminance levels.

The Histogram palette shows the distribution of pixels throughout an image. You can see the distribution of the red, green, and blue pixels as well as the distribution of the luminance. In Figure 8.5, I've chosen to view all of the values.

You can see that the image this histogram represents is a high-key image. A *high-key image* is a bright or fairly light image. This is true because the Luminance value, represented by the black line (which will be harder to distinguish from the other lines in the black-and-white figure) is much higher toward the right. A darker, or *low-key*, image would have the Luminance higher toward the left. High-key and low-key are terms used in photography.

The image that this histogram represents also appears in Figure 8.5. The bird is mostly white, and a lot of highlights are on the water. You can use the histogram to help decide how to adjust an image.

Armed with the histogram, you can decide whether you need to adjust the highlights, the shadows, the midtones, or a combination of the three.

As stated earlier, you choose Colors, Adjust, Highlight/Midtone/Shadow to make the tonal adjustments. In the Highlight/Midtone/Shadow dialog box (see Figure 8.6), you can adjust each tonal range separately.

FIGURE 8.6

The Highlight/Midtone/Shadow dialog box.

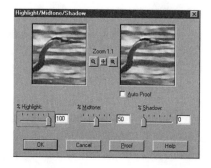

Because you can adjust the different ranges separately, you can use this dialog box to emphasize the highlights or shadows and to darken or lighten the midtones.

You're provided with a real-time preview so that you can see the results of the changes you make. You can also turn on the Auto Proof option, which enables you to see the changes in the actual image.

Having the Auto Proof option on can affect the speed at which your changes take place. If this option slows you down, you can leave the Auto Proof option off and simply click the Proof button when you want to see the effect of your changes on the image.

If you've ever scanned images into your computer only to find that they are too light or too dark, you can use the Highlight/Midtone/Shadow dialog box to adjust the images.

Adjusting Hue, Saturation, and Luminance

Just as you can affect the tones of an image with the Highlight/Midtone/Shadow dialog box, you can adjust the hue, saturation, and luminance (or lightness) of an image with the Hue/Saturation/Lightness dialog box (see Figure 8.7). You access this dialog box by choosing Colors, Adjust, Hue/Saturation/Lightness.

FIGURE 8.7

The Hue/Saturation/ Lightness dialog box.

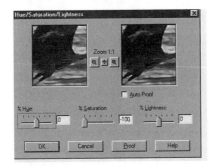

If an image has a color cast, is too bright overall, or is dull or overly saturated, you can use the controls in the Hue/Saturation/Lightness dialog box to make adjustments to the image.

Again, you're provided with a real-time preview so that you can see the results of the changes before applying them to the image.

You can use the Hue/Saturation/Lightness adjustments to create a sepia-toned image. If you have a color image you'd like to try this technique on, open it in Paint Shop Pro. Then follow these steps:

1. Choose Colors, Adjust, Hue/Saturation/Lightness.
2. Set Hue to around 50 and Saturation to about –70.
3. Click the Proof button, and you should see your image take on a sepia tone.

What has happened is that you removed a lot of the saturation so that the image is more like a black-and-white photo. There is still enough color to show the hue, though, which you've changed to a brownish shade. This effect was, and still is, a popular photo effect. Give it a try!

Summary

In this hour, you learned how to choose colors from an existing image and how to effectively use the Color dialog boxes to set new colors. Also, you learned a little about correcting and enhancing an image's highlights, midtones, and shadows. You saw how to adjust the hue, saturation, and luminance of an image. Try experimenting with these setting until you are comfortable using them.

Hour 21, "Preparing Your Graphics for the Web," covers the color issues that you'll need to understand to reproduce your images effectively on the Web. In the next hour, you'll learn how to create some really cool text effects with Paint Shop Pro.

Workshop

The Workshop contains a question and answer section to help answer the most commonly asked questions and quiz questions to help you solidify your understanding of the material covered.

Q&A

Q When I'm following along with the examples in the book, how can I enter the exact colors you're using?

A You can enter the exact RGB values I use in the RGB area of the Color dialog box.

Q Why would I want to toggle the foreground and background colors?

A Toggling the colors makes it easier to use two colors. With the foreground and background color swatches available in the Color palette, you can swap colors with one mouse click.

Q You said that you preferred the Paint Shop Pro Color dialog box to the Windows Color dialog box. Why?

A I just find it easier to get exactly the color I want with the Paint Shop Pro color wheel and Saturation/Lightness box. You can try both and see which one works best for you. The goal is the same—choosing the right color for the job.

Q How do I interpret the graph in the Histogram palette?

A The histogram depicts the colors and luminance of an image, and the graph varies for each image. The graph represents the distribution of pixels in an image. The lighter pixels are represented at the right, and the darker ones at the left. If an image is too light, the graph rises at the right. If an image is too dark, the graph rises to the left. Based on the graph, you can decide how to adjust an image. Then you can use the Highlight/Midtone/Shadow controls to adjust your image.

Quiz

1. What's one way to quickly choose a new foreground color?

2. How can you quickly set an exact foreground or background color?

3. What is the difference between the Paint Shop Pro Color dialog box and the Windows Color dialog box?

4. How can you enhance the shadows of an image without affecting the midtones and highlights?

Answers

1. By clicking the main color swatch in the Color palette.

2. By clicking either the foreground or background color swatch and setting the values manually in the RGB section of the Color dialog box.

3. The main difference is how you select a color. You use a swatch and a slider in the Windows Color dialog box; you use a color wheel and a Saturation/Lightness box in the Paint Shop Pro Color dialog box.

4. By adjusting the Shadow slider in the Highlight/Midtone/Shadow dialog box.

8

HOUR 9

Creating Cool Text Effects

This hour introduces the following issues regarding cool text effects:

- Using the Text tool
- Creating wood-textured text
- Creating chrome text
- Adding a drop shadow
- Adding glow to your text
- Creating text on a path

Paint Shop Pro enables you to enter text into your images via the Text tool. No explicit special effects are built into the Text tool. However, with a little ingenuity and the application of some of the other Paint Shop Pro tools and effects, you can create some amazing effects with text.

Using the Text Tool

The Text tool itself is straightforward and easy to use. To add text to your images, simply select the Text tool (the button with the big "A" on it) and click where you want the text to be in your image. Doing so brings up the Add Text dialog box (see Figure 9.1).

FIGURE 9.1

The Text Entry dialog box.

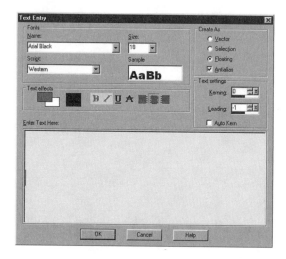

In the Text Entry dialog box, you can select the name, size, and script of a font. You can choose whether or not to add bold, italicize, underline, strike out, or anti-alias your text, and you can set the color. You also can adjust the *kerning* and *leading* (pronounced "ledding") or use auto kerning. Adjustable kerning and leading are new to version 6.

NEW TERM *Kerning* refers to the spacing between letters, and *leading* refers to the spacing between lines of text.

> If the color resolution of your image is 256 colors or fewer, the Antialias option is grayed out, and you won't be able to select it. You should generally create your images and work on them with higher color resolution, preferably 16.7 million colors.

Figure 9.2 shows four lines of text with carriage returns between the lines. The first and last lines have the leading set to 0, and the second line has the leading set to 10 (notice the difference in the spacing between the first and second and the second and third lines).

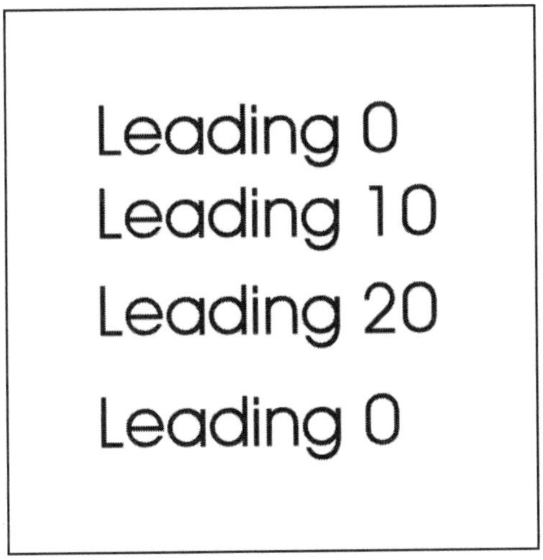

FIGURE 9.2

Several lines of text showing different leading values.

Leading 0

Leading 10

Leading 20

Leading 0

The difference between the third and fourth is even greater with the leading set to 20.

Kerning works similarly, except that the spacing affected is that between each letter. Kerning can make text more readable. Figure 9.3 shows two lines of text; the first has no kerning, and the second has auto kerning enabled.

FIGURE 9.3

Two lines of text, showing no kerning and auto kerning.

No Kerning
Auto Kerning

Note how, in the second line, the *e* in *Kerning* snugs in closer to the *K* and that there is a little less space on either side of the *i*.

To activate the Kerning option, click between two letters in the text entry area and enter a value in the Kerning option box. Negative numbers move the letters together and positive numbers move the letters apart.

You also can choose the alignment of your text and decide whether it should be created as a vector or a selection or whether it should float. Last, but not least, you can enter the text itself. The Add Text dialog box shows a preview of the text as you enter it. You can see the font and style, and you can get an idea of the size of the text, as well.

You may notice that the predefined sizes in the Add Text dialog box are limited. However, you can simply enter whatever value you want in the window above the Size box. This method helps if, for example, you want to use a font size that's bigger than the largest predefined size of 72 points.

After you've chosen your font, its size, style, and script; decided whether it should be antialiased; and entered the actual text, what then? Why, you get to play around with it and see what kind of weird and wonderful things you can do to it.

The next few techniques will illustrate the different "Create As" types. Again, these are Vector, Selection, and Floating.

Creating Wooden Textured Text

This first technique uses the Selection type of text.

You can use some of the built-in textures along with a filter or two and some selection manipulation to create some pretty cool text effects. This next exercise shows you how to create a textured wood effect. Follow these steps:

1. Open a new 500×200–pixel image with the resolution set to 72 pixels per inch. Set the background color to white and the image type to 16.7 million colors.

2. Set the foreground color to a medium brown. I chose R: 172, G: 114, B: 68 RGB values and a white background color. If you need to refresh your memory on how to set the foreground and background colors, refer to Hour 8, "Using Color Effectively."

3. Select the Text tool and, in the Text Entry dialog box, set the options as follows:

   Name: Arial Black

   Size: 72

   Script: Western

   Create As Selection (this will give you a selection in the outline of your text rather than text in a specific color) and Antialias (this setting makes the text nice and smooth)

   Alignment: Left (although this setting really matters only when you're entering more than one line of text)

4. Type in the text that you want to use. With a little thought, I came up with the word *Wooden*.

In Figure 9.4, you can see that the text comes into the image surrounded by the selection marquee.

FIGURE 9.4

Text surrounded by the selection marquee.

This effect is perfect for your immediate purposes because you will be painting over the text. With the selection marquee around the text, you won't be able to paint outside the lines. This feature would have been great back in the days of the coloring book.

> If you need to move the text around, you can do so by moving the mouse pointer over the text until the pointer turns into a four-headed arrow. All you need to do then is click and drag the text into position. If doing so leaves behind text in a visible color, you don't have the background color set to white. Choose Edit, Undo, reset the background color, and move the text again.

It's time to add some texture and color to the text. Follow these steps to do so:

5. Select the Paint Brushes tool.

6. Click the Paint Brush Options (second) tab in the Tool Options window and set Paper Texture to Woodgrain.

7. Click the Paint Brush (first) tab and set the options as follows:

Shape: Round

Brush Options: Normal

Size: 200

Opacity: 100

Hardness: 50

Density: 100

Step: 25

8. Move the mouse pointer to the left of the text and, while holding down the left mouse button, sweep the mouse over the text and back again.

You should get a good covering of paint, but not to the point where the grain disappears (see Figure 9.5).

FIGURE 9.5

Brown woodgrain texture painted onto the text.

This text already looks good, but the job isn't finished yet.

9. Choose Selections, Modify, Feather; then enter a value of 5 for the number of pixels. This setting expands the selection a little and changes the overall effect. Click OK to apply the Feather setting.

Feathering a selection not only expands the selection but also softens the edges. This option can be useful for creating certain effects and for softening the edges of shapes and other objects that you select with the selection tools. I sometimes use this option. To see the difference feathering makes, try following along with an exercise where I use feathering and, at the same time, create the same effect without the Feathering option. You can also try different values for the Feathering option to see the changing overall effect. In fact, this type of experimenting has resulted in many of the techniques that I use when creating digital images.

A higher Feathering value gives you more softness, and a lower value gives you less softness. Play around to see exactly what the effect will be when you change the value.

10. Swap the foreground and background colors by clicking the small, bent, two-headed arrow to the lower left of the foreground and background color swatches. Choose Image, Other, Hot Wax Coating. Adding Hot Wax Coating brings out the grain, makes the wood texture look a little aged and a bit more realistic and, because of the feathering, adds some definition to the edges of the text.

Your final result should resemble Figure 9.6. Not a bad effect for the amount of work involved.

FIGURE 9.6

Final wooden-textured text created with Paint Shop Pro.

9

Creating Chrome Text

Chrome text is one of the most popular effects. I've received many emails asking how to accomplish a chrome effect with different software. The next exercise shows you one way to create this effect in Paint Shop Pro.

Have you ever looked at something that's chrome plated? Not just seen something in chrome, but really looked at it? Take a moment now to step into your kitchen and take a really good look at the faucet fixtures. Go ahead, I'll wait.

What did you see? I'll bet you saw that the fixtures were mostly shades of pale gray (almost but not quite white), with some darker shades (heading into shades that were almost black) that defined the shape of the fixtures, right?

I discovered a Paint Shop Pro technique that mimics true chrome quite closely. To see how this technique works, follow these steps:

1. Open a new 500×200–pixel image with the resolution set to 72 pixels per inch.
2. Set the background color to white and the image type to 16.7 million colors.
3. Set the foreground color to white.
4. Select the Text tool and click somewhere in the image to bring up the Text Entry dialog box. Enter the following options in the Add Text dialog box:

   Name: Arial Black

   Script: Western

   Size: 72

   Create As: Floating and Antialias

   Alignment: Left

   Also, click the foreground color swatch to set the text color
5. Enter some text and click OK. I, quite naturally, entered the word *Chrome*.

If the text from the previous exercise or some other session is still visible, just highlight the existing text with the mouse before you enter the new text to replace the old text.

The text should be white on white, and it should be visible only because it's surrounded by the selection marquee (see Figure 9.7).

FIGURE 9.7

White-on-white text surrounded by the selection marquee.

6. Choose Image, Other, Hot Wax Coating.

7. Repeat the process to add another coat of Hot Wax. You should see your text starting to appear in a light shade of gray (see Figure 9.8).

FIGURE 9.8

A coat of Hot Wax added to the white-on-white text.

The next step is part of the trick to getting the text to appear as if it is chrome plated.

8. Choose Selections, Modify, Feather; then enter 8 for the value in the Number of Pixels spin box.

9. Click OK to feather the selection around your text.

10. Apply another coat of Hot Wax by choosing Image, Other, Hot Wax Coating. Apply a few more coats until your text looks like that in Figure 9.9.

FIGURE 9.9

Final chrome text, created by manipulating the selection and applying multiple coats of the Hot Wax filter.

I applied six coats of Hot Wax to arrive at the final image you see in Figure 9.9. Two were applied before feathering and four more after feathering.

If you look at the text and remember your recent trip to the kitchen, I'm sure you'll agree that the effect does a pretty good job of mimicking true chrome plating.

Adding a Drop Shadow

9

Adding a drop shadow to text used to be a cumbersome process requiring several steps. However, Paint Shop Pro and many other imaging companies have added drop shadows to their standard repertoire.

To effectively use the Drop Shadow filter to create interesting effects with your text, follow these steps:

1. Open a new 500×200–pixel image with the resolution set to 72 pixels per inch. Set the background color to white and the image type to 16.7 million colors.

2. Select the Text tool and then click your image to bring up the Text Entry dialog box.

3. Leave most of the settings from the last two exercises, but choose a different font if you'd like and set the color to what you want the text to be (this time we'll actually use the color of the text as the color of the text). I chose Staccato BT and set the size to 96 points (see Figure 9.10).

FIGURE 9.10

Text added to a new image and still surrounded by the selection marquee.

 You can enter values for the text size that are different from the ones you see in the pull-down menu. To do so, simply click in the Size window and enter a new value.

The selection marquee surrounds the text. Don't deselect the text. (You may not have this font on your system but the results you get will be similar, regardless of the font you choose.)

4. Choose Image, Effects, Drop Shadow to open the Drop Shadow dialog box (see Figure 9.11).

FIGURE 9.11

The Drop Shadow dialog box.

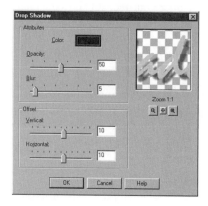

5. Click the Color button to bring up the Color dialog box and choose a color for your drop shadow. I'll stick with black.

6. To arrive at the image in Figure 9.12, set the options in the Drop Shadow dialog box as follows: Color is Black, Opacity is 50, Blur is 5, Vertical Offset is 11, and Horizontal Offset is 8.

FIGURE 9.12

Drop Shadow added to text.

You can use drop shadows to give the appearance of depth to your text. A closer, darker, sharper-edged shadow (as shown in Figure 9.13) gives the appearance of the text being just slightly above the screen (or printed page).

FIGURE 9.13

Sharp-edged, dark drop shadow added to text.

To achieve the hard-edged, close shadow, I used the following values:

Opacity: 80

Blur: 3

Vertical Offset: 7

Horizontal Offset: 5

The following values produced the drop shadow effect in Figure 9.14:

Opacity: 60

Blur: 15

Vertical Offset: 15

Horizontal Offset: 11

FIGURE 9.14

Softer-edged, lighter drop shadow added to text.

Note how the text appears to hover higher in Figure 9.14 than it does in Figure 9.13. This effect is due to the softness and different offsets of the shadow in Figure 9.14.

You should experiment with the various settings in the Drop Shadow dialog box to see how they affect the appearance of your text.

Adding a Glow to Your Text

With the popularity of the television show *X-Files*, people have been asking how to create the glowing text effect seen in the opening credits.

The following exercise shows you how to create the glow. Follow these steps:

1. Open a new 500×200–pixel image with the resolution set to 72 pixels per inch. Set the background color to black and the image type to 16.7 million colors.

2. Select the Text tool and click in the image to bring up the Text Entry dialog box.

3. Use the settings from the previous exercise and choose a font that resembles a typewriter font. I chose Times New Roman (see Figure 9.15). Also, set the text color to a bright green. I used R:30, G:255, and B:45 for the RGB values.

FIGURE 9.15

Bright green text on black.

4. Choose Selections, Select None to deselect the text (or you can right-click the image when the Selection tool is selected).

5. Choose Image, Blur, Gaussian Blur; then set Radius to 5.00. Click OK.

6. Apply the Gaussian Blur one more time with the same settings. The text should now have very soft edges and be blurry (see Figure 9.16).

FIGURE 9.16

Bright green text on black blurred with two applications of the Gaussian Blur filter.

7. Click in the image again to bring up the Add Text dialog box. Change the color to black and, to add the same text, just click OK.

8. The text comes into the image in black this time. All that you need to do is position it over the blurry green text from the preceding steps.

Move the mouse pointer over the text until the four-headed cursor appears and click and drag the black text into place over the green text.

9. Choose Selections, Select None to remove the marquee, and you should end up with text that resembles Figure 9.17.

FIGURE 9.17
Final glowing, X-Files–type text.

9

Creating Text on a Path

New to version 6 is the ability to produce vector shapes and, using that option, create text on a path such as a circle. The following exercise will show you how that's done.

1. Open a new 500×500–pixel image with the resolution set to 72 pixels per inch. Set the background color to white and the image type to 16.7 million colors.

2. Set the foreground color to black.

3. Select the Preset Shapes tool and, in the Tool Options window, set Shape Type to Circle, Style to Outlined, and Line width to 2. Place a check mark in both the Antialias and Create as Vector check boxes.

4. Place the cursor near the middle of the image and, while holding down the left mouse button, drag the mouse outward to draw a circle (see Figure 9.18).

FIGURE 9.18
Vector circle.

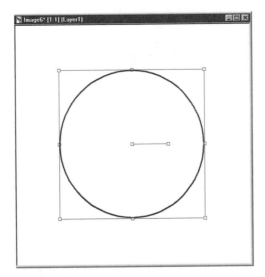

5. Select the Text tool and move the mouse pointer over the circle until the cursor changes to a plus sign with an *A* and a small semi-circle (see Figure 9.19).

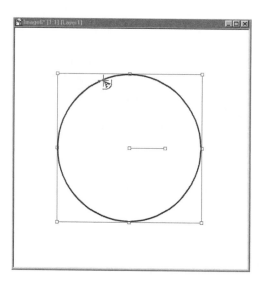

6. Click the left mouse button to bring up the Text Entry dialog box.

7. In the dialog box, enter your text. Make sure that Floating and Antialias are checked in the Create As option.

8. Your text should come in around the circle that you drew in step 4 (see Figure 9.20).

After some experimentation, you may notice that the text always comes in at the same orientation. At first, this would seem to be a problem. However, it's a simple matter to rotate the text. Simply select the Deformation tool, move the cursor over the selected text and rotate it, move it into place, and click Apply in the Tool Options window.

All that's left is to remove the circle. To do so, right-click the Circle layer in the Layer palette.

Choosing Selections, Select None will leave you with perfect text along a circular path (see Figure 9.21).

9

FIGURE 9.21

Completed text in a circle.

Vector Text

Although vector text is not in and of itself an effect, I thought I'd illustrate one of the properties of creating text as a vector.

To demonstrate the difference between vector text and regular bitmap text (Selection and Floating), I'll have you enter some text as a vector and enlarge it. I'll then have you do the same using bitmap (Floating text).

When you compare the two at the end of the exercise, you'll have a good idea of how they differ.

1. To see the differences, open two new 500×500–pixel images at 72dpi with the background set to white and Image Type set to 16.7 million colors.

2. Select the Text tool and left-click in one of the images to bring up the Text Entry dialog box.

3. In the Text Entry dialog box, set the color to black, change the size to 96, place a check mark next to Floating, and then enter the word `Bitmap`.

   The text should almost fill the horizontal space of the image.

4. Move the text into the center of the image and select the Deformation tool. Click and drag down on the control handle at the center of the bottom of the bounding box until you've reached nearly the bottom of the image window.

   Repeat the process by dragging upward on the top center control handle. The text should almost fill the image at this point.

5. Choose Selections, Select None, and you should have something that resembles Figure 9.22.

FIGURE 9.22

Deforming (especially enlarging) bitmapped text changes the quality.

Notice the poor quality of the enlarged text? This is what happens when you enlarge a bitmap.

Repeat the whole process on the second image but this time set Create As to Vector in the Text Entry dialog box.

You'll notice that this time the text comes in with a bounding box already around it.

Drag the bottom handle down and the top handle up again to enlarge the vector text.

To finish (and this is an option you'll need to do often before applying any kind of effect to vector text), you'll need to convert the text to bitmap.

I know, it seems kind of funny to do so, but this will enable you to compare the two images and see the true difference between them.

To convert the text, choose Layers, Convert to Raster.

See how smooth the (formerly) vector text is (see Figure 9.23)? Compare that to the text you entered and deformed as bitmap. Quite a difference.

FIGURE 9.23

Deforming vector text makes no noticeable change to the quality of the text.

9

There will be times when you'll want to create the text as bitmap, other times when you'll want to create it as vector, and still others when you'll create it as vector and convert it to raster (raster is another word that describes bitmapped images).

Using combinations of the types of text and the different filters available, Paint Shop Pro can produce a nearly unlimited number of text effects. All you need to do is play around, try new things, apply filters, and have some fun.

There are probably enough text effects to be the subject of a whole book. We've still got plenty of other topics to cover, however.

To learn a few more text effects, visit my Web site at http://www.grafx-design.com. You'll find some other text effects, along with some more advanced Paint Shop Pro techniques.

Summary

In this hour, you learned how to enter text with the Text tool and how to create some cool effects, including wooden textures, chrome, and drop shadows, using Paint Shop Pro options.

At this point, it's time to start covering more advanced topics, the first of which is layers.

Workshop

The Workshop contains a question and answer section to help answer the most commonly asked questions and quiz questions to help you solidify your understanding of the material covered.

Q&A

Q Can I use some of the filters, such as the Drop Shadow filter, on objects other than text?

A Yes, you can use all the various filters and effects in Paint Shop Pro on virtually any object you create. Some filters require you to make a selection first. To review how selections work, flip back to Hour 4, "Creating and Working with Selections."

Q How can I enter text in the current background color?

A The Text tool doesn't work the same way as other tools, in that you can't right-click to enter text in the background color. Instead, you simply enter the color for the text in the Text Entry dialog box.

Q I don't seem to have the same fonts as you do. Why not?

A Paint Shop Pro uses the fonts installed on your system. Many products, both software and hardware, ship with packages of fonts these days. It's quite possible that you have some fonts that I don't have, as well. If I use a certain font that you don't have, hunt through the ones you do have until you find something that comes close.

Quiz

1. How can you enter text in a larger point size than the predefined 72 points?
2. How can you make text appear to float higher off the screen?
3. Why would you want to apply a filter more than once?
4. Why would you need to set the alignment of text in the Add Text dialog box?

Answers

1. You can enter the value manually in the window above the predefined values in the Add Text dialog box.
2. You can use drop shadows to make the text appear to float higher or lower, depending on the edge hardness and offset of the shadow. Text appears higher as you soften the shadow and enter larger numbers for the offsets.
3. Multiple applications of a particular filter can result in spectacular results that wouldn't be possible otherwise. Playing with filters and learning how they work, even in multiple applications, will make your work stand out from the crowd.
4. The Alignment option is useful only when you enter more than one line of text—this option aligns all lines of text.

PART III

Tools to Work Efficiently

Hour

HOUR 10

Working Progressively with Layers

This hour introduces the following issues about layers:

- Understanding layers
- Using the Layer palette
- Using the Layers menu
- Using layers effectively
- Understanding the blending modes

Layers, a powerful new addition with version 5, enable you to do much more with Paint Shop Pro than was possible with earlier versions. With version 6, layers have been updated and are even more powerful. There are now several types of layers available. These include the raster layers (for bitmaps) from version 5 and two new types: vector and adjustment layers. Vector layers can contain vector objects and adjustment layers, which enable you to make easily changeable adjustments to your photographs. These are extremely powerful tools that enable you to create and edit your images with more precision and flexibility. I'll demonstrate vector layers in Hour 13, "Working with Flexible Vector Tools," and adjustment layers in Hours 17, "Retouching Your Images," and 18, "Coloring and Color Correction."

Understanding Layers

You can think of *layers* as separate drawing surfaces that lay on top of one another, much like sheets of paper in a sketchbook (see Figure 10.1).

FIGURE **10.1**

The concept of layers.

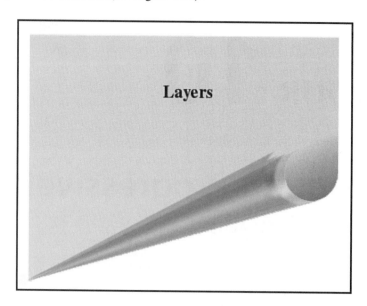

Layers are quite similar to sheets of paper, yet they perform many additional functions. Imagine having a digital sketchbook and being able to see each layer through the others above it. Further, imagine being able to move or edit the objects on any given layer without disturbing the objects on other layers.

Now imagine if you could blend the different layers in ways that enable you to see selected portions of one layer through another. This description suggests just how powerful layers are.

All that power is hidden behind a relatively easy-to-use interface. The interface I'm talking about is the Layer palette (see Figure 10.2).

Figure 10.2 shows the Layer palette for an image that has two layers: the background layer and another layer, Layer1, above the background layer.

Figure 10.2

The Layer palette.

Regardless of the file format, each image that you open in Paint Shop Pro has at least one layer, called the *background layer*. You can, and I think you should, add subsequent layers as you work on an image. I discuss why you should do so as I progress through the remainder of this hour.

The Layer Palette

If you take another look at Figure 10.2, you'll see the various parts of a layer that you can adjust.

From the left, you can see the layer's name. The layer you are currently working on is seen in the color you've chosen for window title bars, and the inactive layers are shaded.

When you add a layer, you have the option of naming it. You can name a layer anything you want. If you're working on a simple image, naming the layers may not be necessary. However, when you get to working on an image with more than four or five layers, giving descriptive names to them helps keep things organized.

If you choose not to name the new layer, Paint Shop Pro assigns a generic name such as Layer1, Layer2, and so on. If you decide to name a layer after you've created it, you can do so. Simply double-click the layer's name in the Layer palette to bring up the Layer Properties dialog box. You can enter a name for your layer there.

You can see a thumbnail view of a layer's contents by holding the mouse pointer over the layer's name in the Layer palette. The thumbnail view appears just below the mouse pointer as a small, floating window.

To the left of the layer name is a small icon that represents the type of layer. A white-and-black triangle combination is used for adjustment layers, a red rectangle is used for vector layers, and a set of red, green, and blue circles is used to represent raster layers.

To the right of the name is the Layer Visibility Toggle button (the icon resembles a small pair of eyeglasses). You can use this button to turn the layer on and off. This feature can be a big help when you're positioning other layers and when you're trying to see what effect one layer has on the others.

10

Along the top of the palette, above the layer names, are three icons: the Create Layer icon, the Delete Layer icon (I sometimes refer to this as the trashcan), and the Create Mask icon. You can drag and drop layers onto these icons. Dragging a layer onto the Create Layer icon will duplicate the layer, and dragging a layer onto the trashcan will delete it (you'll first be asked to verify that you want to delete the layer).

To the right of the three icons are three tabs—the Appearance tab, the Mask tab, and the Group tab. Clicking one of these changes the area to the right of the layer names.

- The Appearance tab shows the Layer Opacity, the Layer Blend Mode, and the Lock Transparency settings.

  The opacity of a layer can be set to allow the lower layers to show through, and blending modes allow layers to interact in weird and wonderful ways. I demonstrate some of these throughout the rest of this book. The Lock Transparency option enables you to change areas of a layer while making sure that the changes do not affect areas that have no pixel information. For example, you could fill every part of a layer except those areas that are transparent. You'll see examples of this used in several places throughout the book.

- Clicking the Mask tab changes the area to show you whether a layer has a mask attached to it and if the mask is linked. I'll describe masks in Hour 11, "Utilizing Masks for Precision."

- Finally, the Group tab shows you which, if any, layers are grouped together.

The Layers Menu

Many options are available to you via the Layers menu. They are:

- The New menu creates a new layer the same way the Add New Layer icon does. You can create a new raster, vector, or adjustment layer.

- The Duplicate menu duplicates the current layer. This has the same effect as dragging and dropping a layer onto the Add New Layer icon.

- The Delete menu deletes the current layer. The difference between the menu command and dragging the layer onto the small trashcan is that the menu option doesn't ask you to verify the operation.

- The Properties menu brings up the Layer Properties dialog box.

- The Matting menu has a submenu. You can use this option to remove the black or white fringes that can come from antialiasing from the edges of objects on a layer.

- The Arrange menu enables you to arrange the order of the layers that make up your image.

- The View menu enables you to view all layers or only the current layer. This menu is a great shortcut for viewing a single layer when you're working on a multilayer image.

- The Merge menu enables you to merge all visible layers or flatten the image. Flattening the image converts a multilayer image into an image with one layer.

> Flattening an image will remove the properties of vector and adjustment layers. This means that you'll no longer be able to adjust any vector objects that you've created or make further adjustments to adjustment layers. Before flattening an image, you might want to save it in the native PSP format to preserve the layer information.

Using Layers Effectively

Now that you've had a look at the Layer palette, it's time to play around with, and get used to, the layers themselves. Follow these steps to do so:

1. Open a new image at 500×500 pixels with the resolution set to 72 pixels per inch, the background color set to white, and the image type set to 16.7 million colors.

2. Select the Text tool and click somewhere in the image. In the Text Entry dialog box, choose a large font, set the color to black, set Create As to Floating and type the letter **B** for background. I set the size to 150 and used Arial Black for the font (see Figure 10.3). Click OK.

3. Move the letter to the upper-left corner of the image and choose Selections, Select None.

FIGURE 10.3
Some text on the back-ground layer.

4. Now add a new layer by clicking the Create Layer icon at the upper-left corner of the Layer palette (the Create Layer icon looks like a couple of blank pages).

5. When the Layer Properties dialog box pops up (see Figure 10.4), click OK to accept the defaults.

FIGURE 10.4

The Layer Properties dialog box.

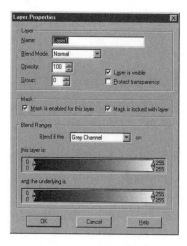

Most of the options in this dialog box can be set from the Layer palette and were discussed previously in this hour. The Blend Ranges option is discussed in more detail in the upcoming section, "Understanding the Blending Modes."

6. Select the Text tool again and enter the number 1.

7. Move the 1 to the lower-left corner of the image (see Figure 10.5).

FIGURE 10.5

A new layer containing a 1 is added.

8. Repeat the process of adding a new layer; this time add the number **2** to the new layer. Move the 2 to the upper-right corner of the image.

9. Add one last layer and add the number **3** to it (you should end up with four layers: background, Layer1, Layer2, and Layer3).

10. Move the 3 to the lower-right corner of the image and choose Selections, Select None.

You should have an image that resembles the one shown in Figure 10.6.

FIGURE **10.6**

Four layers with text and numbers.

Moving Layers

Hmmm. There seems to be a problem with the order of the numbers, though. The 1 and the 2 are in the wrong places and should be switched.

If you had created this image in an older version of Paint Shop Pro (prior to version 5 when layers were introduced), you'd pretty much have to start over. There would be no easy way to change the placement of the numbers. With layers, though, the process is easy.

To see how easy, select the Mover tool (it's the four-headed arrow icon and is the fifth one down in the Tool palette) and then follow these steps:

1. Click the Layer2 button in the Layer palette and click and drag the 2 down to the lower-left corner of the image. Don't worry about it covering the number 1. Because the numbers are on different layers, it doesn't matter.

Actually, with layers that have information, such as the numbers you've entered, surrounded by transparent areas, you can just click and drag the number. If you do so, you'll notice that the layer the number is associated with becomes the active layer.

2. Click the Layer1 button in the Layer palette and click and drag the number 1 to the upper-right corner.

Notice how only the number 1 moved, even though it appeared to be covered by the number 2. Again, this trick is possible because the numbers are on different layers. The numbers seem to be in better order now (see Figure 10.7).

FIGURE 10.7
Four layers with text and numbers in better order.

Grouping Layers Together

What if you need to move two or more layers as though they were a single layer? That's where the Group tab comes in (recall that it's the third tab along the top of the Layer palette).

To move the number 3 and the number 1 together, click the Group tab and then click the Layer Group Toggle icons for Layer1 and Layer3 once each. The word None should turn into the numeral 1, signifying that both layers now belong to group 1. If you use the Mover tool now, both the 1 and the 3 move together.

You can create different groups with different layers. You can also toggle back to where the layers are all ungrouped by repeatedly clicking the Layer Group Toggle button for any of the layers until they all display the word None.

Changing the Opacity and Visibility Options

Let's have some more fun. Try these steps:

1. Drag and drop Layer3 onto the Delete Layer icon (the small trashcan at the bottom-left side of the Layer palette).

2. Paint Shop Pro, through a dialog box, asks you to verify that you want to delete the layer. Click Yes.

3. Add another new layer and add the number **3** to it via the Text tool, using a color other than white or black. A bright red or a pale blue will work nicely.

4. Choose Selections, Select None to remove the selection marquee from around the number.

5. Move the number 3 over the number 1 (use the Mover tool). Note how the 3 completely covers the number 1.

6. Click the Appearance tab and drag the Opacity slider for Layer3 to the left and watch the image as you do so. You should notice the number 3 getting fainter and allowing the number 1 to show through (see Figure 10.8).

FIGURE 10.8

Adjusting the opacity of one of the layers to allow a lower layer to show through.

Amazing! What feats of magic!

7. Now click the Layer Visibility Toggle button (the first icon to the right of the layer's name; it resembles a small pair of eyeglasses) for Layer3. Whoa! The number 3 has disappeared.

   You can bring it right back, though, by clicking the Layer Visibility Toggle button once more. Wow, more magic!

8. Bring the opacity of Layer3 back to 100 so that the 3 covers the 1 again. Now click and drag Layer3 (you can do so by clicking and dragging the layer name) from its position at the top of the Layer palette (see Figure 10.9) so that it's below Layer1 (see Figure 10.10).

FIGURE 10.9

The original layers in the order in which they were created.

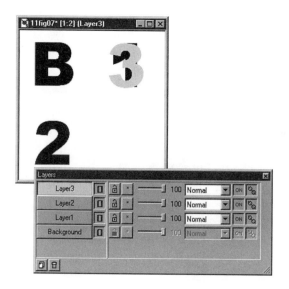

Now the 1 is covering the 3. This change is due to the reordering of the layers.

It's like magic! But wait, there's more! Next you learn about the use of blending modes within layers.

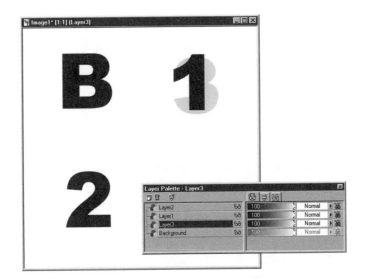

FIGURE 10.10

The layers with their order rearranged.

10

Understanding the Blending Modes

Blending modes enable you to blend layers in weird and wonderful ways.

Just as you've seen how you can change the opacity of a layer so that the layer(s) below shows through, you can change how layers interact with each other. The blending modes in the Layer palette control the blending function.

Several blending modes are available, and they combine layers in different ways. I could, as do some books, simply show you a couple of images stored on two layers and then show you how the different modes affect the image. This approach wouldn't work too well in black and white, though, and you really wouldn't learn anything from the demonstration. Instead, I'll describe the modes and then show you a cool effect you can create with one of the blending modes.

You can access the various layer-blending modes by clicking the pull-down menu for each layer in the Layer palette.

The available blending modes and their effects are as follows:

- **Normal**   Blends the modes only with the Opacity slider in the Layer palette.
- **Darken**   Pixels in the current layer that are darker than the pixels in the underlying layer are applied; lighter pixels disappear.
- **Lighten**   Pixels in the current layer that are lighter than the pixels in the underlying image are applied; darker pixels disappear.
- **Hue**   Applies the hue of the current layer to the pixels in the underlying layers.
- **Saturation**   Applies the saturation of the current layer to the pixels in the underlying layers.
- **Color**   Applies the hue and saturation of the current layer to the pixels of the underlying layers. This mode does not affect the luminance of the pixels in the underlying layers.
- **Luminance**   Applies the luminance values in the current layer to the pixels in the underlying layers.
- **Multiply**   Combines the color of the pixels in the current layer with the colors of the pixels of the underlying layers to produce a darker color. Multiplying any color with black results in black, whereas multiplying any color with white leaves the color unchanged.
- **Screen**   The opposite of Multiply, in that the pixels combine to form lighter colors.
- **Dissolve**   Randomly replaces some of the pixels in the current layer with those from underlying layers. This mode creates a sparkle effect.
- **Overlay**   Preserves patterns or color in the current layer while allowing the highlights and shadows from the underlying layer to show through.
- **Hard Light**   Adds highlights or shadows but is a little harsher than the Overlay mode.
- **Soft Light**   Adds softer highlights and shadows than the Overlay and Hard Light modes.
- **Difference**   Subtracts the current layer's color from the color of the underlying layers, depending on which is lighter.
- **Dodge**   Lightens underlying layers, using the current layer's pixel lightness values.
- **Burn**   Darkens underlying layers, using the current layer's pixel lightness values.
- **Exclusion**   Creates an effect similar to but softer than the Difference mode.

To see the effects these blending modes have, follow these steps:

1. Open two images and copy the first one as a new layer on the second. To do so, choose Selections, Select All. Then choose Edit, Copy.

2. Make the second image current by clicking its title bar and then choose Edit, Paste as New Layer.

3. With the two images combined as one image with two layers, cycle through the blending modes to see the effect each has on the image.

A Real-World Blending Mode Example

1. To see how you can put the blending modes to real-world use, create a new image at 500×500 pixels with the resolution set to 72 pixels per inch, the background color set to white, and the image type set to 16.7 million colors.

2. Set the foreground color to a medium brown. I used R:195, G:154, B:11.

3. Select the Paint Brushes tool and set Paper Texture to Woodgrain (you can do so in the Tool Options window). Set the Paint Brushes options as follows:

Shape: Round

Brush Options: Normal

Size: 200

Opacity: 100

Hardness: 50

Density: 100

Step: 25

4. Sweep the paint brush back and forth over the image to get a dark woodgrain texture.

5. Set the foreground color to white and choose Image, Other, Hot Wax Coating to give the grain more depth (see Figure 10.11).

6. Add a new layer by clicking the Create Layer icon in the Layer palette.

7. Fill the new layer with white using the Flood Fill tool.

8. Select the Text tool and add a large @ (*at* sign) to the layer. I set the font size to 300. Make sure you set the text color to black and that Create As is set to Floating.

9. Choose Selections, Select None.

10. Emboss the text by choosing Image, Other, Emboss.

10

FIGURE **10.11**

Background layer filled with a woodgrain texture.

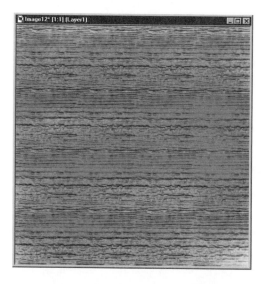

11. Blur the embossed text by choosing Image, Blur, Gaussian Blur and using a value of 2.00. The upper layer should resemble Figure 10.12.

FIGURE **10.12**

Upper layer containing embossed, blurred text.

12. Set the blending mode of the top layer (the one with the embossed, blurred text) to Hard Light.

Wow! Even more magic (see Figure 10.13).

FIGURE 10.13

The two layers, combined with the Hard Light mode, yield a nice woodcut image.

10

The Hard Light blending mode allows the highlights and shadows to show through, yet the woodgrain texture is preserved. You should take the time to play around with the various blending modes to see how they affect the layers that make up your image.

The great part about the changes the blending modes create is that they aren't permanent (unless you flatten the layers). You can always go back and try another blending mode. In fact, try setting the blending mode of the image you just created to Soft Light or Overlay. See the difference?

I use layers a lot more throughout the rest of this book—so much so that you'll be an expert with layers by the time you work through the remaining hours.

Summary

In this hour, you learned about layers. You learned to create and delete layers. You saw how easy it is to move objects around when they're on separate layers. You saw how the Opacity feature works and how to change the order of the layers in an image. Finally, you saw firsthand how blending modes work.

I believe that you're ready to see how masks work. I cover them in the next hour.

Workshop

The Workshop contains a question and answer section to help answer the most commonly asked questions and quiz questions to help you solidify your understanding of the material covered.

Q&A

Q I've added a layer and placed an object on it, but now I don't want the layer any more. What can I do?

A You can delete any layer by making it current and then clicking the Delete Layer icon. You also can drag and drop the layer onto the Delete Layer icon or choose Layers, Delete.

Q I want to change the order of the layers in my image. How do I do so?

A You can drag and drop layers to change the layer order. You can also use the Layers, Arrange option to change the order of your layers.

Q I'd like to be able to see an underlying layer through one that's on top of it. Is this possible?

A Yes. You can change the opacity of any layer by moving the Opacity slider. Doing so will enable you to see underlying layers through the layer whose opacity you adjust.

Quiz

1. How do you move two or more layers as though they were one?
2. How do you toggle off a layer's visibility?
3. How do you combine two or more layers into one?
4. How do you create a new layer?
5. How do you duplicate a layer?

Answers

1. You can group layers using the Layer Group Toggle button on the Layer palette.

2. You can use the Layer Visibility Toggle button on the Layer palette to toggle a layer on and off.

3. You can combine two or more layers by making them visible (and all others invisible) and choosing Layers, Merge, Merge Visible. You can also flatten the image, essentially merging all layers, by choosing Layers, Merge, Merge All (Flatten).

4. You can click the Add New Layer icon, or you can choose Layers, New.

5. You can drag and drop a layer onto the Add New Layer icon, or you can choose Layers, Duplicate.

10

Hour 11

Utilizing Masks for Precision

This hour introduces the following issues about Paint Shop Pro masks:

- Understanding what masks are and what they do
- Using the Masks menus
- Creating your first mask
- Creating a more complex mask
- Delving into advanced mask topics

Masks were available in previous versions of Paint Shop Pro, but starting with version 5, this feature is now more powerful. A mastery of masks and masking techniques marks the difference, I believe, between a casual user and the accomplished one. After working your way through this hour, you'll certainly be a more accomplished Paint Shop Pro user.

In this hour, I show you what masks are and how they can be used. Also, I show you several examples of the digital magic that masks can help you create.

What Are Masks?

Masks are grayscale images that work with existing layers. They enable you to create special effects that would be difficult, or even impossible, to create otherwise.

Masks are analogous to masking tape, but they are far more powerful. If you've done any painting around the house, you probably used masking tape to mask off doorframes and windows. This is similar to what you would do with masks in Paint Shop Pro. Masks enable you to control how the changes you make affect your image.

Because masks are grayscale, you can save them in Alpha channels. This feature enables you to save a mask along with your image so that you can use the same mask in later sessions. Recall that *Alpha channels* are areas where you can store selections. These Alpha channels are stored with an image if you save the image in PSP, TIF, or TGA format.

Masks can also be saved separately and loaded into the same image in a later session or used with other images. Because masks are images in their own right, you can edit them using any of the painting and drawing tools in Paint Shop Pro.

Masks enable you to "mask out" areas of images. These areas can then be selected and removed from the image to be placed into another, for example.

You can use masks to blend objects on one layer with objects on other layers in ways that you might see in magazine ads and product brochures. These are just some of the ways that professionals use masks to their advantage.

The Masks Menu

The Masks menu (see Figure 11.1) contains all the options you need to access your masks.

FIGURE 11.1

The Masks menu.

From within the Masks menu, you can create a new mask, delete an existing mask, invert a mask, edit a mask, and view a layer's mask. You can also load a mask from disk or an Alpha channel, and you can save a mask to disk or an Alpha channel.

Because masks are similar to selections, they can be saved (and loaded) in much the same way that selections can. You can save masks as separate files or in Alpha channels. Saving a mask as an Alpha channel has the advantage that the mask remains with the image that it was created for.

When you choose the New option, you get a submenu that enables you to create the new mask and either Show All or Hide All. You can also create the mask from a selection, choosing to show or hide the selection. Finally, you can create the mask from an image. This option enables you to create a mask from any image that you have open in Paint Shop Pro.

Creating Your First Mask

Recall that masks allow changes to show through where the mask is black and block changes where the mask is white.

However, because masks are grayscale, the changes can show up partially in an image where the mask is gray rather than black or white. If the mask is a lighter gray, the changes will be less visible. Where the mask is a darker gray, the changes will be more evident.

To get a feeling for how masks work, you can create a new mask. Follow these steps to create an image with a simple mask:

1. Open a new image at 500×200 pixels with the resolution set to 72 pixels per inch, the background color set to white, and the image type set to 16.7 million colors.

2. Create a new layer by clicking the Create Layer button at the top of the Layer palette. You can open the Layer palette (if it's not already visible on your screen) by clicking the Toggle Layer Palette button in the toolbar.

3. Use the Text tool to enter some text. I entered the word *Mask* in 100-point, bold, Arial Black, using blue for the color and setting the Create As option to Floating (see Figure 11.2).

FIGURE 11.2
Text entered with the Text tool.

4. Choose Selections, Select None to deselect the text.

5. Choose Masks, New, Show All to create a new mask. However, you won't see any changes to the image at this point.

6. Choose Masks, View Mask. You still won't see any changes because you chose Show All. With the Show All option, the mask is completely white, and no changes to your image occur. (*Show All* refers to showing the image, not the mask. More specifically, it refers to showing the image through the mask, in effect creating a totally white mask.)

7. Choose Masks, Edit. Now any changes you make to the current layer affect the mask, rather than the object(s) on the layer.

8. Choose the Selection tool and set Selection Type to Rectangle in the Tool Options window.

9. Draw a rectangular selection that encompasses the top third of the image.

10. Select the Flood Fill tool.

11. Set the foreground color to black and click in the selection to fill it with black. Make sure that Fill Style is set to Solid color in the Tool Options window.

Whoa! What happened? The selection was filled all right, but it wasn't filled with black. It was filled with a reddish color, right? What you're seeing is the mask itself. You're seeing the mask because you've toggled on the View Masks option. You can also tell that you're viewing the mask and the image through the mask because *(*MASK*)* appears on the image's title bar.

To turn off the view of the mask, choose Masks, View Mask. Hey! What happened this time? The mask has disappeared but so has the top third of the text. The text hasn't really disappeared; rather, it has been "masked out" and is now invisible. Now follow these steps:

1. Select the Selection tool again and draw another selection that encompasses the middle third of the image. You may have to click the Selection tool outside of the currently selected area first.

2. Set the foreground color to a medium gray.

3. Select the Flood Fill tool again and fill the selected area with gray.

Okay, okay, what's going on, here? The gray color doesn't show up, and this time the text seems to fade out to a pale blue (or a paler version of the color you used for the text—see Figure 11.3).

FIGURE 11.3

Text masked off with black, gray, and white.

To see how the mask looks now, choose Masks, View Mask again.

Now the top third is filled with red; the middle third is red, but you can see the text through it; and the lower third is not red at all, and the text is completely visible.

This step proves my earlier explanation about how the black portion of a mask allows the lower layer to show through completely, the gray portion allows some of the lower layer to show through, and the white portion of a mask allows none of the lower layer to show through.

Now you may be asking, "What exactly is showing through?" You may also wonder why I didn't just color the text this way instead of going through all of the work of creating the masks.

Well, it's true that this text could have been created in a much easier fashion if you look at just the text on white. But what if the text was on a textured layer?

If the text was on a separate layer above a textured layer, you'd be able to see the texture through the text; this effect could not be easily re-created without using masks.

To see how the mask would work with the text and a textured background, it's time to create a more complex mask.

Creating a More Complex Mask

Masks can be used to blend textured layers together to yield results that would not be possible any other way. To see how this technique works, follow along with the next exercise.

1. Open a new image at 500×200 pixels with the resolution set to 72 pixels per inch, the background color set to white, and the image type set to 16.7 million colors.

2. Set the foreground color to a pale yellow. I used R:239, G:244, B:164.

3. Select the Paint Brushes tool and set the options as follows:

Paper Texture: Woodgrain

Shape: Round

Brush Tip: Normal

Size: 200

Opacity: 100

Hardness: 50

Density: 100

Step: 25

4. Draw the paint brush back and forth across the image a couple of times to get a good texture.

5. Choose Image, Other, Hot Wax Coating to apply Hot Wax Coating and increase the woodgrain texture.

6. Add a new layer by clicking the Create Layer icon at the top of the Layer palette.

7. Select the Text tool and add some large black text to the image (make sure that you set Create As to Floating). I used 100-point, bold, Arial Black and entered the word *Mask* (see Figure 11.4).

FIGURE 11.4

Black text on a separate layer above a woodgrain texture.

8. Choose Selections, Defloat. This option drops the text but leaves it selected.

9. Choose Masks, New, Hide Selection. The text seems to disappear, and the selection marquee is visible over the texture background.

If you choose Masks, View Mask, you'll see that the mask is covering the text with a partially transparent red color.

10. Choose Masks, Edit so that you'll be painting on the mask and not on the actual image.

11. Select the Flood Fill tool.

12. In the Tool Options window, set Fill Style to Linear Gradient. Click the second tab in the Tool Options window and choose Black—White.

13. Set Angle to 180 degrees.

14. Click each letter to fill its mask with the gradient.

15. If the View Mask option is still on, toggle it off by choosing Masks, View Mask.

Your final image should resemble Figure 11.5.

FIGURE 11.5

Black text masked with a linear gradient to allow the textured layer below to show through.

An effect such as this would be almost impossible to accomplish without the use of a mask.

You could have text on a layer above the texture and adjust its opacity, but that would affect all of the text. What you've done here is use a gradient mask to allow the text to gradually blend into the texture.

Saving and Loading Masks

You can save and load your masks after you've created them. Masks such as the two you created in the previous exercises are not hard to re-create, and you probably wouldn't need to save them. If you spend more than a few minutes creating a mask, though, you'll probably want to save it.

To save a mask, simply choose Masks, Save to Disk or Masks, Save to Alpha Channel. Saving the mask to disk saves the mask separately; saving it to an Alpha channel saves the mask with your image.

If you save your mask as an Alpha channel, though, you'll need to save your image in PSP, TIF, or TGA format to preserve the channel.

If you choose to save the mask to disk, you'll be prompted for a filename. Leave the default extension .msk so that Paint Shop Pro will recognize the file when you decide later to load the mask.

Understanding Advanced Mask Topics

In the last exercise, you saw that masks can be made from selections. The reverse is also true. You can create selections from masks.

Because you can use the drawing and painting tools to create a mask, those you create can be very complex. When you finish "painting" your mask, you can create a selection from it.

What can you do with this complex mask/selection? Digital magic!

Have you ever wondered how to isolate someone from an image? Have you ever thought that it might be fun to cut someone from one image and place him into another? These effects, and more, are possible with the following technique.

For this exercise, I need some help from my assistant, Zöe (see Figure 11.6).

FIGURE 11.6
Zöe on her blankie.

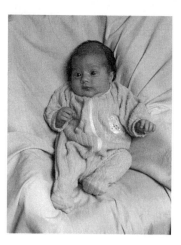

My niece, Zöe, was just under a year old when this photo was taken, but her mom said she could help with this lesson. You won't have this particular photo, so load one of your own photos from which you want to remove an object or a person. Then follow these steps:

If you don't have access to an image for this exercise, load one of the image files from the Paint Shop Pro CD-ROM.

1. Create a new layer by clicking the Create Layer icon in the upper-right corner of the Layer palette.
2. Fill the new layer with white and drag it down so that it's below the layer with the photo on it.

If you have trouble dragging the new layer below the layer with your photo on it because the photo is on the "background" layer, you can double-click the background layer and accept the defaults in the Layer Properties dialog box. Doing so will promote the background to a layer and enable you to rearrange the layers.

3. Choose Masks, New, Hide All.

4. Choose Masks, Edit.

5. Choose Masks, View Mask. You should see your photo behind the red mask (see Figure 11.7).

FIGURE 11.7

Zöe with the full mask in place.

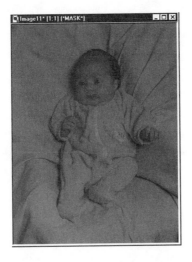

6. Set the foreground color to white and the background color to black. (Either click the foreground and background color swatches and set the colors or choose the colors from the color picker.)

7. Now you're ready to start working on the mask. Select the Paint Brushes tool and set the options to the following:

Brush Type: Normal

Size: 5

Shape: Round

Paper Texture: None

You may want to zoom in a little (see Figure 11.8), and you'll probably want to change the brush size from time to time.

FIGURE 11.8

Zöe with some of the mask removed.

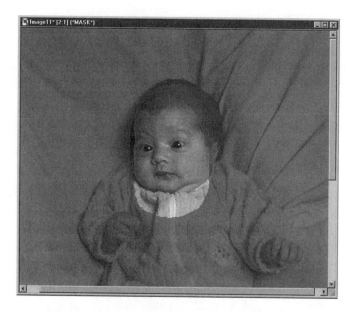

8. The goal here is to remove the red masked area from the portion of the photo that you want to select. I want to select Zöe and leave out the blanket. Painting or drawing with white removes the mask; painting or drawing with black replaces it. Because you can replace the mask, it doesn't matter if you draw outside the lines, as it were. Try to come as close as possible, though, so that there'll be a smooth transition from the object to its new background.

   If you make a mistake, swap the foreground and background colors by clicking the small, bent, two-headed-arrow icon below the current foreground and background color swatches. You can go back and forth like this, removing and replacing the mask, until you've removed the mask completely from the object you want to select (see Figure 11.9).

9. You can create the selection from the completed mask by choosing Selections, From Mask. Doing so creates a selection from the mask you just "painted" (see Figure 11.10).

   You should now have a selection that exactly matches the object or person you want to copy.

10. Choose Masks, View Mask to toggle off the mask, and you'll see that the object you masked out is selected.

11. Make the layer with the photo active and choose Edit, Copy.

FIGURE 11.9

Zöe with the completed mask.

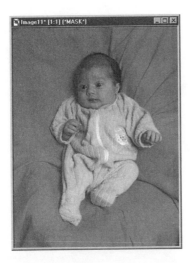

FIGURE 11.10

Selection created from the finished mask.

11

12. Open the new image you want to paste the selected object or person onto. I created an image of clouds to depict what a little angel my niece is.

13. With the new image active, choose Edit, Paste as New Layer and move the selection into place (see Figure 11.11).

FIGURE 11.11
Zöe in the clouds.

That's it! There's much more digital magic that you can accomplish with masks. I use masks again later in the book when I discuss composites in Hour 19, "Compositing."

Summary

In this hour, you discovered masks. Masks are images that work with existing layers and enable you to create special effects that are otherwise difficult or impossible to create. You learned how to create simple and complex masks and how to save and load masks. You saw how masks do their magic. The best way to become more comfortable with masks is to play around and practice using them. They are worth the time and effort!

I believe that you're ready to learn about channels and see how they work. I cover them in the next hour.

Workshop

The Workshop contains a question and answer section to help answer the most commonly asked questions and quiz questions to help you solidify your understanding of the material covered.

Q&A

Q Why can't I see the new mask I added?

A You must choose Masks, View Mask to see the current mask.

Q I tried to change the mask, but I changed the image instead. Why?

A You must choose Masks, Edit to edit the mask instead of the image.

Q When I add a mask and choose Masks, Edit, I can't set any colors other than black, white, and shades of gray. How come?

A The reason you can use only black, white, and shades of gray when working on a mask is that masks are grayscale and, therefore, cannot contain any color information.

Quiz

1. How do you create a new mask from a selection?

2. How many colors can you use to "paint" a mask?

3. How do you delete a mask?

4. How can you save a mask?

5. If you create a mask from an object and decide to move the object, can the mask follow the object as you move it? (This is a trick question, and the answer depends on remembering what you learned about the Layer palette in Hour 10, "Working Progressively with Layers.")

Answers

1. After creating the selection, you can create a mask from it by choosing Masks, New, Hide Selection or by choosing Masks, New, Show Selection.

2. Technically, none (masks are grayscale). You can use black, white, and all the shades of gray, though, for a total of 256 colors.

3. You can delete a mask by choosing Masks, Delete. You'll be asked if you want to merge the mask into the current layer. You should select No to delete the mask.

4. You can save a mask by choosing Masks, Save to Disk or by choosing Mask, Save to Alpha Channel.

5. Yes, the layer can be linked to the mask via the Link Mask Toggle button in the Layer palette. When you link the mask to the layer, the mask moves with the object (if you move the object with the Mover tool), keeping the object properly masked.

11

HOUR 12

Using Channels Effectively

This hour introduces the following issues about understanding and using channels:

- Understanding what channels are and how they are used
- Splitting and combining channels
- Identifying information in channels
- Making channels work for you

Channels are not new to Paint Shop Pro version 6. Channels have been available in previous versions. Like layers and masks, though, channels are quite mysterious and powerful.

In this hour, I show you what channels are and how they can be used.

What Are Channels?

Every image you create, whether it's layered or not, whether it's 16.7 million colors or grayscale, can be broken down into its component channels. How an image breaks down into channels depends on how you want to use the channels. For example, if you want to use the channels to create color separations so that a service bureau can print your image, you need to split your image into C, Y, M, and K channels.

Essentially, *channels* are grayscale representations of the information that makes up each image. Each grayscale channel holds part of the information that makes up an image.

If, for example, you split an image into its red, green, and blue components, the Red channel will contain the red information in the original image. Likewise, the Green channel will hold the green information, and the Blue channel will hold the blue information.

Splitting Channels

Note that splitting an image into channels does not affect the original image. Splitting an image into channels creates completely new images—one for each channel. Even recombining these images (or channels) into an image doesn't affect the original.

You split the channels of an image when you want to work on an individual channel. For example, sometimes digital cameras don't do a great job (although they're constantly getting better), and the resulting photos sometimes need correction.

One way to correct the problems inherent with images taken with a charged couple device (CCD) such as a digital camera is to examine each channel and fix the one that has problems. The Blue channel is usually the biggest culprit, and fixing the Blue channel (sometimes with just a little softening) and recombining the channels into an RGB image often helps tremendously.

Splitting (and combining) channels in Paint Shop Pro is easy. To split an image into its separate channels, simply choose Colors, Channel Splitting and then choose the type of channels you want to split the image into. You can choose RGB, HSL, or CMYK.

Do these acronyms look familiar? They should. These are the different ways you have of looking at the colors that make up your images in Paint Shop Pro.

For the most part, you can ignore the CMYK format. This format is most useful when you need color separations for high-end printing, which is beyond the scope of this book. If you plan on doing lots of high-end printing, you should consult with the personnel at your local service bureau.

Ignoring CMYK leaves you with two choices, RGB and HSL. Which one is best for a specific use depends on many factors, including what exactly you'll be using the channels for. In the following sections, I explain how to use channels to help you create masks.

Combining Channels

After splitting an image into separate channels to do some work on it via the channels, such as removing blemishes in a photo, you need to recombine the channels into a full-color image. Combining channels into an image requires a little more work but is still relatively easy.

To combine channels into an image, choose Colors, Channel Combining. Then choose Combine from RGB, HSL, or CMYK, depending on what the image was split into.

Paint Shop Pro displays a dialog box in which you enter the filenames of the channels. Normally, these files would already be open and onscreen from previous channel splitting.

Identifying the Information in Channels

Now that you've seen how to split an image into its component channels and know how to recombine the channels, it's time to see what channels look like.

Figure 12.1 shows an image with a medium gray background with the words Red, Green, and Blue on it.

12

FIGURE 12.1
Red, green, and blue text on a gray background.

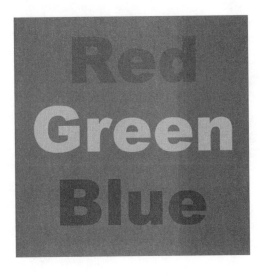

Each word is in its own color. That is, the word *Red* is colored red (R: 255, G: 0, B: 0); the word *Green* is in green; and the word *Blue* is in blue. Figures 12.2 through 12.4 show the Red, Green, and Blue channels of Figure 12.1.

FIGURE 12.2
The Red channel of Figure 12.1.

FIGURE 12.3
The Green channel of Figure 12.1.

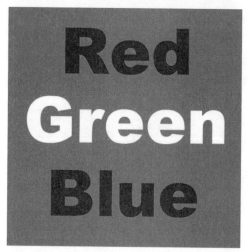

Each channel shows its associated word (color) in white and the other words in black because each color shows up this way in its own channel. If I had left the background of the image white before splitting it into the separate RGB channels, the words in the color of each channel would not be visible.

FIGURE 12.4
*The Blue channel of
Figure 12.1.*

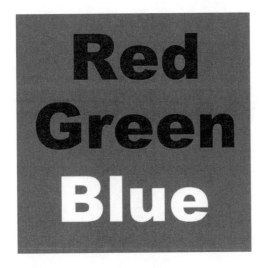

In other words, a color shows up very brightly in its own channel. The example I used has each color in its purest form, but the theory holds true for any image.

For example, the skin of a Caucasian is made up of mostly red and green with almost no blue at all. Given that, how would you expect the three RGB channels of a portrait to look? If you think that the skin would be lighter in the Red and Green channels and darker in the Blue channel, you would be right.

Putting Channels to Work

Take a look at the photo of Zöe again (see Figure 12.5).

FIGURE 12.5
A color photo of Zöe.

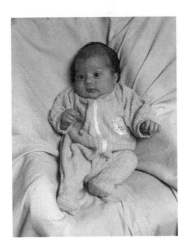

12

Of course, you can't see the colors here, but you know what Caucasian skin tones look like. Figures 12.6 through 12.8 are, respectively, the Red, Green, and Blue channels from this photo.

FIGURE 12.6

The Red channel from the photo of Zöe.

FIGURE 12.7

The Green channel from the photo of Zöe.

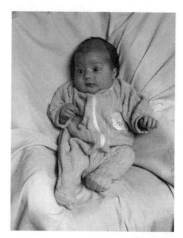

Notice how the Red and Green channels are quite light and the Blue channel is very dark around Zöe's face? This effect confirms what I said about Caucasian skin being mostly red and green. (Remember that the brighter an area is in the photograph, the more of that color that appears there. When viewing the Red and Green channels, Zöe's face is very bright. Therefore, in the original image her face contains a lot of red and green. However, when viewing the Blue channel, Zöe's face appears very dark, which shows that her face contains very little blue.)

FIGURE 12.8
The Blue channel from the photo of Zöe.

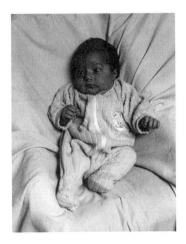

Testing Your Understanding of Channels

Here's a little exercise to test your knowledge of channels so far. Take a look at the three channels and see whether you can guess the color of Zöe's pajamas. You may not get the exact color, but you should get close.

The pajamas contain a lot of red, as evidenced by how light that portion of the photo is in the Red channel. There's also just a little blue and almost no green.

If you said pale red, pink, or a light pinkish mauve, you'd be right on the money.

Using Channels to Create Masks

So how do channels help you, the digital artist? You now know that channels are grayscale representations of the components of an image. You also know what a channel looks like in relation to other channels, and you know a little about reading a channel's information. But what can you do with a channel?

One really good use is to help you make selections and masks that are otherwise somewhat difficult to create. Finding the channel with the greatest contrast between the area you want to mask and the rest of the image enables you to create better masks with less work.

Remember how much work was involved in creating the mask around the subject in Hour 11, "Utilizing Masks for Precision"? Take another look at Figures 12.6 through 12.8.

Can you spot a channel that would make the mask creation easier? What about Figure 12.6? A lot of contrast appears along the edges between Zöe and the blanket. It might be easier to work on that channel.

12

Because splitting an image into its component channels doesn't affect the actual image, you can do so and work on just one of the channels without harming the original.

For example, I could take the Red channel from the photo of Zöe and further manipulate it to prepare it for building the mask. Figure 12.9 is the result of adjusting the brightness and contrast of the Red channel.

FIGURE 12.9

The Red channel from the photo of Zöe with the brightness and contrast adjusted.

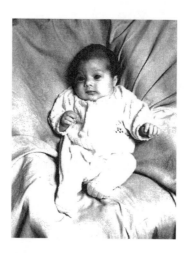

I've added to the brightness and the contrast to boost the difference between Zöe and her blanket. This is still not as good as it could be, though. Instead of trying this channel, I'd rather look for a better way. I'll try splitting the image into the HSL channels.

To see the HSL channels of an image, choose Colors, Channel Splitting, Split to HSL.

In the Saturation channel, the difference between Zöe and her blanket is even greater than in the Red channel. I'll go with the Saturation channel for the mask creation.

Figure 12.10 shows the Saturation channel from the photo of Zöe.

By adjusting the brightness and contrast of this channel, you can almost create the mask just by making a selection with the Magic Wand tool.

Figure 12.11 is the result of adjusting the contrast to its highest setting and playing with the brightness a little.

Notice the black area surrounding Zöe? You could just select this area with the Magic Wand tool; convert the selection to a Mask (Masks, New, Hide Selection); and clean up the mask a little with the Paint Brushes tool.

This approach would be easier and result in a better mask than the steps used in Hour 11. Figure 12.12 shows the result of the preceding process.

FIGURE 12.10
The Saturation channel from the photo of Zöe.

FIGURE 12.11
The Saturation channel from the photo of Zöe with the brightness and contrast adjusted.

12

FIGURE 12.12
The Saturation channel, adjusted and turned into a mask.

Aside from some cleanup in the lower-left corner, this mask is almost ready to go. Most of the edges have been selected without having to paint along them with the Paint Brushes tool.

Summary

In this hour, you learned how to read the information stored in channels, how to split an image into channels, and how to combine channels into an image. You also saw how channels can help you create complex masks.

In the next hour I take you on a tour of the new vector tools.

Workshop

The Workshop contains a question and answer section to help answer the most commonly asked questions and quiz questions to help you solidify your understanding of the material covered.

Q&A

Q Why are channels grayscale?

A Channels are grayscale because they represent only one portion of an image—for example, the Red channel (from an RGB split) or the Lightness channel (from an HSL split). The information in any one channel can be described with eight bits. Eight-bit grayscale images are perfectly suited for holding the information that makes up an image's channel.

Q Why would I choose RGB channels over HSL channels?

A The type of channels you split an image into depends on what you hope to accomplish with the channels. As an example, I first looked at RGB channels to create the mask in the last example. However, I ultimately decided to use HSL channels because the Saturation channel came closest to the mask I was trying to create.

Q Does splitting an image into channels affect my original image?

A No. Splitting an image into channels creates completely new images—one for each channel. Even recombining these images (or channels) into an image doesn't affect the original.

Quiz

1. Why would you want to split an image into CMYK channels?

2. Name a good reason for splitting an image into its separate channels.

3. How are channels helpful in creating masks?

4. Do you necessarily need to recombine the channels into an image?

Answers

1. Splitting an image into CMYK channels is necessary for creating color separations for high-end printing.

2. Splitting an image into channels helps you create complex masks more easily than using other methods, such as the ones outlined in Hour 11.

3. By finding the channel with the greatest contrast between the area you want to mask and the rest of the image, you can create better masks with less work.

4. Not if you need the channels for purposes such as creating masks.

12

Hour 13

Working with Flexible Vector Tools

This hour covers the following:

- Using vector tools
- Creating vector shapes
- Editing nodes
- Creating vector lines
- Type as vectors
- Vector object properties

Starting with version 6, Paint Shop Pro includes a selection of vector-based tools. I described some of the differences between vector-based and raster-based (bitmap) tools throughout other sections of the book. For example, I described the differences you can expect when resizing the two types of objects in Hour 9, "Creating Cool Text Effects."

The main difference is that you can easily manipulate vector objects after creating them. Although you also can manipulate bitmapped objects, you cannot do so with the same flexibility as you can with vector objects.

Using Vector Tools

The various vector tools available are

- The Text tool
- The Draw tool (formerly the Line tool)
- The Preset Shapes tool
- The Vector Object Selection tool

Along with the tools, there is a new layer type. This, of course, is a vector layer. Any vector object, line, shape, or text will reside on a vector layer. In fact, if a raster layer is current and you select a vector tool and start to draw with it, a new vector layer will be created above the current raster layer.

You'll note that selecting a tool does not automatically mean that you'll be drawing with a vector object. Each vector tool described in the previous list, with the exception of the Vector Object Selection tool, must be activated from either the Tool Options window (for the Draw tool and the Preset Shapes tool) or the Text Entry dialog box (for the Text tool).

Both of these dialog boxes have options that must be selected for the tool to operate in vector mode.

Other than setting the options, drawing a vector object isn't really any different from drawing with a bitmap tool. The exception, though, is the Draw tool. Drawing lines as vectors is a bit tricky, but this tool is quite powerful.

After drawing vector text or shapes, you will notice a distinct difference, though. Say, for example, you draw a bitmap shape using the Preset Shapes tool. The shape is drawn and that's the end of it. If, on the other hand, you draw a shape with the Create As Vector option selected, that's a whole other matter.

Creating Vector Objects

After you draw a vector shape and release the mouse button, you'll notice a bounding box surrounding your shape. Also, you'll note that there are control points and a control handle. The points are at and between each corner of the object. The control handle is a line originating from the center and extending toward the right (see Figure 13.1).

FIGURE 13.1

A vector object with its control handle, its control points, and its layer, and the Tool Options window.

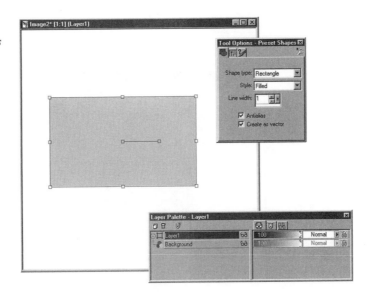

You can drag any of the points to resize the object. Dragging one of the corner points will resize the height and width simultaneously.

You can also distort the object by holding down the Shift or Ctrl key and clicking and dragging a corner point. Doing so will skew (Shift key) or change the perspective of (Ctrl key) the object. You also can click and drag the rightmost point of the control handle to rotate the object.

The most fun, though, comes when you start editing nodes.

Editing Nodes

Nodes are similar to control points but much more powerful. Rather than being on the bounding box, though, they are on the object itself.

To see how nodes work, follow along with this exercise:

1. Open a new 500×500-pixel image with the background set to white.

2. Set the foreground color to red.

3. Select the Preset Shapes tool.

4. In the Tool Options window, set the Shape Type to Ellipse, the Style to Filled, and make sure the Create As Vector option is checked.

13

5. Place the mouse near the middle of the image and click and drag to draw a vertical ellipse (see Figure 13.2).

FIGURE 13.2

An ellipse drawn with the vector-based Preset Shapes tool.

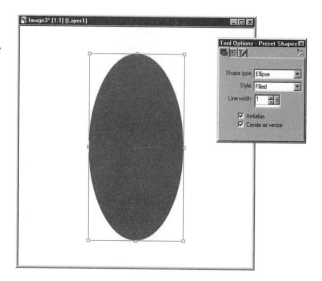

6. Select the Vector Object Selection tool (it's the tool at the very bottom of the tool-bar, or the rightmost one if you've set your toolbar horizontal).

   You'll notice that the Tool Options window has changed (see Figure 13.3) and that there is a Node Edit button visible.

FIGURE 13.3

After selecting a vector object, you can edit its nodes.

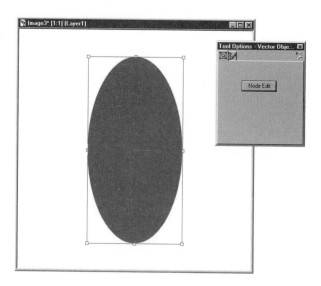

7. Click the Node Edit button (here's where the real fun begins).

   You'll note that the ellipse loses its fill and that instead of a bounding box there are points along the ellipse itself: one at the top, the bottom, the left, and the right (see Figure 13.4).

FIGURE **13.4**

A vector object in node editing mode.

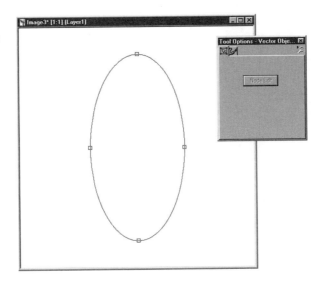

8. Move the mouse over each node. You'll notice that as you do so, the mouse pointer describes several of the nodes. The top node is called start and the leftmost node is called close. These nodes are the start and the end of the curve that makes up the ellipse. When you move over the other two nodes, the cursor is a small plus sign with an arrowhead at each end. Along the curve, the mouse pointer has a small curve associated with it. Anywhere else in the image, the pointer has a small plus sign. When the pointer is a plus sign, you can add nodes; when it's a curve you can move the object. When you see the start, close, or plus sign with the arrowheads, you can move the nodes. Also, by right-clicking a node, you can change the node's behavior. You can choose from asymmetric, symmetric, cusp, and smooth/tangent (see Figures 13.5 through 13.8).

13

FIGURE **13.5**

An asymmetric node.

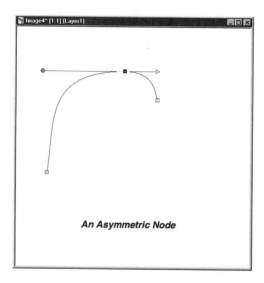

An asymmetric node connects two dissimilar curves. You'll note that the beginning and ending points of the control line can be different lengths.

FIGURE **13.6**

A symmetric node.

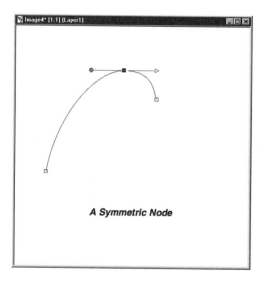

A symmetric node joins two similar curves. The ending points of the control line are always the same distance from the node.

FIGURE 13.7

A cusp node.

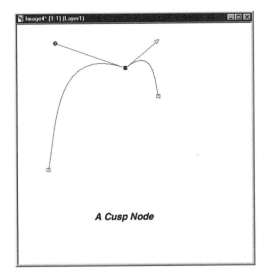

A cusp node joins two lines. Each control handle determines the angle and distance of its associated line.

FIGURE 13.8

A smooth/tangent node.

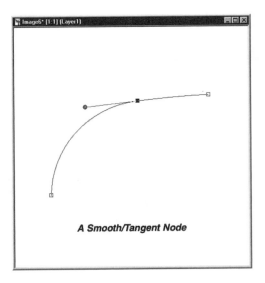

A smooth/tangent node connects a curve and a line. The control line determines how smoothly the line and the curve connect. Note that you can only choose a smooth/tangent line where a curve meets a line. You can change the curve on either side of a node by right-clicking the node and choosing Node Type, and then choosing either Convert to Line, Line Before, or Line After from the floating menu that appears.

13

To change a node from one type to another, select the node and right-click it to bring up the floating menu. From the menu, choose Node Type and then choose the type of node you want.

Entirely new shapes can be drawn by editing nodes on existing shapes. By following along with the next exercise, you will see how a heart shape can be created from an existing ellipse. To get started, open a new 500×500 image and draw a vector ellipse.

1. On the ellipse, select the top node and right-click it.
2. To change the node to a cusp, Choose Node Type, Cusp from the floating menu. If the Cusp choice is grayed out, the node is already a cusp.
3. Drag both control handles up and toward the outside (see Figure 13.9).

FIGURE 13.9

Changing a symmetri-
cal node to a cusp
node and editing it.

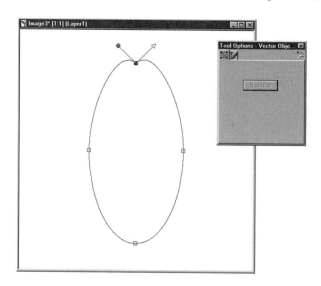

4. Drag the node down toward the middle of the image (see Figure 13.10).
5. Click the bottom node and change it to a cusp node.
6. Move its handles upward and outward, too (see Figure 13.11).

FIGURE 13.10

Moving the top node.

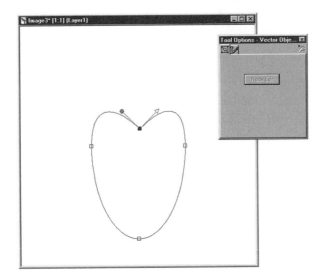

FIGURE 13.11

Moving the bottom node.

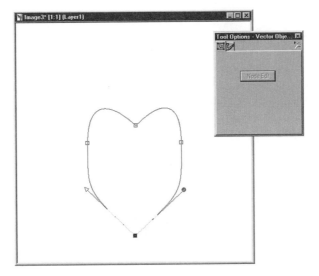

I think we're getting to the heart of the matter, now.

7. Click and drag the left node to the left.

8. Click and drag the right node to the right (see Figure 13.12).

13

FIGURE 13.12

Moving the left and right nodes.

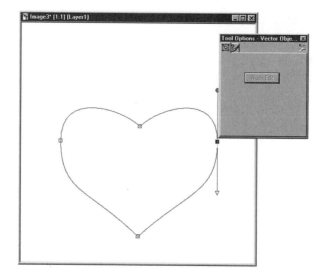

9. Right-click a node and choose Quit Node Editing. You should have a red heart (see Figure 13.12).

FIGURE 13.13

A heart shape created by editing the nodes of an ellipse.

Amazing! Try that with a bitmap object.

This should give you an idea of the types of things you can do with vector shapes and their nodes. You can also manipulate lines as vector objects.

Creating Vector Lines

Vector lines have some mysterious properties, similar to the properties associated with vector shapes. While vector shapes are closed, though, vector lines are open-ended objects. Vector lines also contain nodes that can be manipulated.

To draw a vector line, select the Draw tool and, in the Tool Options window, choose a type.

You can choose from Single Line, Bezier Curve, Freehand Line, and Point to Point Line.

Drawing Single Lines

Single Line is a straight line that begins where you first click the mouse and ends where you release the mouse.

You can restrict the angle to multiples of 45 degrees by holding down the Shift key as you click and drag.

You can also see the coordinates of the starting and ending points, the angle, and the length of the line displayed along the bottom-left corner of the main window. This is very helpful.

In the Tool Options window, you can set the width of the line and whether it will be antialiased, whether it will be a vector (which we'll be using for the lines in this hour), and whether it will be closed.

The Closed option doesn't apply to straight lines but will close any curve you draw as a Bezier or a curve.

Drawing Bezier Curves

I described and demonstrated Bezier curves in Hour 6, "Drawing Tools and Techniques." Drawing them as vector objects is exactly the same except that you have the added benefit of being able to change them either by using the control handles of the bounding box or by editing their nodes.

Drawing Freehand Lines

The Freehand line tool enables you to draw freehand curves. They can be open ended, antialiased, and created as vectors.

When drawing a freehand line, you can also set the tracking. This option is available under the second tab of the Tool Options window with the Draw tool selected and Type set to Freehand.

Figure 13.14 shows the tracking set to 2.

13

FIGURE **13.14**

A freehand curve drawn with the tracking set to 2.

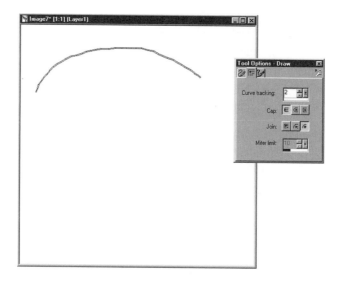

Figure 13.15 shows a similar curve drawn with the tracking set to 60.

FIGURE **13.15**

A freehand curve drawn with the tracking set to 60.

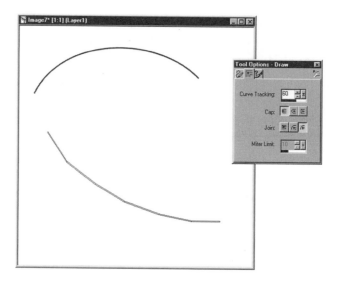

The difference is the distance between the straight lines that will make up the final curve. It does make a difference in how smooth the curve will be as you draw it, but it makes no difference in the smoothness of the final curves, as you can see in Figure 13.16.

FIGURE 13.16

Two freehand curves drawn with different tracking values.

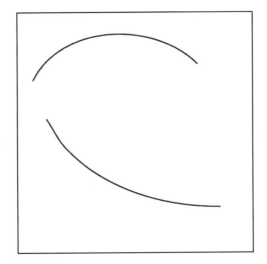

Drawing Point to Point Lines

The Point to Point line tool is quite powerful. You can draw straight lines going from one point to another, and you can use this tool to create multifaceted shapes. To do so, simply click, move the mouse, click, move the mouse, click, and so on. Each click will set another point in the shape. To end the shape, simply select another tool. You can close the path by selecting the two end nodes using the Vector Object Selection tool, right-clicking one of the nodes, and choosing Edit, Close from the floating menu.

Besides drawing straight lines with the Point to Point tool, you can draw curves similar to the Bezier tool. However, the point-to-point lines remain editable as you draw them and can contain many nodes.

You can draw a point-to-point curve by clicking, moving the mouse, and clicking and dragging. You can continue to click and drag as needed to create the curve you want (see Figure 13.17).

Don't worry if the curve isn't exactly the shape you want; it can be edited at the node level, just as the shapes were earlier in this hour.

13

FIGURE 13.17

A multinode curve, drawn with the Point to Point Line tool.

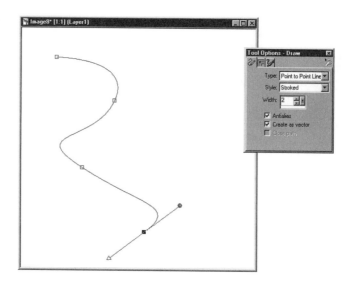

Type as Vectors

You saw earlier, in Hour 9, that text can be entered as either a bitmap or a vector. At that time I demonstrated how resizing text entered as vectors yields better results than resizing bitmap text. But vector text has more going for it than just being resizable. You can also create editable curves from any text you enter.

To do so, enter some text using the Text tool and make sure that you place a check mark in the Vector option under Create As in the Text Entry dialog box.

To convert the text to editable curves, select the text using the Vector Object Selection tool and right-click the text.

From the floating menu, choose Convert Text to Curves, and then choose either As Single Shape or As Character Shapes.

Either choice will activate the Node Edit button in the Tool Options window.

Both choices are similar except that the As Single Shape option activates the Node Edit button right away and keeps all the text as one shape. On the other hand, the As Character Shapes option separates the text into separate characters that can be moved and manipulated singly as well as with node editing.

Whichever option you choose, you now have the ability to edit your characters at the node level, just as you did with the shapes and lines described earlier in this chapter.

Vector Object Properties

All vector objects are created on vector layers. You can have more than one vector object on a vector layer, and each is separately selectable and is easily manipulated. You can select any current vector object from its layer. When a vector object is added to a vector layer, it creates a sublayer (see Figure 13.18).

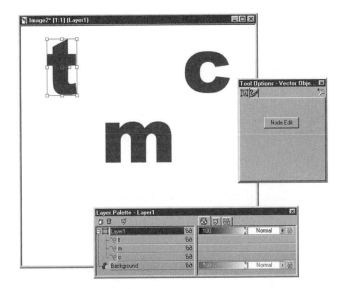

You can select each object by clicking it with the Vector Object Selection tool or by clicking its name in the Layer palette.

You can also manipulate any vector object's properties by right-clicking its name in the Layer palette. Doing so brings up a floating menu from which you can choose Properties. This brings up the Vector Properties dialog box (see Figure 13.19), which enables you to change the properties of the currently selected vector object.

You can see in Figure 13.19 that I've changed the properties of the letter *m* to Stroked instead of Filled and changed the line width from 1 to 5. The result is an outlined (stroked) letter, rather than a solid one.

You can also change the aliasing, whether the object layer should be visible, its color, its cap, and its join and miter limits. All of these options and their effects have been previously discussed.

13

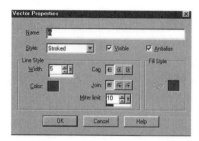

FIGURE 13.19
The Vector Properties dialog box.

Rasterizing Your Vector Objects

One drawback to vectors, as powerful as they are, is that you can't apply the same filters to them as you can to bitmap objects. For example, you can't add a bevel to vector-based text or apply a texture to a vector shape. There is a solution, though. You can convert your vector objects to bitmap by rasterizing them.

To convert any object, though, means converting all objects on the same vector layer. This has its drawbacks, as well. If you want some objects to remain as vectors, you should create them on their own layers or copy and paste them to a new vector layer before proceeding with the conversion process.

You can cut, copy, and paste vector objects as you would any other object you create in Paint Shop Pro.

To convert a vector layer and its associated vector objects to bitmap, right-click the layer name in the Layer palette and choose Convert to Raster. Note that, having done so, you can reverse the process only by choosing Edit, Undo.

Figure 13.20 shows two of the letters, the *t* and the *c*, converted to raster with an Inner Bevel filter applied.

FIGURE 13.20

Two letters converted from vector to raster with an effects filter applied.

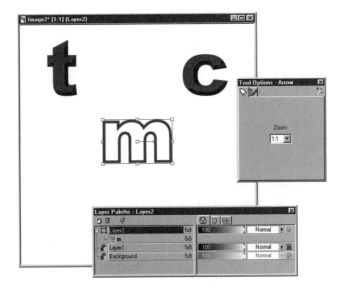

Before I converted the layer, I copied the *m* and then pasted it to a new vector layer.

Talk about flexibility!

Summary

This hour introduced you to some of the wonders of vector objects. These are powerful tools and will take some time, patience, and effort on your part to master. Any time spent will be well rewarded, though.

I encourage you to play around with as many of these tools as time permits. When creating a new image, for example, stop for a moment and try to decide whether a vector object might serve your purposes better than a bitmapped one.

Workshop

The Workshop contains a question and answer section to help answer the most commonly asked questions and quiz questions to help you solidify your understanding of the material covered.

13

Q&A

Q How do I return to a vector object to edit it?

A Clicking a vector layer's name in the Layer palette will select the vector object. You can also select an object using the Vector Object Selection tool.

Q How do I add a node to a vector object?

A You can add nodes by Ctrl+clicking a segment, whether that segment is a line or a curve.

Q What is a cusp node?

A A cusp node is one that has separate curves emanating from either side. This property means that a cusp can be a sharp point.

Q How do I quit editing nodes?

A Right-click a vector object and choose Quit Node Editing or press Ctrl+Q.

Quiz

1. How do you change the properties of a node?

2. How do you change the properties of a vector object, such as Fill, Stroke, and Stroke & Fill?

3. How do you convert a vector object to a raster (bitmap) object?

4. How do you arrange vector objects?

Answers

1. You can change the properties of a node by right-clicking the node and choosing Node Type. From the pop-up menu, you can change the type of node and the type of segment (line to curve or curve to line).

2. You can change the Stroke and Fill properties, such as line width and fill color, by right-clicking a vector object and choosing Properties. Doing so will bring up the Vector Properties dialog box, where you can make the desired changes.

3. You can convert a vector object to a raster (bitmap) object by selecting the object with the Vector Object Selection tool and choosing Layers, Convert to Raster.

4. Vector objects can be arranged by clicking and dragging their layers in the Layer palette.

Hour **14**

Using and Creating Picture Tubes

This hour introduces the following issues:

- Understanding picture tubes
- Using picture tubes
- Finding picture tubes
- Creating your own picture tubes

Picture tubes, new from version 5, are a fun-to-use addition to Paint Shop Pro. They are so much fun, in fact, that many new Web sites have sprung up just to offer picture tubes to Paint Shop Pro users. You learn about where you can get more picture tubes later in this hour.

Let's get started by learning what picture tubes are and how they can help you.

What Are Picture Tubes?

Picture tubes, in their most basic form, are really just a form of the Paint Brushes tool. The Picture Tube tool is almost like a rubber stamp, in that it allows you to reproduce the same image, or set of images, again and again across a background. The images within a picture tube are set and cannot be modified, but they can be reproduced with ease. You can use this technique to create seamless backgrounds, backgrounds for logos, or anything else that follows a theme.

You use the Picture Tube tool much as you do any of the other painting and drawing tools—by selecting it and clicking and dragging the mouse. Figure 14.1 shows the Picture Tube Tool icon.

Using Picture Tubes

The Picture Tube tool is available in the Tool palette. It's the seventh icon from the bottom (or right, depending on how you have your Toolbar positioned) and looks like a brush with a small blue rubber stamp above it.

After selecting the Picture Tube tool, you can choose the actual tube and the scaling for the image that the tool creates from within the Tool Options window (see Figure 14.1).

FIGURE 14.1

An image created with the Picture Tube tool and the Tool Options window. The Picture Tube tool icon is shown on the right.

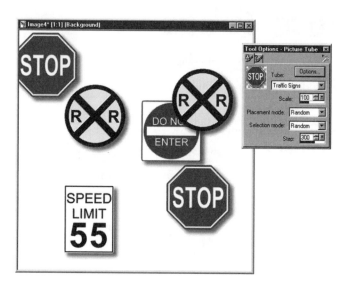

To create the image you see in Figure 14.1, follow these steps:

1. Choose the Traffic Signs tube selection from the Tube menu under the Picture Tube tab in the Tool Options window and set the scaling to 100% in the Scale slider.

2. Simply click a few times within the image to draw the traffic signs using the tool.

All the information that a tube needs is stored within the tube itself. The good news here is that you can create amazingly complex tubes.

Figure 14.2, for example, is a picture of a tarantula, created with one single stroke of the Picture Tube tool.

FIGURE 14.2

A complex image created with a single stroke of the Picture Tube tool.

Some of the other options available when you're painting with tubes are accessible by clicking the Options button in the Tool Options window after you've selected the Picture Tube tool.

From within the Picture Tube Options dialog box (see Figure 14.3), you can set the following settings:

- The Placement mode determines whether the objects in the tube image appear at random or fixed intervals as you're painting with the Picture Tube tool.

- The Selection mode determines how an object is selected from among the other objects that make up the tube. The Selection modes you can choose from are Random (an object is chosen randomly from among all of the objects); Incremental (objects are chosen in the order in which they are laid out in the tube); Angular (objects are chosen based on the angle at which you click and drag the tool);

14

Pressure (objects are chosen based on the amount of pressure you apply with a pen and tablet); and Velocity (objects are chosen based on how fast you move the mouse pointer over the image you are painting on).

FIGURE 14.3

The Picture Tube Options dialog box.

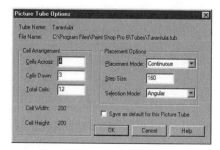

Take a moment to try out the various tubes. Play with the scaling, change the tubes, and paint a few strokes with each. You may be amazed at the cool artwork that can be created by combining some of the different tubes.

Finding New Picture Tubes

Even with the substantial number of tubes available when you install Paint Shop Pro, you'll probably find yourself wanting more.

> You can find tons of tubes on the Web. As a starting point, visit Jasc Software, Inc.'s site at http://www.jasc.com and go to the Resources pages. You'll find plenty of sites listed there that offer free tubes.

Tubes are stored as separate files with the Paint Shop Pro folders on the hard drive of any Paint Shop Pro user. This means that users can trade tubes with ease.

> The tube file format changed between version 5 and version 6 of Paint Shop Pro. The two formats are not compatible. However, there is a conversion utility provided with version 6. You can find it under Start, Programs, Paint Shop Pro 6. Simply run the program (it's called Picture Tube Converter) and specify the directory where the version 5 files are and where the version 6 files should go and all of your tubes will be converted. This will come in handy if you should receive tube files from a friend who's still using version 5 or if you find some older tube files on the Web.

You can find the tube files in the Tube folder on your hard drive. To do so, if you installed Paint Shop Pro in its default directory, double-click the My Computer icon on the main Windows desktop. Double-click the C: drive icon, the Program Files icon, the Paint Shop Pro icon, and, finally, the Tubes icon (this order depends on your having installed Paint Shop Pro to the default directory).

After all the double-clicking, you'll see the Tubes folder (see Figure 14.4).

FIGURE 14.4

The Tubes *folder on the author's hard drive.*

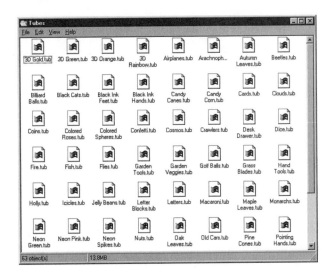

The icons with the .tub extension are tube files. You can copy any of these, or any you create, to a floppy or add them to an email attachment to send to a friend.

Note that the .tub files you see in this folder are available to you under the Tool Options window when the Picture Tube tool is selected.

You can also view the tube file using the PSPBrowse program. To do so, choose File and point the program to the same folder as outlined in the preceding steps. This has the advantage of giving you a visual representation of the tube files (see Figure 14.5).

If you are having trouble finding the Picture Tube files on your hard drive (or someone else's), use the Find Files option in the Start menu and search for *.tub. This search finds any files on the current hard drive with the .tub extension.

14

FIGURE 14.5

The Tubes *folder on the author's hard drive, seen with PSPBrowse.*

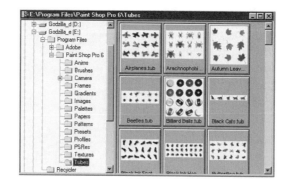

Also, you can zip them up singly or in groups and store them on a Web site so that anyone in the world can access them. Before you do so, though, you have to create some of your own tubes.

Creating Your Own Picture Tubes

Creating your own picture tubes is, naturally, more complicated than just painting with them. It's not all that difficult, though.

There are just a few things to keep in mind. You must create your tubes on a transparent background, and the image must be 24-bit color. Also, you must break up the main tube image (the image that will hold the various tubes or objects) into a grid and place each separate image into one of the squares formed by the grid.

You'll need to set up the grid so that it has enough squares to hold your images. You can use as few as one square and as many squares as you'll need to accommodate the various objects you'll be using. I'm not sure what the limit on squares is, but without going through each built-in tube, I came across some that went as high as 36 squares.

The first step is to decide which objects to use. Normally, you want a theme of some sort. For the following exercise, I use a few letters, but you can draw images, scan images or objects, copy portions of photographs, or use anything else you'd like.

After you decide on the subject and gather up the objects you need, it's time to build the tube image. Follow these steps:

1. Open a new image that'll be large enough to hold all of the objects you'll be using. Start with a 600×200 image.

   Remember to set Background Color to Transparent. If you don't, you won't be able to export your image to a tube file—and you'll find this out only after putting all the time and effort into creating and arranging your objects.

You also won't be able to export the image to a tube file if you have more than one layer in the image. If you keep these things in mind before starting out, you'll be okay.

2. With your new image file open, you should turn on the grid to help with the placement of your various objects. To turn on the grid, choose View, Grid.

Of course, the grid may not be set up with the dimensions you need. To correct this problem, follow these steps:

   A. Choose File, Preferences, General Program Preferences. You will get the Paint Shop Pro Preferences dialog box.

   B. Click the Rulers and Units tab to display these options (see Figure 14.6).

FIGURE 14.6

The Rulers and Units tab.

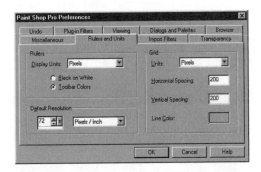

   C. You'll need to set the Horizontal and Vertical setting to the size you need for your grid. Because I'll be creating three objects in a 600×200 image, I set the spacing to 200. This setting gives me three 200×200 squares across.

   D. I also set Line Color to a bright red. I did so because the default, gray, which works nicely on a white background without getting in the way, isn't too visible on the transparent background. To change the color of the grid's lines, click the line color swatch and select a color from the Color Picker dialog box.

   E. Finally, click OK to set the new grid preferences.

Figure 14.7 shows my image with the grid turned on and set up with the dimensions and color I selected.

After you open the new image and set up the grid, you can start placing or drawing your objects.

3. Place your objects. I chose to use the letters *A*, *B*, and *C*. To place these letters (or any image) into the grid, you simply move the object into place while it's still selected.

14

FIGURE 14.7

Empty image file with the grid visible.

4. After placing the letters into the grid, I decided to jazz them up a bit.

   I used the Blade Pro plug-in (a demo is available at `http://www.flamingpear.com/`) on the letter *A* (I show you more about this and other plug-ins in Hour 15, "Applying Filters"), played around with some noise and some motion blurring to get a metallic effect for the letter *B,* and used the woodgrain texture effect from Hour 9, "Creating Cool Text Effects," to create the letter *C*.

   The final image appears in Figure 14.8.

FIGURE 14.8

The ABC image file, ready to be exported to a tube file.

All that's left is to export the image as a tube file, as follows:

1. Make sure that the image you want to export is open and that it's the current image. Then choose File, Export, Picture Tube to open the Export Picture Tube dialog box (see Figure 14.9).

FIGURE 14.9

The Export Picture Tube dialog box.

2. The only settings you'll need to change are the numbers for Cells Across and Cells Down. Change these to reflect the number of cells that your image contains. For this example, I would choose three cells across and one cell down. The total number of cells will be updated automatically for you. You can pretty much ignore the other options; the tube's user can set them. However, you do need to give your tube a name.

3. After you make the changes and enter a name, you can click OK in the Export Picture Tube dialog box to save your tube.

Your tube will be available immediately. To test it, open a new file (you can change the background from transparent to any color you choose at this point), select the Picture Tube tool, choose your tube from the pull-down menu in the Tool Options window, and start painting.

That's it!

You should have lots of fun with tubes. Remember that you can change the size of the squares when you create a tube image; you don't need to use the 200×200 size that I used. You can use from 1 to 36 (at least, maybe more) squares, and you can fill the squares with just about anything you want.

Try rotating your objects or resizing them (see Hour 5, "Working with Deformations," for a refresher on using deformations) as you place them in the grid. Try using similar objects but with different colors, and so on.

Summary

I hope you enjoyed this hour as much as I did. I think tubes are fun, and you should have some fun using and creating them. In this hour, you learned how to use existing tubes, how to find new ones, how to create your own, and how to share the tubes you create with others.

The topic of filters, both built-in and third-party, is one of my favorites, and you'll see why in the next hour.

Workshop

The Workshop contains a question and answer section to help answer the most commonly asked questions and quiz questions to help you solidify your understanding of the material covered.

14

Q&A

Q I get an error when I try to export my tube image; why?

A You must make sure that the image is 24-bit color, that it contains only one layer, and that the objects are placed over a transparency. Improperly setting these options is the most common reason for such an error message.

Q Can I use pictures of people for tubes?

A Yes. Anything that can be scanned in or drawn can be used. All you need to do is copy the portion of the image you want and paste it into the image that you'll be exporting as a tube.

Q When I try drawing with some tubes, only one object shows up. Why?

A Check to see if the tube contains more than one image and what the Selection mode is. You can check these settings by clicking the Options button in the Tool Options window with the Picture Tube tool selected. If the Pressure setting is set for the Selection mode and you're using a mouse instead of a tablet, you might get only one of the objects from the tube to show up.

Quiz

1. How do you view the grid to help you place objects when creating a tube file?
2. How do you change the dimensions and color of the grid lines?
3. How many grids can you use when creating a tube file?
4. How can you share your tube files with others?
5. How can you convert the version 5 tube files you created or downloaded from the Web?

Answers

1. Choose View, Grid.
2. Choose File, Preferences, General Program Preferences. The grid settings can be changed in the Paint Shop Pro Preferences dialog box under the Rulers and Units tab.
3. You can create from 1 to 36 (and possibly more) grids. You just need to create the grid and store your objects in it. When you export the file, enter the appropriate numbers in the Cells Across and Cells Down windows.

4. Tube files are stored on your hard drive in a folder under the `Paint Shop Pro` folder. Any of the `.tub` files can be copied to floppy, attached to email messages, or placed on a Web site where others can access them.

5. You can convert any of your older version 5 tube files by clicking the Start button in Windows and then choosing Programs, Paint Shop Pro 6, Picture Tube Converter.

14

Hour **15**

Applying Filters

Filters, a type of built-in or third-party plug-in, are extensions to a program. Filters add functionality to a program by allowing you to create an effect that you otherwise could not create. Some filters come with Paint Shop Pro, and other filters (often referred to as plug-ins) are available from third-party software companies.

In this hour, I show you some of the built-in filters and some of my favorite third-party plug-ins. I also show you some of the cool effects you can accomplish with these filters. The following issues are covered:

- Understanding filters
- Using Paint Shop Pro's built-in filters
- Finding cool plug-ins
- Installing plug-ins
- Using third-party plug-ins

Why Filters?

As I mentioned, filters and plug-ins extend the capabilities of a program such as Paint Shop Pro.

Many of today's imaging programs are written to be *extensible*, which means that they can have their functionality extended through the use of add-on software. This technology enables other programmers to write software that literally can be plugged into the main program.

If you've purchased and installed a plug-in program, it should be available under the Image, Plug-in Filters menu in Paint Shop Pro.

Where You Can Get Plug-ins

As mentioned earlier, some filters come with Paint Shop Pro, and others are available from third parties. Most, if not all, of the companies that write plug-ins are on the Web, and some offer free demos of their plug-ins.

Plug-ins range from free (or nearly free) to shareware (priced from $15 to $25) to commercial products (priced from $50 to $200 or more).

The Web addresses of several companies mentioned in this hour follow:

- Alien Skin at http://www.alienskin.com. Alien Skin makes the very popular Eye Candy plug-in.
- Auto F/X at http://www.autofx.com. Auto F/X makes plug-ins such as Page Edges, Photo/Graphic Edges, Typo/Graphic Edges, The Ultimate Texture Collection, and more.
- Flaming Pear at http://www.flamingpear.com/. Flaming Pear is the creator of BladePro, a relatively new but increasingly popular plug-in that enables you to add textures and bevels to objects.
- MetaCreations at http://www.metacreations.com. MetaCreations, widely known for its 2D and 3D imaging products, also produces Kai's Power Tools (KPT). KPT is a collection of awesome filters that enable you to create gradients and textures and manipulate images.
- RAYflect at http://www.rayflect.com. RAYflect products include Four Seasons, which enables you to add realistic and otherworldly atmospheric backdrops (skies such as sunsets, storms, and so on) to your images.
- Wacom at http://www.wacom.com. If you're lucky enough to own a Wacom graphics tablet, you should also have a copy of PenTools. This product, which ships with every tablet from Wacom, offers a collection of cool effects that work with your pen and tablet.

15

I don't cover all the filters available on the market (there are just too many, with more coming to market weekly, it seems). Whole books could be written on the subject. I don't even cover each separate filter in any given package (again, there are just too many). However, I do show you some of my favorites, give you an idea of how to use them, and suggest what you can accomplish with them.

Using Built-In Filters

You've already seen examples of at least one of the built-in filters. I've used the Hot Wax Coating filter in a couple of examples to add even more texture to the woodgrain texture and to create a chrome effect. Paint Shop Pro has a few more built-in filters, though, and the nicest are the Effects filters, many of which are new to version 6.

The Effects filters consist of the Black Pencil, Blinds, Buttonize, Charcoal, Chisel, Chrome, Colored Chalk, Colored Pencil, Cutout, Drop Shadow, Feedback, Glowing Edges, Inner Bevel, Kaleidoscope, Mosaic-Antique, Mosaic-Glass, Neon Glow, Outer Bevel, Pattern, Sculpture, Texture, Tiles, and Weave. Some of these are discussed in the following sections. For the rest, I encourage you to experiment. Load a photo, create an image, or make a selection, and try some of the different filters on it.

Buttonize Filter

The Buttonize filter (choose Image, Effects, Buttonize) enables you to instantly create rectangular buttons from any image. Figure 15.1 shows the Buttonize dialog box.

FIGURE 15.1

A button being created with the Buttonize filter and the Buttonize dialog box.

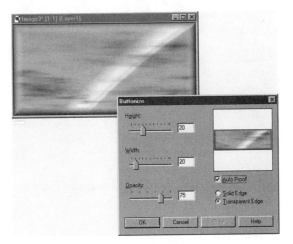

You can see the settings I've chosen for the button and the result of applying those settings in Figure 15.1.

You can change the height, width, and opacity of the bevel. You also can choose a solid or transparent edge. You can use the Auto Proof feature so that you can see the changes you're applying in real time.

Both the Solid Edge and Transparent Edge options use the current background color for the bevel. The difference is that the solid edge is a solid color, using only shades of the background color, whereas the transparent edge allows the image to show through, as seen in Figure 15.1.

Chisel Filter

The Chisel filter (choose Image, Effects, Chisel) adds an outer bevel around the current selection. This bevel can be transparent or in the background color. You can also adjust the size of the bevel.

You can see the effect of the bevel in the preview window of the dialog box in Figure 15.2.

FIGURE 15.2

The Chisel effect being applied to some text.

In this dialog box, you can set the size of the bevel and whether it should be transparent or created with the current background color.

Cutout Filter

The Cutout filter (choose Image, Effects, Cutout) makes selections appear to be cut out of the background. Essentially, this filter adds a shadow to the inside of the object (see Figure 15.3).

FIGURE 15.3

The Cutout effect being applied to some text.

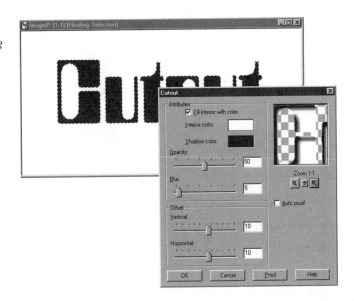

You can fill the area with white if you like. You also can set the interior and shadow colors, the opacity and blur of the shadow, and the vertical and horizontal offsets of the shadow.

The vertical and horizontal offsets enable you to move the shadow around to get different effects.

The Blur setting also affects this feature. A softer blur makes the cutout appear higher than the same effect done with less blurring.

The Opacity setting affects how opaque or transparent the resulting shadow will be.

Drop Shadow Filter

The Drop Shadow effect adds a drop shadow to selected objects. This effect is often used on text.

You can set the color, the opacity, and the blur of the shadow. You also can set the vertical and horizontal offsets of the shadow (see Figure 15.4).

FIGURE 15.4

*The Drop Shadow
effect being applied to
some text.*

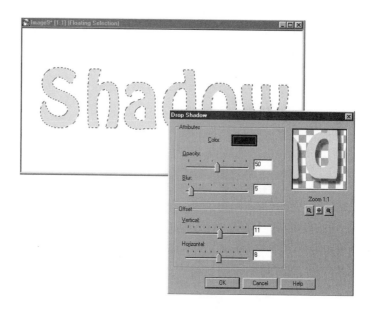

One effect that I like is to apply the drop shadow to white text on a white background
(see Figure 15.5).

FIGURE 15.5

*The Drop Shadow
effect applied to white
text on a white back-
ground.*

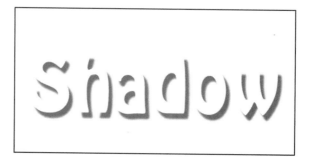

To create this effect, open a new image with a white background and follow these steps:

1. Select the Text tool.

2. Add some text to your image, making sure that you set the color to White in the
   Text Entry dialog box or, as an alternative, set the Create As option to Selection to
   have the text come in as a selection.

3. Instead of seeing filled text, you'll see just a selection. (The text is still filled; it's
   just filled with white and is against a white background.)

4. Choose Image, Effects, Drop Shadow and set the options to your liking.

5. After clicking OK to apply the drop shadow, you should end up with a result similar to that shown in Figure 15.5.

   I've seen this effect used recently on television and in magazine ads. It is hard to believe that it's so simple.

Recall also that many of the filters discussed in this hour are used throughout various parts of the book. In Hour 9, "Creating Cool Text Effects," for example, I used the Gaussian Blur filter for the *X-Files* text and in Hour 10, "Working Progressively with Layers," I used the Emboss filter to give a relief effect to an object on woodgrain.

Filters Effects with Layer Blending Mode Variations

Sometimes you can apply a filter to a layer and, with the help of a layer blending mode change, get a truly awesome effect.

To see an example of this technique, open a scan of a photo and follow along with the next example:

1. Choose Selections, Select All and Edit, Copy to copy the photograph.

2. Choose Edit, Paste As New Layer.

3. Choose Image, Effects, Black Pencil (this is a new filter that comes with version 6). This filter will give your photograph the effect of being drawn with a black pencil. But wait, the best is yet to come!

4. Change the layer blend mode in the Layer palette to Softlight.

Your photograph should resemble a softly colored, hand-drawn sketch (see Figure 15.6).

FIGURE 15.6

Applying the new Black Pencil effect to a copied layer and changing the layer blend mode to achieve the look of a hand-drawn sketch.

Figure 15.6 shows all three stages of the photograph. You can see the original photo, the layer with the Black Pencil filter applied, and the final image with the layer blending mode changed to allow the two layers to interact.

Examples of how some of the other built-in filters can be applied are shown throughout this book.

Using Third-Party Filters

Along with the filters that ship with Paint Shop Pro, numerous third-party filters (often referred to as *plug-ins*) are available.

Installing Plug-Ins

Installing a plug-in package so that it can be used with Paint Shop Pro is a multistep process:

1. The first step is to install the software according to the manufacturer's instructions. These days, that mostly involves inserting a CD-ROM into the drive and following a couple of short instructions.

   The most important point to note is where on your hard drive the plug-ins are installed.

   Normally, you'll want to keep all your plug-ins in separate folders under one main folder. For example, you might create a Plug-ins folder under the Paint Shop Pro folder and store all your plug-ins in separate folders there.

2. The second step to installing your plug-ins is to tell Paint Shop Pro where they are on your hard drive, which is the reason behind making a Plug-ins folder. After you've installed your plug-ins, choose File, Preferences, General Program Preferences.

3. Choose the Plug-in Filters tab to bring up the Plug-in Filters options (see Figure 15.7).

4. Enter the folder(s) where the filters are stored in the text box(es) at the bottom of the dialog box. For example, in Figure 15.7, I have entered C:\Program Files\Paint Shop Pro 6\Plugins in the first folder area. You also can click the Browse button to find the appropriate folder instead of typing in the name. I've enabled two entries because I own Paint Shop Pro (in Folder 1) as well as Photoshop (in Folder 2). I keep most of my filters under the Photoshop folder.

FIGURE 15.7

The Plug-in Filters options.

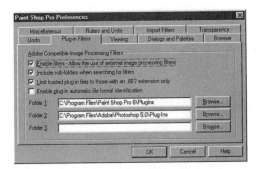

15

The options you can set in the Plug-in Filters tab are as follows:

- **Enable Filters**   This option allows the use of external image processing filters. You should, of course, place a check mark next to this option if you want to use the filters you've installed.

- **Include Subfolders when Searching for Filters**   This option should be checked if you did as I recommended and stored each plug-in package in its own subfolder.

- **Limit Loaded Plug-In Files to Those with an .8B? Extension Only**   This option should be checked if all the filters are 100 percent Photoshop compatible (which most of those available are). Paint Shop Pro enables you to use external plug-ins that are compatible with the industry standard. That standard is set by Adobe, the maker of Photoshop. Photoshop-compatible filters have a file extension that starts with 8B and ends with one other character. Normally, using only this type of filter results in fewer compatibility problems.

- **Enable Plug-In Automatic File Format Identification**   You can leave this option unchecked as I have done, or you can let Paint Shop Pro try to identify the file format of your filters.

- **Folder Names** As mentioned previously, the next three entries in the dialog box are the most important. They tell Paint Shop Pro where to find your plug-ins.

With your plug-ins installed and with Paint Shop Pro aware of where they are, you should be able to find them under Image, Plug-in Filters.

If you've installed Export filters, such as Ulead's SmartSaver, they will also be available under File, Export, Plug-in Export. Note that if you install filters while Paint Shop Pro is running, you might have to restart the program before the filters are available.

Alien Skin's Eye Candy

Eye Candy has long been one of my favorite plug-ins. It has some cool filters, such as
Inner Bevel, Chrome, Fire, and Smoke. Figure 15.8 shows the Eye Candy dialog box for
the Smoke filter.

FIGURE 15.8

*Alien Skin's Eye
Candy dialog box for
the Smoke filter.*

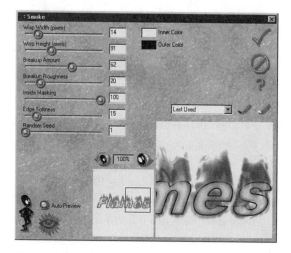

The Eye Candy dialog boxes are pretty much the same for all filters. The only changes
are the particular options you can set.

One nice touch with the Eye Candy filters is the real-time preview window, which you
can see in the lower-right corner of Figure 15.8. Figure 15.9 shows the result of applying
both the Fire and Smoke filters.

FIGURE 15.9

*Alien Skin's Fire and
Smoke filters applied
to some text in Paint
Shop Pro.*

I've seen many tips on applying a fire effect to text, but none comes close to the Eye Candy filter. You can get a demo of the Eye Candy filters at Alien Skin's Web site (http://www.alienskin.com).

Auto F/X's Photo/Graphic Edges

Auto F/X is the creator of several amazing filter packages. One of my favorites is Photo/Graphic Edges.

Starting with the latest version, Photo/Graphic Edges operates as a standalone as well as a plug-in. That is, you can run it separately as well as from within Paint Shop Pro.

The Photo/Graphic Edges filter enables you to add complex edges to your photographs. You can also add certain effects, such as Sepia Tones, Grain, and Burns. Figure 15.10 shows the Photo/Graphic Edges dialog box.

FIGURE 15.10

Auto F/X's Photo/Graphic Edges dialog box.

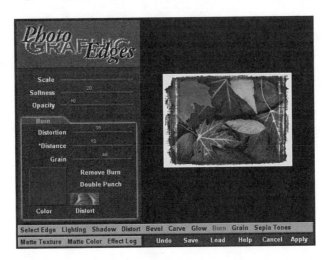

Figure 15.11 is the result of adding both an edge and a burn effect to a photograph of some fall leaves.

Along with the various effects that can be applied to an image with the Photo/Graphic Edges filter, you can select from a large gallery of edges that come with the plug-in.

Visit Auto F/X's Web site at http://www.autofx.com for more information and to download a demo of this cool plug-in.

15

FIGURE 15.11

Auto F/X's Photo/Graphic Edges filter applied to a photograph of some fall leaves.

Flaming Pear's BladePro

There is a lot of fuss over this "new kid on the block" on the Paint Shop Pro Internet newsgroup (`comp.graphics.apps.paint-shop-pro`), and rightly so. This really cool plug-in enables you to add textures, lighting, and bevels to your images. All you need to do is select an object and call up the filter (Image, Plug-in Filters, Flaming Pear, BladePro).

Figure 15.12 shows a template I created for my Web site, GrafX Design (`http://www.grafx-design.com`) a while back.

FIGURE 15.12

Radioactive symbol template created for the GrafX Design Web site.

15

After selecting it with the Magic Wand tool, I used BladePro (see Figure 15.13) to add a texture called Lizard to the symbol.

FIGURE 15.13

Flaming Pear's BladePro dialog box.

The result of applying the texture can be seen in Figure 15.14.

FIGURE 15.14

The Lizard texture from Flaming Pear's BladePro plug-in, applied to the radio-active symbol.

In addition to the extra textures and environments supplied with BladePro, many more are available from the Flaming Pear Web site (http://www.flamingpear.com/) and from other sites springing up all over the Web.

Typing **BladePro** into your favorite Internet search engine will undoubtedly turn up hundreds of sites where you can find more textures and environments for BladePro.

Of course, you can play around with the settings of the various options to create your own effects. These can be saved and passed on to friends or placed on your own Web site to be shared with the rest of the world.

To save a setting, click the bottom button at the middle of the interface. Clicking this button will bring up a dialog box where you can name and save your settings file.

RAYflect's Four Seasons

RAYflect's Four Seasons is an atmospheric generator. Huh? Okay, let's try this again. The Four Seasons plug-in enables you to create sky scenes such as sunsets, sunrises, and even rainbows. In fact, the rainbow effect in Figure 15.1 at the beginning of this hour was created with the Four Seasons plug-in.

You can use this filter to fill in those terribly plain or washed-out, pale blue skies that you sometimes get in photographs. For example, the train in Figure 15.15 was shot on a cloudy, rainy day in New Hampshire.

FIGURE 15.15

Shot of an old railway engine.

Although the gray day did wonders for bringing out the saturated colors of the engine, the sky itself really detracts from the overall feel of the photograph. No problem—Four Seasons to the rescue.

Using the selection and masking techniques described in Hour 2, "Opening, Saving, and Printing Files," and Hour 11, "Utilizing Masks for Precision," I selected the sky and was then able to run the RAYflect plug-in to give the sky a major facelift (see Figure 15.16).

FIGURE 15.16

*RAYflect's Four
Seasons dialog box.*

15

You can use the Four Seasons plug-in to adjust the sun, the moon, and the clouds. You can add haze and fog or use one of the preset skies. I used one of the Daytime presets to enhance the sky behind the engine (see Figure 15.17).

FIGURE 15.17

*Shot of an old railway
engine with an
enhanced sky, courtesy
of RAYflect's Four
Seasons plug-in.*

Visit RAYflect's Web site at http://www.rayflect.com to download a demo of this plug-in when you want to add a bit of color to the sky in a photograph.

Other Plug-Ins

You can start finding cool plug-ins by checking out the demos of the ones I've mentioned here and the others listed at the beginning of this hour. You're sure to find a product that meets your needs, whether it's to enhance your photographs or to help in the creation of Web graphics.

Summary

I hope you enjoyed this hour. It was more of a reading and visual adventure than a hands-on experience. I wanted to use this time to give you an idea of what's available out there in the way of plug-ins, rather than just walk you through one or two examples.

I hope that you got an idea of why the topic of filters, both built-in and third-party, is one of my favorites. Filters really are fun to play with and, more than that, they can really add to your images in many ways.

Workshop

The Workshop contains a question and answer section to help answer the most commonly asked questions and quiz questions to help you solidify your understanding of the material covered.

Q&A

Q I tried to apply a filter but the option was grayed out. Why?

A Most filters need you to be running in 16.7 million color mode and won't work otherwise. Choose Colors, Increase Color Depth, 16.7 Million Colors. If this method doesn't work, make sure that you're trying to apply the filter to an object or selection on the current layer and that the object or selection contains the needed information. (Make sure that the selection is not empty or transparent.)

Q I don't understand the difference between filters and plug-ins. What is the difference?

A Filters are the built-in effects that come with Paint Shop Pro, and plug-ins are usually add-ons. These terms are often interchanged, though.

Q I installed a filter, but it doesn't show up in the menu. Why isn't it there?

A The most likely cause is that you haven't told Paint Shop Pro where the filter is stored on your hard drive. Choose File, Preferences, General Program Preferences and click the Plug-in Filters tab. Enter the folder where you installed the plug-in filter into one of the three Folder entries in the dialog box. After doing so, your filter should show up. If it doesn't, chances are that you installed the filter while Paint Shop Pro was running. Exit and restart Paint Shop Pro to see whether this step solves the problem.

Quiz

1. Where can you get plug-ins for Paint Shop Pro?

2. How do you install a plug-in?

3. What do plug-ins do?

4. Why would you want to use a filter or plug-in?

Answers

1. Plug-ins are available from many different companies. Many of these companies have Web sites. See the list at the beginning of this hour for a starting point.

2. First, install the software according to the manufacturer's instructions. Then open Paint Shop Pro and choose File, Preferences, General Program Preferences. Click the Plug-in Filters tab and enter the folder where the filters are stored into one of the text boxes at the bottom of the dialog box.

3. Essentially, plug-ins extend the functionality of Paint Shop Pro. They do so by enabling you to apply new effects, depending on the plug-in.

4. Plug-ins and filters enable you to create certain effects that would be hard to accomplish, if not impossible, without their use.

HOUR 16

Special Effects

You should pretty much be at the point now where you can start to take advantage of what you've learned so far. You can start applying your knowledge to create some effects that produce more advanced images.

In this hour, I show you how to create a page curl effect, how to mimic gold and other metallic effects, and how to add bevels to give your images a more 3D look. The following issues are covered:

- Adding a page curl effect
- Creating metallic effects
- Using bevels effectively

Adding a Page Curl Effect

This effect, like many others, is actually easier to accomplish with version 6 than it was with previous versions. First, you have to create a new Gradient fill. Follow these steps:

1. Open a new image in the size that you want the final image to be. If you're going to use it for a Web graphic, I suggest keeping it around 200×250. I'll be working with a 400×500 image so that it appears at a good size printed in the book.

2. Set the resolution to 72 pixels per inch, the background color to white, and the image type to 16.7 million colors.

3. Add a new layer by clicking the Create Layer icon at the top of the Layer palette.

4. Select the Selection tool and set the Selection Type to Rectangle in the Tool Options window.

5. Make a selection near the bottom that extends most of the width of the image (see Figure 16.1).

FIGURE 16.1

A Rectangle selection made at the bottom of a new layer.

6. You'll need to create a new gradient. If you're not sure of the steps required, look back to Hour 7, "Painting Tools and Techniques."

The gradient I used can be seen in Figure 16.2. The colors, from left to right, are as follows:

R: 192 G: 192 B: 0 - Dark Yellow

R: 255 G: 255 B: 0 - Bright Yellow

R: 255 G: 255 B: 255 - White

R: 255 G: 255 B: 0 - Bright Yellow

R: 192 G: 192 B: 0 Dark Yellow

FIGURE 16.2

Multicolored dark yel-low, bright yellow, and white Gradient fill.

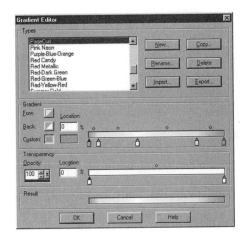

7. Set Angle to 180 in the Tool Options window.

8. With your gradient created, click in the rectangular selection to fill it with the gradient.

> I used different shades of yellow because I'll be creating an image that mim-ics yellow sticky notes. You can, however, choose other colors for your page curl effect.

9. Select the Deformation tool. Move the mouse pointer over the upper-left corner of the selection and, while holding down the Ctrl key (to create perspective rather than to change the size of the selection), click and drag the mouse toward the cen-ter of the left side. You should end up with something that resembles Figure 16.3.

10. Double-click within the area or, optionally, click the Apply button in the Tool Options window to complete the deformation.

11. Choose Selections, Select None.

12. Select the Selection tool and set Selection Type to Ellipse.

13. Make a selection similar to the one I've made in Figure 16.4.

FIGURE 16.3

Creating the curl with a deformed, filled rectangle.

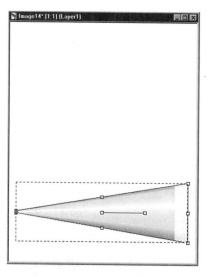

FIGURE 16.4

Making an elliptical selection to complete the curl.

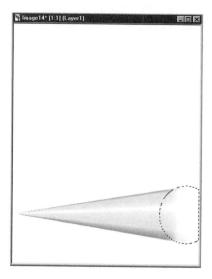

14. Press the Delete key to remove the selected elliptical area and choose Selections, Select None. The completed layer is the curled portion. All that's left to do is rotate it a little.

15. Select the Deformation tool and use it to rotate the curl counterclockwise a little (see Figure 16.5).

FIGURE 16.5

*Rotating the curl coun-
terclockwise.*

16. Now that the curl is complete, it's time to add the rest of the sticky note behind it. Make the Background layer active; this is where you'll add the yellow rectangle to complete the effect.

17. There are a couple of ways to create the shape behind the curl; some are more elegant than others. The method I'll use here is quicker than most, if not as nicely executed. Select the Preset Shapes tool and set Shape Type to Rectangle and the Style to Filled. Make sure that the Create As Vector option is unchecked.

18. Set the foreground color to bright yellow (R: 255 G: 255 B: 0).

19. Place the mouse pointer at the point of the curl effect and drag it upward and to the right until you've got a large rectangle. The right edge should line up with the lower outside edge of the curl effect (see Figure 16.6).

20. Here comes the inelegant part: Set the background color to White and select the Eraser tool.

21. Drag the Eraser tool (click and drag, that is) over the lower portion of the yellow rectangle to remove the area below the curl and complete the effect.

You can use the Text tool to add some text, if you like. Your image should resemble the one shown in Figure 16.7.

FIGURE 16.6

Adding the rectangle behind the curl effect.

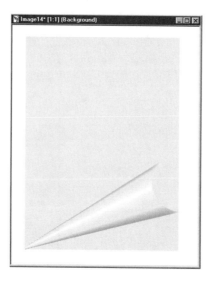

FIGURE 16.7

The completed page curl effect.

Mastering Metallic Effects

Since I first started GrafX Design, I've received a lot of email asking how to create a metallic effect. Here's one way that's quick and easy:

1. Open a new 600×600–pixel image with the resolution set to 72 pixels per inch, the background color set to white, and the image type set to 16.7 million colors.

2. Choose Image, Noise, Add.

3. In the Add Noise dialog box, set %Noise to 100 and choose Random. Click OK. These settings will fill the image with thousands of small, colored pixels.

4. To create the metallic effect, though, you'll want the noise to be grayscale. To change the image from color to grayscale, choose Colors, Gray Scale. Your noise will now be in shades of gray.

5. It's time to make the noise look like brushed metal. Before you do so, though, you should return the color depth to 16.7 million colors. To do so, choose Colors, Increase Color Depth, 16.7 Million Colors.

6. Choose Image, Blur, Motion Blur.

7. In the Motion Blur dialog box, set the direction to about 120 degrees, the intensity to about 25 pixels and click OK.

You should end up with something like Figure 16.8.

FIGURE 16.8

A brushed aluminum effect.

You can color the metallic effect so that it resembles other brushed metals. Try this:

1. Choose Colors, Colorize and set Hue to 173 and Saturation to 120.

2. Choose Colors, Adjust, Brightness/Contrast and lower the brightness to about –6 and the contrast to about –6. This will give you a blued-steel effect. This can be used as a blended layer over something such as the button bar shown in Hour 7 (Figure 7.10) to give you a really believable metallic effect.

16

This texture and other versions of it can be used for all types of features, from interfaces to text.

Using Bevels

It used to be that you had to resort to third-party plug-ins if you wanted a good inner bevel effect for interfaces, oddly shaped buttons, and text. With version 6's capabilities, though, you can now add bevels to any shape you want. Here's how:

1. Open a new 600×300–pixel image with the resolution set to 72 pixels per inch, the background color set to white, and the image type set to 16.7 million colors.

2. Use the Text tool to add some text to the image, making sure that the Create As option is set to Floating. I used Cosmic Two at 120 points (see Figure 16.9).

FIGURE 16.9

Blue Cosmic Two text on a white background.

3. With the text still selected (it should be selected after you add it to the image), choose Image, Effects, Inner Bevel.

4. You can use this new filter to add all types of bevels to your text or other objects. In Figure 16.10 you can see that I'm using the Angled preset to give the text a hard-edged bevel.

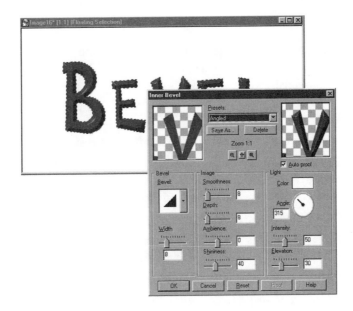

FIGURE 16.10
Bevel effect added to the text with the Inner Bevel filter.

Summary

I hope you enjoyed this hour. Paint Shop Pro also enables you to create many other special effects. Examples appear throughout this book; many more are in my other Paint Shop Pro book, *Paint Shop Pro Web Techniques*, New Riders Publishing, ISBN: 1-56205-756-1. (Even though that book was written with Paint Shop Pro 4, a lot of the techniques still apply.) Tons more are on the Web. You can start with some of the effects on my GrafX Design Web site (http://www.grafx-design.com), find others at Jasc Software, Inc.'s Web site (http://www.jasc.com), and still others at links from Jasc and GrafX Design.

As you become more familiar with Paint Shop Pro and with digital imaging in general, you'll probably come up with many more effects yourself.

Workshop

The Workshop contains a question and answer section to help answer the most commonly asked questions and quiz questions to help you solidify your understanding of the material covered.

Q&A

Q Where can I find more effects that can be created with Paint Shop Pro?

A A good starting place is the Web. You can visit Jasc Software's site at http://www.jasc.com and GrafX Design at http://www.grafx-design.com. Both sites contain tips and links to other sites with even more tips.

Q Can I make different colored metals such as gold and bronze?

A Yes. One way is to experiment with colorizing the image. Choose Colors, Colorize and play around with the Hue and Saturation settings.

Q Is there an easier way to do page curls?

A Yes. A third-party filter is available in Kai's Power Tools from MetaCreations.

Quiz

1. Is it possible to create special effects by using more than one filter?
2. What is a bevel?
3. Can I create different materials with Paint Shop Pro?
4. How does the Magic Wand tool help build special effects?

Answers

1. Yes. In fact, I encourage you to play around with different filters, brush settings, and so on—whatever helps you come up with new effects.

2. A bevel, at least in real life, is an angled area around the edges of an object. This effect can be "faked" in a paint program such as Paint Shop Pro to add apparent depth to an image.

3. Yes. In this hour I demonstrated how to create metallic effects, but I've also demonstrated how to create wood textures in other chapters. The possibilities are limited only by your imagination and how much time you're willing to dedicate to creating a texture. You can also use plug-ins, built-in filters, and even brush textures to create interesting effects.

4. You can use the Magic Wand tool to select portions of various objects according to their colors.

PART IV

Advanced Paint Shop Pro Tasks

Hour

HOUR 17

Retouching Your Images

We all have collections of snapshots that we cherish, right? Or we have collections of old family photos, a few of which we'd like to frame and put up on a wall. Some of them are in good shape but, more often than not, some of them need at least some retouching.

Paint Shop Pro has the tools you need to fix all but the worst of your images. This hour covers the following issues:

- Using the retouching tools
- Fixing brightness and contrast
- Removing dust marks and scratches
- Removing portions of an image

Using the Retouching Tools

Several problems usually need correcting. Old snapshots often have scratches, dust spots, and bad brightness or contrast. Sometimes they have a less-than-sharp image because of the quality of the older camera lenses.

You can fix the dust spots and scratches by using a combination of the Dropper, Paint Brushes, Retouch, and Clone Brush tools. In addition, you can fix most brightness and contrast problems by using the Brightness/Contrast feature, and you can fix the sharpness by using the Unsharp Mask filter.

I show you how to use each of these tools as I walk you through the process of fixing the image you see in Figure 17.1.

FIGURE 17.1
An old family photograph in need of repair.

You can see that all the problems mentioned earlier exist in this particular photo. There are dust spots and a couple of scratches, the brightness and contrast are off, and the photo is not as sharp as it could be. I'll fix each of these problems in this hour, starting with the brightness and contrast.

Fixing the Brightness and Contrast

To adjust the brightness and contrast of an image, choose Colors, Adjust, Brightness/Contrast.

Using the preview window, I bumped up the contrast of this image to +12, and I left the brightness alone. You can see the result, along with the Brightness/Contrast dialog box, in Figure 17.2.

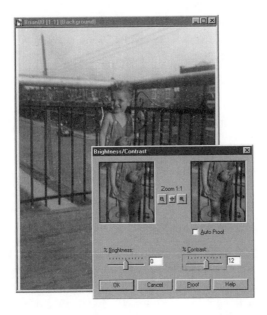

FIGURE 17.2

Adjusting the brightness and contrast.

17

You can see the original image to the left in the dialog box, and you can see the effect of the changes in the preview window to the right. You can click and drag the preview window, so that you can see different areas of the image.

You can also zoom in and out on the preview by clicking either of the zoom icons (they both resemble magnifying glasses; one has a small plus sign and the other has a small minus sign). Also, you can move around the image quickly by clicking the icon between the zoom icons. Doing so will bring up a thumbnail of the image, with a small rectangle cursor that you can use to quickly home in on an area of the image.

If zooming doesn't show you as much of the image as you'd like, you can place a check mark in the Auto Proof check box as I've done, so that the changes will be visible in the image itself.

With the brightness and contrast adjusted, the next step is to remove the dust spots and scratches.

Removing Dust Marks and Scratches

You'll want to remove as many of the dust marks and scratches as you can before using the Unsharp Mask filter, because this filter can actually accentuate the bad spots of a photograph.

Removing the spots is tedious but fairly easy. I recommend a combination of the Dropper and Paint Brushes tools. (This process involves switching between the two tools, picking up nearby colors with the Dropper, and applying them with the Paint Brushes tool.)

> Before you get down to the hard work of removing spots by hand, you might want to try the Despeckle filter (choose Image, Noise, Despeckle). The Despeckle filter can remove some of the smaller spots and reduce the work you have to do manually.

Follow these steps to remove dust and scratches manually:

1. Zoom in on the image so that you can easily spot the dust marks you need to fix.

2. Select the Dropper (its icon resembles a small eyedropper) and use it to select a color near a spot that needs to be repaired. Switch to the Paint Brushes tool to paint over the dust mark. First make sure that the brush is set to a small size, that the hardness is low (even setting it to 0), and that the opacity is about 50%.

   You'll be constantly switching between the Dropper to pick up a new color and the Paint Brushes tool to paint over a dust mark. Like I said, tedious…. It's worth the effort, though.

> To help relieve the tedium, you can switch back and forth to the Dropper tool rapidly by holding down the Ctrl key with the Paint Brushes tool selected.

Figure 17.3 is the result of running the Despeckle filter on the image.

Figure 17.4 is the result of removing all but the worst (the largest) of the remaining spots with the Paint Brushes and Dropper tools.

Any remaining marks, such as the scratches, will have to be removed with the Clone Brush tool. As you may recall from Hour 7, "Painting Tools and Techniques," the Clone Brush tool (which resembles two brushes together) copies one portion of an image over another.

Select the portion you want to copy by right-clicking and then clicking and dragging to copy the area you've selected onto another area. As you draw with the Clone Brush tool, you'll see two cursors: One cursor shows you where you're copying from, and one shows you where you're copying to.

FIGURE 17.3

The Despeckle filter removes most of the dust spots.

17

FIGURE 17.4

The rest of the spots have been removed manually with the Dropper and Paint Brushes tools.

As with the Dropper/Paint Brushes combination, you should constantly change where you're copying from by right-clicking in a new area.

As with the Dropper/Paint Brushes combination, you'll want to zoom in to get a clear view of the areas that need work. You'll also want to adjust the Clone Brush settings in the same manner as you adjusted the Paint Brushes tool. That is, you'll want a fairly small, soft, slightly transparent brush. Remember, you're correcting an existing image, not painting a new one.

You'll also want to keep changing the area you're cloning from, depending on the area you want to cover. Just right-click when you want to select a new area and keep working.

Figure 17.5 is the result after using the Clone Brush tool on some of the worst marks.

Figure 17.5

The worst marks were removed manually with the Clone Brush tool.

Compare Figure 17.5 to the original image in Figure 17.1. Quite an improvement already, but there's more. The final touch-up is to sharpen the image with the Unsharp Mask filter.

Using the Unsharp Mask Filter

To fix the sharpness, or lack thereof, I'll use the Unsharp Mask filter. The Unsharp Mask filter mimics a traditional film compositing technique used to sharpen the edges of an image.

The Unsharp Mask works by increasing the contrast between adjacent pixels. The edges it works on are based on the difference of the pixels in the image, using the values you enter for the different options. All of this sounds complex, and it is. Using the filter is not as complex, though.

To apply the Unsharp Mask, choose Image, Sharpen, Unsharp Mask. This brings up the Unsharp Mask dialog box (see Figure 17.6).

FIGURE 17.6

The Unsharp Mask dialog box and the image to which the filter is being applied.

Aside from the usual Zoom, Auto Proof, and Preview options, you'll see three options that you can set: Radius, Strength, and Clipping.

- The Radius setting determines how many pixels in an area will be affected by the filter. As this number increases, so does the apparent sharpness of the image. Setting too high a number, though, simply increases the overall contrast of the image, especially if you also increase the Strength setting.

- The Strength setting affects how much the contrast will change over the areas affected by the filter. Setting this number too high simply makes the image appear to have too much contrast.

- The Clipping setting is important. This option determines how much contrast must exist between the pixels before the filter will be applied to an area. If "dust marks" (that is, white specks and small scratches) show up as you lower this value, you'll want to adjust it a little higher.

Basically, the values you enter depend on a particular image and the results you're after. I used 2.00 for the Radius setting, 100% for the Strength setting, and 3 for the Clipping value to arrive at the final retouched image shown in Figure 17.7.

17

FIGURE 17.7
FIGURE 17.7

The final retouched image with the contrast improved, all of the dust marks and scratches removed, and the sharpness corrected.

Compare this image to the original in Figure 17.1, and I'm sure you'll agree that it's a big improvement. This image could now be printed and hung.

Retouching to Remove Portions of an Image

Besides retouching older images, you may simply need to work on an area of a photograph to change some portion of the image. For example, you may want to remove someone's braces or make minor corrections to a person's complexion.

Retouching tricks such as these are certainly possible with Paint Shop Pro. Figure 17.8 shows a close-up of a portrait in which the model is still wearing braces.

FIGURE 17.8

A portrait with the braces showing.

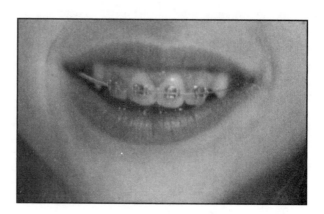

You can correct this lovely smile by using some of the same techniques you used to retouch the old photo in the previous exercise.

To remove some of the smaller offending areas, you can use the Dropper/Paint Brushes technique.

Remember to lower the opacity of the Paint Brushes tool so that you gradually cover an area as you work, rather than trying to speed things up by painting quickly over an area. It is better to work an area over several times than to make too large an adjustment that glaringly shows that the image has been retouched.

The whole idea is to do the retouching in a way that fools the viewer into believing that the image is in its pristine original condition. Use a "light hand," in the form of smaller, softer, more transparent brushes.

Figure 17.9 shows the result of using the Dropper/Paint Brushes technique to remove the braces on the bottom teeth and at the sides of the mouth.

17

FIGURE 17.9

Initial retouching with the Dropper/Paint Brushes technique removes some of the braces.

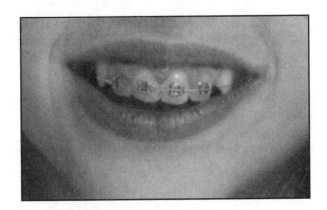

I think that's about as far as the Dropper/Paint Brushes technique will carry me, though. It's time for the Clone Brush tool.

Using the Clone Brush tool, I can copy portions of the teeth where there are no braces over areas where the braces exist. Again, working with the Clone Brush tool, it's wise to make frequent backups.

You'll also want to constantly change the area from which you're cloning, so that you don't just copy large areas over existing areas. Doing so would be a dead giveaway that the image had been retouched.

Sometimes you'll unavoidably make a bit of a mess of an area with the Clone Brush tool. Don't panic, though. Here's a trick you can use to help fix some of those problem areas.

Figure 17.10 shows one such area caused by overworking the Clone Brush tool. You can see how the front tooth that I've been working on is slightly speckled.

FIGURE 17.10

A problem area caused by overworking the Clone Brush tool.

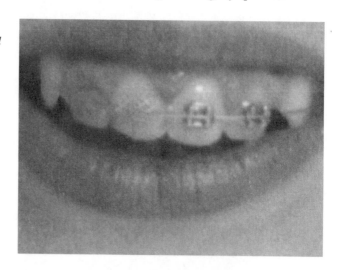

To fix this area, select the Freehand tool and set the feathering value to 2 or so. Use the Freehand tool to select the offending area (see Figure 17.11).

FIGURE 17.11

The problem area, selected with the Freehand tool.

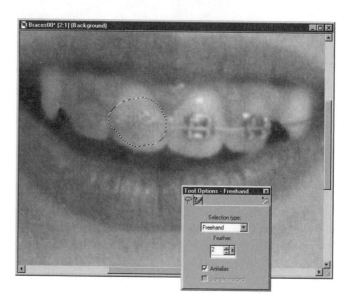

With the area selected, choose the Gaussian Blur filter (Image, Blur, Gaussian Blur) and turn on the Auto Proof option. Adjust the Radius setting until the area is corrected.

What you're going for is the removal of the marks made with the Clone Brush tool while maintaining the same graininess and appearance as the surrounding image.

Figure 17.12 shows the Gaussian Blur dialog box with the settings I used and the result of applying Blur to the image.

FIGURE 17.12

The problem area, corrected with the application of the Gaussian Blur filter.

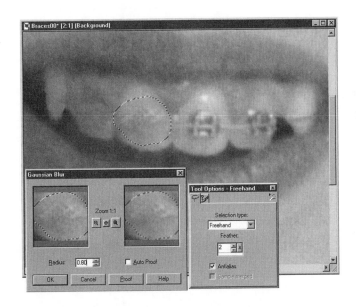

17

Figure 17.13 shows the image with the braces totally removed from the portrait.

FIGURE 17.13

Braces totally removed from the portrait.

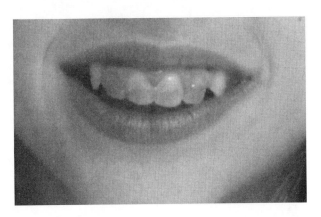

A few problem areas remain. The retouching has left some of the areas of the teeth a little darker than they should be. Fortunately, this defect is easy to correct.

To lighten up the areas that were darkened with the Clone Brush tool, I selected the Retouch tool (it resembles a small hand with one finger pointing downwards). Again, I set a soft brush with a low Opacity setting (these are in the Tool Options window). I set the Tool controls to Lighten RGB and moved the brush around the offending area.

> The Retouch tool can be used to change areas of an image selectively. You can choose Lighten RGB, Darken RGB, Soften, Sharpen, Emboss, Smudge, Push, Dodge and Burn (*dodge* and *burn* are photographic darkroom terms meaning lighten and darken), Saturation Up, Saturation Down, Lightness Up, Lightness Down, Hue Up, Hue Down, Saturation to Target, Lightness to Target, Hue to Target, and Color to Target. That's a lot of options!
>
> Once you've selected the Retouch tool and set the Retouch mode, you can adjust the Brush Tip, as I've done in this exercise, to retouch small areas of the image.

As I worked, I changed the brush size and worked lightly over the areas I wanted to lighten. Figure 17.14 shows the final brace-less smile.

FIGURE 17.14
Final retouched smile.

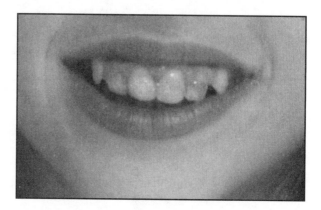

Perfect!

Work like this takes time and practice. Done properly, though, it's certainly worth the effort.

Summary

This hour was a bit tough. Don't stop here, though. Retouching photographs is an art form that requires lots of time and practice to get right. As you can see from the results, it's worth the time and effort.

As with any other art form, you'll get better with practice. I've shown you a couple of tricks and a shortcut or two. The rest is up to you. If you have images that need work, get them out and start playing around with the techniques I've described. You'll be amazed at the results.

Before getting back into some more of the fun stuff, I tackle one more difficult subject in the next hour: coloring and color correction.

17

Workshop

The Workshop contains a question and answer section to help answer the most commonly asked questions and quiz questions to help you solidify your understanding of the material covered.

Q&A

Q I'm not clear on why you lower the opacity of the brushes when retouching. Can you explain why you do so?

A I lower the opacity to change the amount of effect a brush has. I'd rather apply a subtle effect two or three times than apply an obvious (or overdone) effect once. Lowering the opacity of the brush enables me to make a less obvious retouch.

Q Why do you use such a small brush size when retouching?

A Again, it's a matter of subtlety. What you're trying to do is retouch an image without the image appearing to have been retouched. Making smaller changes as you work enables you to make the changes less obvious.

Q Why do you keep changing the settings of the various tools as you work?

A It's still that subtlety thing. A digital image contains many small pixels of varying color and luminance. Large sweeping changes are usually obvious to anyone who views your work. Changing the size, opacity, and other variables as you work makes the changes far less obvious. With enough practice, the changes will be virtually invisible to anyone who views the results of your work.

Quiz

1. What's a quick way to remove most of the small dust marks that may be present on an older image?

2. How do you remove the remaining dust marks?

3. Is there a trick that can help when the Clone Brush tool makes a mess of an area?

4. Can a graphics tablet help with retouching?

Answers

1. You can use the Despeckle filter (choose Image, Noise, Despeckle) to remove most of the smaller dust marks.

2. You can use the Dropper/Paint Brushes technique. This process involves switching between the two tools, picking up nearby colors with the Dropper, and applying them with the Paint Brushes tool.

3. Yes. You can make a feathered freehand selection and run the Gaussian Blur filter on the area.

4. Yes. As with other digital imaging, a tablet is a much better tool than a mouse.

Hour 18

Coloring and Color Correction

Discussing color in a black-and-white book may seem silly. However, most of the work you do with Paint Shop Pro will be in color, and just because I can't show you color examples doesn't mean that I can't tell you how to use color in your work.

This hour tackles the following issues related to color:

- Understanding the theory behind good color
- Understanding Gamma correction
- Adjusting the hue, saturation, and lightness
- Working with the Hue Map command
- Adjusting the reds, greens, and blues in your colors
- Using adjustment layers
- Grasping color correction in a nutshell

A Little Color Theory

Color on a computer screen is somewhat different from color in other media, such as finger paints. You may remember back to when, as a child, you would mix a couple of primary colors to get a secondary color. For example, you might mix blue and yellow to get green, right?

Well, the idea is the same when it comes to the colors you see on your computer screen. The biggest difference is that the primary colors you worked with as a child were red, yellow, and blue, and the primary colors you'll use for digital work are red, green, and blue.

Here's how it works. If you mix two of the three colors from the choices of red, green, and blue, you'll get cyan, magenta, or yellow.

Sound familiar? You may recall that cyan, magenta, and yellow make up the CMYK color model (used for printing). Forget that for now, though. We'll be concentrating on the color scheme you see on your screen, which is the RGB color model.

To see how the colors mix, take a look at Michael's Modified Color Wheel (see Figure 18.1).

FIGURE 18.1

Michael's Modified Color Wheel.

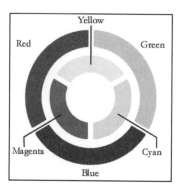

If you take any two of the colors from the outside of the wheel and mix them, you get the color on the inside between the two that you mixed.

Conversely, if you take any two colors from the inside of the wheel and add them, you'll get the color from the outside between the two that you mixed.

Also, the opposite of any color is on the other wheel. In other words, if you want to know the opposite of green, find green on the wheel and then find its opposite on the other wheel. Green is on the outside, so its opposite color is across from it on the inside. Therefore, the opposite of green is magenta.

This system tells you, the digital artist, what colors to add to an image to correct any color cast caused by bad scans, bad photo finishing, and so on. For example, if an image is too green, simply add magenta to correct it.

How much magenta? It really depends on the image. There is no magic formula.

On the other hand, Paint Shop Pro has many tools to help you correct color problems with your images. In fact, some of Paint Shop Pro's color tools make it easy to correct an image's color faults by enabling you to subtract from a color rather than worry about which color to add, and most of them work in the Hue, Saturation, Lightness (HSL) or RGB model.

The first thing you might need to adjust in an image is the brightness and contrast. Rather than immediately going for the Brightness/Contrast option, though, you should consider one other option: Gamma correction.

Understanding Gamma Correction

An image's *Gamma* is a combination of its brightness and its contrast. Consequently, you can adjust both the brightness and the contrast simply by adjusting the Gamma.

18

The Gamma Correction option does a nice job of correcting the brightness and contrast of a color image. Using the Brightness/Contrast image throws away too many shades or colors, in effect leaving gaps in the histogram (discussed shortly) of an image.

Using the Gamma Correction Feature

To use the Gamma Correction feature, choose Colors, Adjust, Gamma Correction. Figure 18.2 shows the Gamma Correction dialog box, along with an image having its Gamma adjusted.

To lighten an image, drag the sliders to the right. To darken an image, drag the sliders to the left.

If the overall image needs to be lightened or darkened, leave the sliders linked. If you want to change the Gamma of only one color, unlink the sliders by toggling off the link option and then moving the slider for that particular color (see Figure 18.3).

The photograph I was working on still had a bit of a green cast to it that was easily corrected by unlinking the sliders and adjusting the Green slider to the left.

FIGURE **18.2**

An image having its Gamma adjusted.

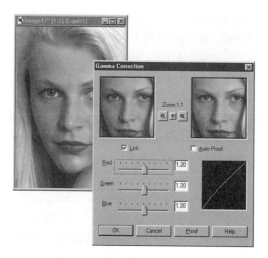

FIGURE **18.3**

An image having its Green channel's Gamma adjusted.

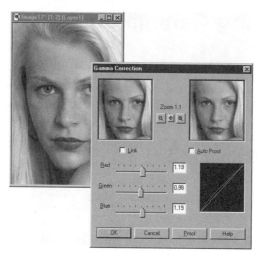

Using the Histogram Palette

With many images, small changes to the Gamma will suffice. However, sometimes more drastic changes are needed. How can you tell when an image needs adjusting and where it needs to be adjusted? That's where the Histogram palette comes in.

To see the histogram, click the Histogram icon. It resembles a small black-and-white bar graph and is located in the standard toolbar. You can use the histogram to see how the colors and the luminance of your image are distributed. Figure 18.4 is the histogram of the image before I started to work on it.

FIGURE **18.4**

*An image that needs
correcting and its his-
togram.*

You can see right away that the image is too dark. The histogram verifies this impression in that the graphs don't go all the way to the right. A good image has a more even distribution in the histogram.

If the histogram graph is higher toward the right, too much of a certain color is present or the image is too light, depending on which graph you're examining.

If the graph is bunched up toward the left, you have too little of the color that is represented or the image is too dark.

Figure 18.5 is the same image as Figure 18.4 after the Gamma corrections.

18

FIGURE **18.5**

*An image that has
been corrected and its
histogram.*

Did you notice the better distribution of the graphs in the histogram? The graphs all go to the right now, and more of the graphs can be seen. This change in the histogram is a result of the changes made to the image with the Gamma Correction tool.

You can use the histogram to read an image's color cast, as well. If one graph is way off in relationship to the others, you'll know that the image has a color cast in that particular color.

Several menu items are associated with the histogram. You can either equalize or stretch a histogram:

- The Equalize command smoothes out the histogram so that the image's brightness is averaged.

- The Stretch command stretches the histogram so that the brightness of an image is spread more broadly across the histogram

Both of these options are available under Colors, Histogram Functions. These commands have limited capabilities, though. If an image is really bad, they'll have almost no effect.

Playing with Other Color Adjustments

After setting an image's Gamma, you can move on to making more color adjustments if necessary.

For example, you can adjust the highlights, midtones, and shadows separately with the Highlight/Midtone/Shadow command (choose Colors, Adjust, Highlight/Midtone/Shadow—see Figure 18.6).

FIGURE 18.6

Adjusting an image's highlights, midtones, and shadows.

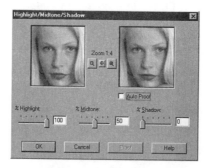

The highlights in an image are the lighter areas, the shadows are the darker areas, and the midtones are the areas in between. This idea may seem a little simplistic, but it basically reflects those areas in an image. In a black-and-white photo, the highlights are the light grays and the whites, the shadows are the dark grays and blacks, and the other middle gray areas are the midtones.

Moving the sliders to the right lightens the highlights, the midtones, or the shadows. Moving them to the left darkens the highlights, midtones, or shadows. As with any of the other color adjustment commands, you'll want to move the sliders in very small increments. Large movements will distort your image.

Adjusting the Hue, Saturation, and Lightness

You also can adjust an image's hue (or color cast), saturation (or amount of overall color), and lightness (overall brightness).

To do so, choose Colors, Adjust, Hue/Saturation/Lightness to bring up the Hue/Saturation/Lightness dialog box (see Figure 18.7).

FIGURE 18.7
Adjusting an image's hue, saturation, and lightness.

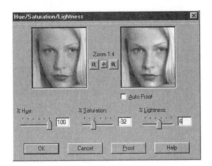

In Figure 18.7, I've lowered the saturation and raised the lightness a little to give the photograph the appearance of a hi-key image.

 A *hi-key image* is one that is very light. You'll see hi-key photographs used a lot in magazine ads for women's cosmetics.

You can get some cool effects with your photographs with this command. For example, you can lower the saturation to the point that the color is barely there. This look would be similar to the effect of a hand-colored photograph.

Working with the Hue Map Command

The Hue Map command is very powerful because it enables you to completely remap, or change, any color to any other. With Hue Map, colors are described in terms of degrees around the color wheel seen in the Color dialog box (*not* Michael's Modified Color Wheel).

If you take a look at the Hue Map dialog box in Figure 18.8 (choose Colors, Adjust, Hue Map), you'll notice that numbers are associated with each of the 10 color sliders.

FIGURE 18.8

The Hue Map dialog box.

The numbers go up in increments of 36 from 0 degrees to 324 degrees. Each color occupies 36 degrees.

This is the way that colors are mapped to the color wheel when you look at colors expressed as HSL.

As you change the settings of a color slider, you'll see a change in the image preview window (the rightmost preview window), which you can compare to the unmodified image in the small preview window to the left. You also can control the saturation and lightness shifts from the Hue Map dialog box. Remember that small changes are best.

Take a look at the color wheel in the Color dialog box (see Figure 18.9), and you'll see how the colors are arranged around the wheel.

At this point you may be viewing the color wheel in a whole new light. If you measure the colors around the wheel in terms of degrees, you'll see how neatly the colors fit onto the wheel.

Getting back to the Hue Map command, you can, as I said, remap any color to any other color. You will want to make these adjustments in very small increments, though, unless you plan on creating strange effects from your photographs.

To remap any color to any other, simply move the slider up or down until you achieve the change you want.

FIGURE 18.9
The Color dialog box.

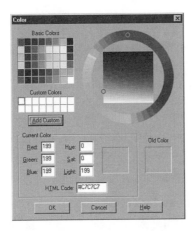

Adjusting the Reds, Greens, and Blues of Your Image

The last choice in the Colors, Adjust menu is the Red, Green, and Blue command. This command enables you to separately change the Red, Green, and Blue values in an image.

As with the other dialog boxes, you'll find a real-time preview, an Auto Proof check box, and the sliders that enable you to change the different values for the red, green, and blue in your image (see Figure 18.10).

18

FIGURE 18.10
The Red/Green/Blue dialog box.

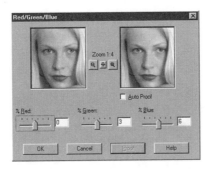

You'll want to use the same amount of caution when moving these sliders as with the others. Even a change of 3 or 4 can make a visible difference in your image.

You can easily remove a color cast by entering negative values in the sliders in the Red/Green/Blue dialog box.

For example, my original image was a little green, and I adjusted it by entering –3 for the Green value in the Red/Green/Blue dialog box.

I obviously can't show you the results here, but that small change fixed the slight green cast that resulted from the photo-finishing process.

Using Adjustment Layers

Here's the good news about correcting your images with Paint Shop Pro 6: You now have access to an incredibly powerful feature known as adjustment layers.

Adjustment layers enable you to make changes to your image that affect things such as brightness and contrast, levels, curves, and more without affecting the actual image. You can apply these changes in conjunction with each other to see how they affect the image and then undo the changes as simply as removing a layer.

Describing all of the options available with adjustment layers would require more than a portion of a chapter in any book and would require you to understand much more than the typical beginner. Instead of trying to give you a crash course in all of the features and what they do, I'll show you how an adjustment layer works and tell you why it's so important in image correction.

To add an adjustment layer, choose Layers, New Adjustment Layer, and then choose from one of the options available. Some of the options will enable you to make some of the adjustments described earlier in this hour and some of them are completely new. Two of the new adjustments that are available are Levels and Curves.

Figure 18.11 shows the image being worked on, the Layer palette (which shows that this image has only one layer—the Background layer), and the Layer Properties dialog box, as I add a new adjustment layer to the image.

The Levels adjustment is similar to the Gamma adjustment, but it enables you to make finer adjustments.

Input Levels modifies the image by darkening the darkest values and lightening the lightest values, resulting in an increase in the contrast.

Output Levels modifies the image by lightening the darkest values and darkening the lightest values, resulting in resetting the lowest and highest ranges for brightness levels.

FIGURE 18.11

Adding a Levels adjustment layer to an image that needs correcting.

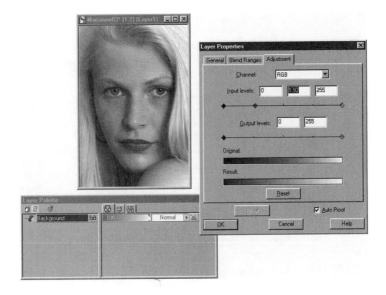

After making the required adjustments and clicking OK, you'll notice that a new layer has been added to the image (see Figure 18.12).

18

FIGURE 18.12

A Levels adjustment layer, added to an image that needs correcting.

You can redo the values by simply double-clicking the adjustment layer in the Layer palette. This is much better than making an adjustment and later changing your mind only to find that the settings you've chosen in a dialog box have been reset to the default values. Also, if you decide to discard the changes, even after saving and re-opening the image, you can simply delete the adjusted layer.

You also can change the way that the adjustment layer interacts with the layer below. For example, you can change the opacity of the adjustment layer in the Layer palette. You also can toggle the adjustment layer's visibility on and off for a quick "before and after" view of how the adjustment affects the image.

Amazing and powerful stuff!

You also can add other adjustment layers to further correct or fine-tune your images. Figure 18.13 shows the Curves adjustment layer at work.

FIGURE 18.13

A Curves adjustment layer, added to an image that needs correcting.

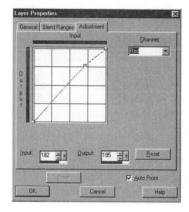

The Curves adjustment layer enables you to fine-tune the lightness of the pixels in your images. You can work on all the channels or each channel separately. Again, this is an incredibly powerful tool that enables you to make professional-level adjustments to your images.

After using adjustment layers, you'll never want to work on image correction without them again.

> Make sure that you save your images, with their adjusted layers, as PSP files. If you flatten an image and save it in any other format without saving a copy with the layers intact, you'll lose the flexibility that the adjustment layers afford you.

Color Correction in a Nutshell

To recap, the first thing you should do after acquiring your image is adjust the Gamma (or Levels via an adjustment layer). This step enables you to lighten or darken and change the contrast without affecting the histogram as much as the Brightness/Contrast command would.

You can test this yourself by loading an image and duplicating it with Edit, Copy and then Edit, Paste as New Image (or press Shift+D) so that you have two images open concurrently. Then follow these steps:

1. Check the number of colors in the image by choosing Colors, Count Colors Used.

2. Turn on the Histogram palette and change one image with the Brightness/Contrast command (Colors, Adjust, Brightness) and change the other using the Gamma Correction command (Colors Adjust, Gamma Correction).

   You may find that the Brightness/Contrast command compresses the histogram, whereas Gamma Correction does not. You may also find, by checking the number of colors in each image, that the number of colors is significantly lower after the application of the Brightness/Contrast command, compared to the application of the Gamma Correction command.

3. When you've corrected the overall Gamma, you can unlink the sliders and, if necessary, change the Gamma of the colors separately.

4. If your image is still in need of some help, you can examine the histogram again. Depending on the particular image, the histogram should show an even distribution of all of the colors and the luminance.

   Recall that if the graph is higher toward the right, too much of a certain color is present or the image is too light, depending on which graph you're examining. If the graph is bunched up toward the left, you have too little of the color that is represented or the image is too dark.

5. If the Gamma correction isn't helping, you can make further adjustments with either the HSL command or the RGB command (Colors, Adjust, Red/Green/Blue or Colors, Adjust, Hue/Saturation/Lightness). You'll want to make these changes in very small increments, though.

6. By adding to or subtracting from the Hue, Saturation, and Lightness or the Red, Green, and Blue sliders in the Hue/Saturation/Lightness or Red/Green/Blue dialog box, you'll be able to make the final adjustments necessary to bring your image into line.

Color and color correction are incredibly complex subjects requiring much time, patience, and study. Many professionals have spent their lifetimes studying these subjects.

If it doesn't seem easy as you start out, don't get too frustrated. With time and practice, you'll certainly be able to adjust your photographs so that they appear properly. Most of the time it's a matter of trial and error—don't forget to use the Undo command!

18

Summary

This tough hour presented some theory and even more options. You'll want to spend some time playing with the different commands to see what effect they have on your images. Correcting an image's color is even more difficult than retouching and will require much time, effort, and practice. One day, though, you'll be able to look at a high-priced magazine ad and wonder why someone didn't add just a little more red.

With the two toughest subjects in digital imaging out of the way, it's time to get back to the fun stuff. In the next hour, I show you how to composite two or more images together. This high-end technique can produce amazing images.

Workshop

The Workshop contains a question and answer section to help answer the most commonly asked questions and quiz questions to help you solidify your understanding of the material covered.

Q&A

Q How is HSL different from RGB?

A HSL and RGB are just two different ways of looking at the same thing—the color wheel. If you check the RGB and HSL settings in the Color dialog box, you'll see that each RGB has a corresponding HSL and vice versa.

Q How would you fix a green tint in a photograph?

A You could lower the green using Colors, Adjust, Red/Green/Blue.

Q How do you replace color hues?

A You can do so via the Hue Map (choose Colors, Adjust, Hue Map).

Quiz

1. Using Figure 18.1 as your guide, what color would you need to add to an image that had too much cyan in it?

2. What does a histogram of an image tell you about the distribution of color within the image? What does it mean if the histogram graph is higher toward the right side?

3. What is the difference between the RGB and HSL color models?

4. What does the Hue Map command do for you?

Answers

1. You would need to add red to compensate for the cyan tint.

2. The histogram reflects the distribution of color and light in an image. A histogram that is weighted too far to the right indicates too much of a certain color or an image that's too light, depending on which graph you're reading.

3. The only difference is in the way that a color is represented. It's like reading a book in one language and then reading it again in another language. It's the same book, but with a different way of looking at it.

4. It enables you to replace one hue (or color) with another.

18

Hour 19

Compositing

Compositing is the art of merging photographs together. There are two basic styles of compositing. The first style—called a *collage*—places images together in a way that makes it obvious that the images are from different sources. This technique is currently very popular. You see collages in magazines and television ads every day. The second style of compositing is the *photomontage* or just *montage*. With a montage, the trick is to fool viewers into believing that what they're seeing is real, even though it's impossible. Examples of this type of composite are flying cars, people placed into older images that might have been taken before they were even born, and so on.

This hour tackles the following issues related to composites:

- Creating collages
- Creating photo montages

Creating Collages

Creating a collage is easier than creating a montage, because you're not trying to fool the viewer. What you want to accomplish with a collage is a nice composition using different images. In doing so, you hope to convey a message of some sort.

Before you start a collage, you should gather your source material and decide on the general layout that will convey your idea. In this exercise, I construct a fictitious brochure for a railway company; the brochure's purpose is to entice the viewer to ride the rails.

To get started, I selected three images of trains that I thought would work well together in the brochure. Figures 19.1 through 19.3 are the three images I selected.

FIGURE 19.1
Photograph of a railway switch.

FIGURE 19.2
Photograph of a loco-motive engine.

Figure 19.3

A close-up of a train's wheels.

I've already resized the images a little so that they all more or less share the same dimensions.

To resize the images after scanning them, choose Image, Resize. The Resize dialog box (see Figure 19.4) has all the necessary options to help you resize an image.

Figure 19.4

Paint Shop Pro's Resize dialog box.

To begin, you should decide on the approximate size for the final composite image and set the dimensions for the first—or *base*—image, on which the other images will be placed.

Because the Resize dialog box remembers the last dimensions you used, it's relatively easy to set the new size for the remaining images. This statement is true even though the third image (the train wheels) is in landscape mode (wider than it is high) and the other two are in portrait mode (higher than they are wide).

When it came to resizing the train wheels image, I just used the Width setting of the first two images. The Resize dialog box enables you to keep the proportions of the image (by placing a check mark in the Maintain Aspect Ratio check box), so after setting the width, I just clicked OK and the image was set to the proper size.

19

After resizing the images, the next step is to place copies of the second and third images into new layers in the first image. You can follow the next sequence of steps with any three images—just modify the procedure for your own images. Follow these steps to create your collage:

1. Select the second image (the engine) and choose Edit, Copy to copy the entire image to the Clipboard.

2. Make the first image current by clicking its title bar.

3. Choose Edit, Paste, As New Layer. You don't need the second image for now, so go ahead and close it.

4. To copy the third image onto the first as a new layer, repeat the above process.

5. At this point, you should have one image with three layers (similar to Figure 19.5).

FIGURE 19.5

A multilayered image, ready to be turned into a collage.

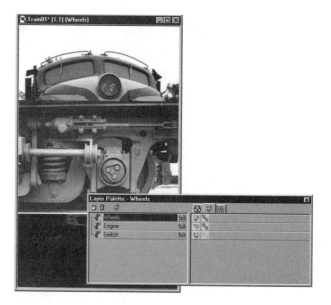

You can see that I've renamed the layers just to keep things easier to manage. You can rename them by double-clicking each layer's name in the Layer palette in turn and renaming it.

6. Now you need to blend the second layer into the first. To help with this process, you can turn off the visibility of the top layer (the one with the wheels). It'll still be there, it just won't be visible. To turn off a layer's visibility, simply click the Layer Visibility Toggle icon in the Layer palette.

7. To help resize and place the engine, I'll reduce its layer's opacity so that I can see through to the layer below. To do so, I can simply adjust the Opacity slider in the Layer palette.

8. To resize the image of the engine, select the entire layer (Selections, Select All) and then select the Deformation tool. (It's the rectangular shaped icon and is the third from the top if your Tool palette is placed vertically and third from the left if horizontally.)

   I used the Deformation tool to resize the Engine layer so that it would fit into the upper-left corner of the image (see Figure 19.6).

FIGURE 19.6

The engine, resized and moved into the upper-left corner.

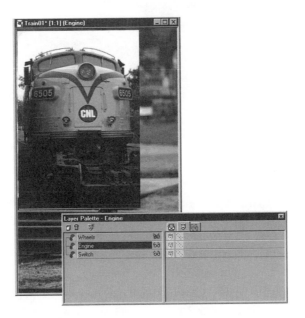

9. I'd like to fade the edges of the Engine layer to make the collage flow more easily. To do so, I selected an oval area around the engine with the Selection tool style set to elliptical and the Feather value set to about 6.

10. Copy the selection to the Clipboard (Edit, Copy) and then paste the selection to its own layer (Edit, Paste, As New Layer).

    This step enables you to have a copy of the entire Engine layer if you decide to change the selection in some way.

11. To continue, turn off the visibility of the original Engine layer and move the elliptical selection into place (see Figure 19.7).

    With the selection in place, choose Selections, Select None.

19

FIGURE 19.7

The engine, fit into a feathered elliptical shape.

I want the switch to show through the engine a little more than it does, though. The answer is to use a mask to change the opacity of the engine and let the switch show through.

12. To create the mask, use Masks, New, Show All. To see the mask as you work on it, choose Masks, View Mask. I then chose Masks, Edit to work on the mask. All that's left now is to paint in the mask.

   Painting in black will add to the mask and let the image below show through, whereas painting in white will bring back any areas you've masked out.

13. After painting in the mask, I decided that the engine was too small. To fix the problem, I chose Masks, Delete and deleted the mask. (Note that a dialog box pops up when you choose to delete the mask—I was deleting the mask because of an error, so I chose not to merge the current mask.) I then used the Deformation tool to resize the engine so that it was a bit larger. I then redrew the mask (sometimes it's a matter of trial and error).

Figure 19.8 shows the engine and its mask in place.

Time to add the wheels. Remember that the wheels are already there on a separate layer; they've just had their layer's visibility turned off. To turn on the layer's visibility, simply toggle the Layer Visibility Toggle icon in the Layer palette.

FIGURE 19.8

The engine and its mask in place.

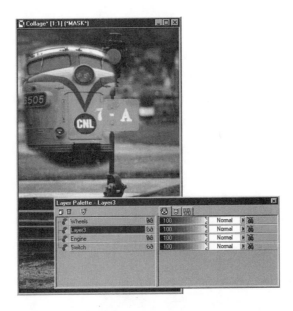

1. I want the wheels at the bottom of the collage with the background slowly blending into them. To accomplish this blend, I first move the wheels into place at the bottom of the image using the Mover tool—its icon resembles a cross with arrowheads. You can see the wheels moved into place in Figure 19.9.

FIGURE 19.9

The Wheels layer, moved into place and its visibility turned on.

19

2. To select the Wheels layer so that I could create the mask, I used the Magic Wand and selected the transparent area above the wheels. I then inverted the selection with Selections, Invert.

3. To create the new Mask, choose Masks, New, Show Selection.

4. Choose Masks, Edit so that you can add a Gradient fill to the mask.

5. To fill the mask with the gradient, select the Flood Fill tool and set the Type option to Linear Gradient.

6. Set the foreground color to black and the background color to white.

7. Set the gradient direction to 180 degrees and then click in the selected area to fill the mask with a black-to-white linear gradient.

8. To turn off editing and the view of the mask, choose Masks, Edit and Masks, View Masks.

Figure 19.10 shows the final collage.

FIGURE 19.10

The final collage, cre-ated in Paint Shop Pro.

All that's needed to turn this into a brochure is some text, as shown in Figure 19.11.

To add text, select the Text tool, place the mouse pointer where you want the text to appear in the image, and click. You then enter your text in the Text dialog box. Remember also that you should add text to a new layer so that you can change the text without redoing the entire image.

I show you how I created the outlined text effect in the next hour.

FIGURE 19.11

The final brochure with the text in place.

Creating Photo Montages

Creating photomontages is a more complex process, or it can be, under certain circumstances. I create a relatively simple photo montage in the next exercise, and along the way I point out things that you should watch for when creating your own.

Figures 19.12 and 19.13 are the two images I'll be compositing in this exercise.

FIGURE 19.12

A graffiti-covered wall.

19

FIGURE 19.13

A self-portrait of the author, shot in his studio.

Figure 19.12 is an outdoor shot of a graffiti-covered wall. The original was shot on color slide film. Figure 19.13 is a self-portrait of the author (that would be me), taken in the studio and shot on black-and-white film stock.

Your *modus operandi* when creating photomontages is to eliminate all differences between the photos so that they appear to be from the same image. You'll have to adjust the images in several areas ("gotchas"): lighting, shadows, film speed (graininess), size, and color, to name a few.

The first gotcha here would be that the two films are different: One is color slide film, and the other is black-and-white negative film. An easy way around this problem, of course, is to convert the color slide to black and white (or "grayscale" as it's called in digital imaging) after scanning it into Paint Shop Pro.

To convert the color photo into grayscale, choose Colors, Grey Scale. You should remember to bump the color resolution back up afterwards. To do so, choose Colors, Increase Color Depth, 16 Million Colors.

For the montage to work, the self-portrait needed a little resizing after it was scanned in so that both images would be the same size relative to each other. The process here is the same as that discussed earlier with the train images.

Essentially, what I want to do is superimpose the studio shot onto the location shot of the graffiti-covered wall. The first step is to isolate the self-portrait:

1. In this particular case, the solid-color background of the studio simplifies the isolation process.

   With the background one solid color, I simply used the Magic Wand to select the background and then inverted the selection (Selections, Invert) to select the self-portrait.

If this image showed the subject against other objects, the process of selecting the subject would be more involved and would require the techniques shown in Hour 11, "Utilizing Masks for Precision."

2. When the subject is selected, copy it to the Clipboard (Edit, Copy) and paste it into a new layer on the Graffiti image.

3. To paste the selection into the Graffiti image, make the Graffiti image current and then choose Edit, Paste, As New Layer (see Figure 19.14).

FIGURE 19.14

The subject from Figure 19.13, pasted into the image from Figure 19.12.

Because the subject is on its own layer, moving it into place with the Mover tool is a simple matter (see Figure 19.15).

FIGURE 19.15

The subject from Figure 19.13, moved into place.

19

Even though these photographs were shot on different types of film, they were both shot with the same ISO (that is, they were both shot with film of the same speed). The lighting in both photographs is also similar enough to not be a problem. If either of these variables is a problem with the images you're trying to composite, though, you may have to consider reshooting.

4. Now you must fix the differences in the photos, such as lighting, shadows, and film speed, to produce a more realistic effect. The only difference in the photos here is that the background should be a little fuzzier than the subject to mimic the effect of distance in a photograph. That situation is easily corrected by running the Gaussian Blur filter against the background image.

Figure 19.16 shows the final montage.

FIGURE 19.16
The subject has been moved to make a better composition, and some Gaussian Blur was added to the background.

Creating montages is an art form and requires much time, patience, and practice. But it's something that you can have fun with, too.

I've barely scratched the surface of what can be done with these techniques. In fact, whole books have been written on the subject. For more information, try *Photoshop Collage Techniques* by Gregory Cosmo Haun. This book is published by Hayden, and its ISBN is 1-56830-349-1.

Summary

This enjoyable hour mixed theory and practice. I hope I've given you some ideas of what you can do with photographs, Paint Shop Pro, and some time and effort. I doubt that you'll be able to look at printed photos in the same way anymore, knowing the magic that can be accomplished with a digital imaging program such as Paint Shop Pro.

In the next hour, I show you how to create more special effects, using combinations of filters and other tools.

Workshop

The Workshop contains a question and answer section to help answer the most commonly asked questions and quiz questions to help you solidify your understanding of the material covered.

Q&A

Q How do I resize an image without changing its relative dimensions?

A The Resize dialog box has a check box called Maintain Aspect Ratio. Placing a check mark in this check box maintains the relative dimensions of an image as you resize it. You can also right-click and drag a corner of your image with the Deformation tool.

Q Can I create an image using both the montage and collage techniques?

A Yes, you can. Of course, the resulting image would be seen as a collage because of the collage elements in it.

Q What tricks can I use to align or correct shadow differences in an image?

A If the sun is on one side in one image and on the other in the other image, one trick would be to flip one of the images. This technique can have its drawbacks, though. For example, if the image that you flip has text, it would be readily apparent to the viewer and might spoil the illusion. Some shadows might be very difficult, if not impossible, to fix. In such cases, you might want to consider reshooting the photo.

19

Quiz

1. Explain the difference between a collage and a montage.

2. When creating a collage in Paint Shop Pro, what happens after resizing your images?

3. Why would you want to turn off a layer's visibility while creating a collage? How do you do this?

4. Why is creating a montage usually a more complicated task than creating a collage?

Answers

1. A collage is a collection of images placed together using layers and masks, so that the final image appears to be created from several images. A montage is also built of several images; however, the objective is to fool the viewer into believing that the image was actually shot on one frame of film, even if the subject matter is unbelievable.

2. After adding each image to a separate layer and resizing it, the next step is to place each layer to get a rough idea of the layout or composition.

3. Turning a layer's visibility on and off helps to cut down on some of the visual static. Sometimes working with less visual information is easier than working with visibility turned on.

4. With a montage, you're trying to fool the viewer into believing that the final image is real and not digitally created.

Hour **20**

Combining Advanced Techniques

Sometimes the difference between a good effect and a great one is simply adding another effect over one that's already present. Other times, you can get a special effect just by trying something that you normally wouldn't think of.

In this hour, I show you how to use some Paint Shop Pro tools in ways you might not have thought of. I cover the following advanced techniques:

- Outlining text and other objects
- Filling text with textures or photos
- Creating an interface

Outlining Text and Other Objects

One technique that Paint Shop Pro doesn't offer is a way to stroke, or outline, objects. Of course, you can stroke rectangles, squares, circles, and ellipses when you create them, but there's no easy way to stroke some odd-shaped object such as text. Or is there?

In Hour 19, "Compositing," you may have noticed the 1-800 number on the final railway brochure (refer to Figure 19.11) and wondered how I did that. Here's how:

1. Open a new 600×300 image with the resolution set to 72 pixels per inch, the background color set to white, and the image type set to 16.7 million colors.

2. Add a new layer for the text by clicking the Create Layer icon at the top of the Layer palette and name it Text. You'll need to add the new layer because you'll be adding another layer later that will go between the layer with your text and the Background layer, and it will help you keep things straight.

3. Use the Text tool to add some text to your image. I added the word "Outlined" in 90-point Arial Black and used a light blue for the color. Make sure you set Create As to Floating.

   The text should still be selected—it should still have the marquee around it.

4. Make the Background layer active by clicking its name in the Layer palette. This technique is a quick way of having the new layer appear above the Background layer and below the Text layer. Alternatively, you can create the new layer and click and drag it into place.

5. Add another new layer and name it Outline.

6. Choose Selections, Modify, Expand and enter a value of 5.

   You should now have three layers: Background, a layer with an active selection called Outline, and another layer on top called Text (see Figure 20.1).

FIGURE 20.1

Background, expanded selection, and text.

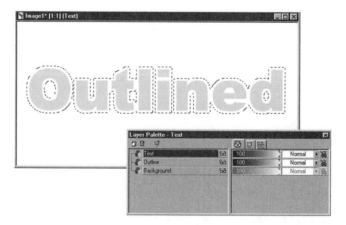

7. With the Outline layer active, set the foreground color to the color you want for the outline. I chose black for this exercise.

8. Select the Flood Fill tool (it resembles a small paint bucket tipped over slightly), set Fill Style to Solid Color, and click inside the selection. You may have to use this technique in several areas to fill the entire outline.

9. Choose Selections, Select None, and you should have text that resembles that shown in Figure 20.2.

FIGURE 20.2
Outlined text.

You can use this technique to stroke, or outline, anything that you can select. In fact, I use a similar technique to outline multiple objects in vector programs such as Illustrator. Figure 20.3 is an example of this popular illustration effect.

FIGURE 20.3
A pen with a dark outline, shown in Illustrator.

20

You can also expand on this technique and have the text in white on a white background so that the text would appear as just the outline (see Figure 20.4).

FIGURE 20.4

White text on a white background, outlined in black.

This technique gives the appearance that the text is outlined and doesn't have anything in its center. I accomplished this effect using the same steps as explained previously except that the text is white instead of blue.

Filling Text with Textures or Photos

You can use the effect described in the last section to fill the text with a texture or even a photo and outline it. Here's how:

1. Start with two photographs. I'm using two photographs of fall leaves (see Figures 20.5 and 20.6).

FIGURE 20.5

Yellow fall leaves.

FIGURE 20.6

Red fall leaves.

2. Make the image that you want to place the text onto active by clicking its title bar.

3. Add a new layer to this image and name it Text.

4. Use the Text tool to add some text.

5. Leave the text selected and select the Flood Fill tool.

6. Under the Flood Fill tab in the Tool Options window, set the Fill Style option to Pattern.

7. Click Flood Fill Options tab to bring up the Flood Fill Options dialog box.

8. Use the New Pattern Source pull-down menu to choose the red leaves as the pattern source. This step will enable you to fill the text selection with the red leaves.

9. One by one, click the letters so that they become filled with the image pattern (see Figure 20.7).

To make the letters more visible, you can use the same techniques as I did in the previous example:

1. With the text still selected, create a new layer above the Background layer.

2. Expand the selection by choosing Selections, Modify, Expand. This time I used a value of 3.

3. Set the foreground to white and click in each letter to fill it with white. Make sure that you've reset the Fill Style to Solid Color under the Flood Fill tab in the Tool Options palette.

4. Choose Selections, Select None.

20

FIGURE 20.7

Letters on one image filled with the pattern of another.

You should have something similar to the image in Figure 20.8.

FIGURE 20.8

Outlined letters on one image filled with the pattern of another.

Creating an Interface

The next technique uses some of the techniques you've already learned, along with a couple of new tricks.

This project demonstrates the step-by-step process that goes into making an interface that you can use for many purposes—from Web page to CD-ROM interfaces to kiosk touch screens and more.

Setting Up the Interface

In this example, I'm using a slightly modified version of the brushed-metal texture that was described in Hour 16, "Special Effects" (refer to Figure 16.10). I'll also use the bevel technique that was used for several other examples in other hours.

To follow along, open a new 600×600 image at 72 pixels per inch with the background color set to white and the image type set to 16.7 million colors. Then follow these steps:

1. Turn on the grid by choosing View, Grid.

2. Select the Selection tool (it's the small dashed-line rectangle icon).

3. In the Tool Options window, set the Selection Type option to Rectangular and the Feather value to 10.

4. Draw a rectangular selection from 50,50 to 550,550. You can use the grid and the coordinates displayed at the lower-left of the screen to help you position the Selection tool.

5. Select the Flood Fill tool (it resembles a small, tipped over paint bucket) and set the foreground color to black.

6. Click in the selection to fill it with black.

7. Save the selection by choosing Selections, Save To Alpha Channel.

8. Choose Selections, Select None.

9. Choose Image, Other, Emboss to add a bevel to the rectangle.

10. Choose Image, Mirror to reverse the bevel (see Figure 20.9).

FIGURE 20.9
Beveled rectangle.

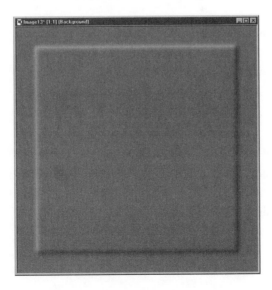

20

11. Add a new layer and name it Steel Plate.

12. Load the saved selection by choosing Selections, Load from Alpha Channel.

13. Fill the selection with white.

14. Choose Image, Noise, Add.

15. Set %Noise to 100 and choose Random.

16. Choose Colors, Grey Scale to turn the noise into grayscale.

17. Choose Colors, Increase Color Depth, 16.7 Million Colors.

18. Choose Image, Blur, Motion Blur, set the direction to 120, and set the intensity to 25 pixels. This setting gives you the same brushed-metal look that was described in Hour 16.

19. To change the look a little, choose Image, Sharpen, Sharpen More. This modification brings out the texture of the metal a little more.

20. Make the Background layer active (you can do so by clicking the layer's name in the Layer palette) and turn off the visibility of the Steel Plate layer. (To turn off a layer's visibility, simply click the Layer Visibility Toggle icon in the Layer palette.)

21. Choose Selections, Select None to turn off the current selection, then select the Selection tool and set the Feather value to 0 in the Tool Options window.

22. Select a rectangular area around the beveled rectangle.

23. Choose Selections, Invert.

24. Set the current background color to white and press Delete to fill the area around the beveled rectangle with white. Choose Selections, Select None to turn off the selection.

25. Make the Steel Plate layer visible again and set its blending mode to Overlay.

    You should have a nice beveled steel plate—perfect for the foundation of the interface (see Figure 20.10).

26. If you turned off the grid, as I have done, turn it back on by choosing View, Grid.

27. Add a new layer and name it Indents.

28. Using the grid as a guide, make a circular selection (set the Feather value to 1) that's about 60 pixels in radius in the upper-left corner of the image.

29. Fill the selection with a black-to-white Linear blend at an angle of 120 degrees (see Figure 20.11).

30. Click and drag the Indents layer onto the Create Layer icon at the upper left of the Layer palette to duplicate it.

FIGURE 20.10

The beveled steel plate.

FIGURE 20.11

An indent added in the upper-left corner.

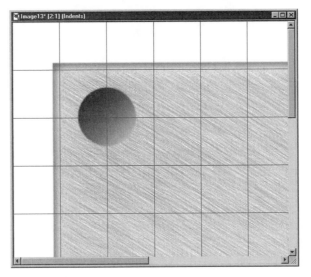

20

31. Use the Mover tool to move the indent on the new layer to the right corner of the plate.

32. Turn off the visibility of the Steel Plate and Background layers.

33. Choose Layers, Merge, Merge Visible to merge the two Indents layers into one layer.

34. Click and drag this layer onto the Create Layer icon to create another layer with the two indents on it.

35. Drag these indents to the bottom of the image (you might need to restore the visibility of the other layers to help you place the indents).

36. Turn off the visibility of the Steel Plate and Background layers again and merge the two Indents layers.

37. Rename the Indents layer Indents, as it has probably been renamed through all of this copying. You should now have three layers: the Background layer, the Steel Plate layer, and the Indents layer. Your image should resemble the one shown in Figure 20.12.

FIGURE 20.12

Steel plate with indents in each corner.

38. Add another layer and name it Screws.

39. Select the Selection tool and, in the Tool Options window, set the Selection Type option to Circular and set the Feather value to 1.

40. Place the mouse pointer in the center of the upper-left indent (use the grid to help you place the pointer) and make a selection that's about 30 pixels in radius.

41. Set the foreground color to a light gray (I used R: 180, G: 180, B: 180) and the background color to a dark gray (I used R: 77, G: 77, B: 77).

42. Select the Flood Fill tool and, in the Tool Options window, set Fill Style to Sunburst Gradient. Click the Flood Fill Options tab and set Gradient to Foreground-Background.

43. Change the Gradient Center by setting Horizontal to 30 and Vertical to 27.

44. Click within the selected area to fill it with the gradient. This will be the screw's head.

45. Click and drag this layer onto the Create Layer icon to duplicate the screw.

46. Drag the screw into place over the upper-right indent.

47. Turn off the visibility of all of the layers except the two layers with the screws.

48. Merge these two layers by choosing Layers, Merge, Merge Visible.

49. Drag the merged layer onto the Create Layer icon to duplicate the layer.

50. Turn on the visibility of all of the layers so that you can position the bottom screws. Position the bottom screws over the bottom indents.

51. Turn off the visibility of all of the layers except the two that contain the screws.

52. Choose Layers, Merge, Merge Visible to merge the two Screws layers. Rename the layers to Screws.

53. Turn on the visibility of all of the layers. Your image should resemble the one shown in Figure 20.13.

FIGURE 20.13

The steel plate with the indents and screws in place.

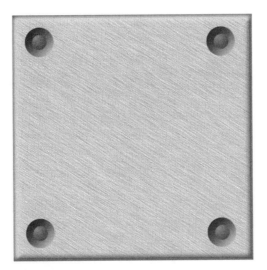

20

Adding the Finishing Touches to the Interface

Now for the finishing touches. If you'd like, you can add a drop shadow (Image, Effects, Drop Shadow) to the screws.

I used the Drop Shadow effect to add a black shadow with the opacity set to 70, the blur set to 5, and both the vertical and horizontal offsets set to 2. The drop shadow adds to the illusion that the interface is three-dimensional (see Figure 20.14).

FIGURE 20.14

Drop Shadow effect added to the screws.

You can leave the screws like this and call them rivets, or you can go ahead and add the slots. To add the slots, I used the same technique of creating one element and then copying its layer and moving the new element into place.

1. To create the first slot, add a new layer, call it Slots, and zoom in on the screw in the upper-left corner of the image.

2. Select the Selection tool and, in the Tool Options window, set the selection type to Rectangular, set the Feather value to 0, and turn off the Antialias option.

3. Draw a rectangular selection over the screw head (see Figure 20.15).

FIGURE 20.15

Making a rectangular selection for the slot in the screw head.

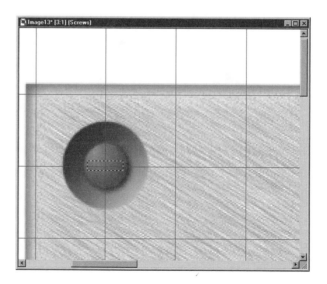

4. Swap the foreground and background colors by clicking the small, bent, two-headed arrow below the foreground and background color swatches.

5. Select the Flood Fill tool and, in the Controls palette, set Fill Style to Linear Gradient.

6. Click the Options button to bring up the Flood Fill Options dialog box.

7. Set the direction to 180 degrees and click OK.

8. Click in the rectangular selected area to fill it with the gradient.

9. Select the Deformation tool (it's the rectangular icon with dots at each corner and the center point of each side, top, and bottom) and use it to turn the slot 45 degrees (see Figure 20.16).

FIGURE 20.16

The slot filled with a linear gradient and rotated 45 degrees.

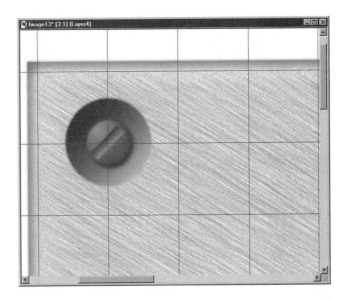

10. Choose Selection, Select None.

11. Copy the Slots layer (drag and drop the layer onto the Add New Layer icon) and drag the second slot into place over the upper-right screw.

12. Merge these two layers by making all others invisible and choosing Layers, Merge, Merge Visible.

13. Drag the merged layer onto the Add New Layer icon and drag the second set of slots into place over the bottom screws.

14. Merge the two Slots layers and rename the layer Slots.

20

15. You should now have five separate layers: Background, Steel Plate, Indents, Screws, and Slots.

16. You should probably lower the opacity of the Indents layer so that some of the steel plate shows through. You can adjust the opacity of any layer by making the layer active (click the layer's name in the Layer palette) and moving the slider to the left. I set mine to about 60%.

Figure 20.17 shows my final image.

FIGURE 20.17

The final steel plate and screws interface.

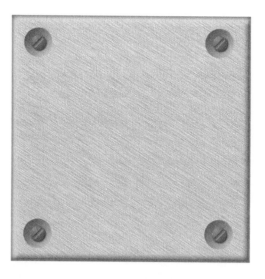

All that's left is to add some text, a logo, or some buttons. I discuss some of the methods for doing so in Hour 22, "Buttons and Seamless Tiles."

Summary

This was another fun hour. I've shown you how to create some neat effects that are not commonly done with Paint Shop Pro. I really hope that you'll see from these examples just how powerful Paint Shop Pro is and that you'll explore some ideas of your own.

In the next hour, I show you how to prepare your graphics for the Web.

Workshop

The Workshop contains a question and answer section to help answer the most commonly asked questions and quiz questions to help you solidify your understanding of the material covered.

Q&A

Q What other kinds of effects can be accomplished using the outline procedure described in this chapter?

A Stroking, or outlining, is a cool technique that has many uses. For example, you could select many different objects at one time, using any number of selection techniques, and apply the effect to outline all the objects.

Q What elements besides screws would be good to add to an interface?

A Basically anything that adds to the illusion that you're after. For example, you might add buttons, dials, animated dials, and more.

Q How do you create the 3D look using gradients?

A Because lighter objects appear to be closer than darker objects, gradients give objects a three-dimensional appearance. Going from light to dark, or vice versa, fools the eye into believing that a flat object has depth.

Quiz

1. Why do you have to use so many layers when outlining an irregularly shaped image or text?

2. Which tool do you use to add a texture or photo to text?

3. How does the Drop Shadow tool help you create a realistic-looking interface?

4. How do you merge two layers? Why would you want to do this?

Answers

1. You use the different layers to keep the objects separate and so that you can outline in one color and fill in another.

2. You can use several tools to achieve this effect. One way is to use the Paint Brushes tool and choose a texture from the Tool Controls tab in the Controls palette.

3. The drop shadow helps create depth in an image, giving a more realistic 3D quality to your images.

4. You can merge two or more layers by turning off all other layers' visibility and choosing Layers, Merge, Merge Visible. You would want to merge layers that won't need to be manipulated separately again to control the size of the file. The more layers an image has, the larger the file size.

20

PART V

Paint Shop Pro for the Web

Hour **21**

Preparing Your Graphics for the Web

Today many digital artists are creating graphics for the World Wide Web. Creating images for the Web, though, means working within certain limitations. You must be aware of things such as color palettes, dithering, antialiasing, and Web file formats.

You must also be aware of file compression. You don't need to know about it at the same level as programmers do, but you must be aware of the difference it can make with your images. The following Web-related issues are covered in this hour:

- Working with file formats
- Adjusting color depth
- Using palettes
- Previewing your images for the Web
- Dithering and antialiasing

Working with File Formats

So what's the best way to compress your images? Currently, and unfortunately, only two file formats are available for Web graphics: GIF and JPG. I say *unfortunately* not because of these two formats, but rather because of the lack of other choices.

Why compress your image files, anyway? Because compressing files saves disk space and because compressed files download faster from your Web pages.

GIFs

GIF, for *Graphical Interchange Format*, is an image compression format originally developed by CompuServe. This format is one of the most popular formats for computer images. It also has a couple of features that make it appealing for Web graphics. Like any other format, though, it also has some shortcomings. In addition to lacking some desirable features, GIF has recently been surrounded by copyright infringement problems. The mathematical algorithm used to compress the image information, called LZW (for Lempel-Ziv & Welch, the mathematicians who developed it), is patented by Unisys. (An *algorithm* is a mathematical formula that can be programmed in computer language to perform a set of steps.)

Unisys has decided to charge developers licensing and royalty fees. This prospect didn't sit well with the Internet community at large. As a result, programmers on the Web have banded together to create the PNG (pronounced "ping") format. This format is not currently supported on today's popular browsers. The situation should change shortly, though, with the Internet community pushing for PNG's inclusion. Despite this controversy, GIF has been and probably will continue to be around for a while.

Although the latest versions of the two most popular browsers do display PNG files, neither fully supports the file format. Paint Shop Pro will save PNG files but does not enable you to fully utilize all of the features that the format supports. The features that are unsupported by the browsers and Paint Shop Pro, alike, are Gamma and Transparency.

GIFs: The Good, the Bad, and the Ugly

Although somewhat limited, GIF has some really good properties. For example, it can compress cartoons, illustrations, and images with large areas of similar color very well. Even with these types of images, though, GIF yields different results because of the way that the GIF compression algorithm works. You can see what I mean by looking at Figures 21.1 and 21.2.

FIGURE 21.1

Thick horizontal stripes: 1,292 bytes.

FIGURE 21.2

Thick vertical stripes: 1,540 bytes.

The figures are similar except that Figure 21.1 has horizontal bars and Figure 21.2 has vertical bars. Aside from that, both are the same size and have the same number of colors. Note the file sizes, though. Figure 21.2 is 248 bytes bigger than Figure 21.2. That's almost 20 percent bigger. Take a look at a few more images (Figures 21.3 and 21.4), and then you can examine why this size difference occurs.

FIGURE 21.3

Thin horizontal stripes: 1,299 bytes.

Wow! There's an even bigger difference between the file size of Figure 21.3 and that of Figure 21.4. The difference is 1,380 bytes—a whopping 106 percent. What's interesting, as well, is that there is only a very small difference in file size between Figure 21.1 and Figure 21.3—only seven bytes.

21

Figure 21.4

Thin vertical stripes: 2,679 bytes.

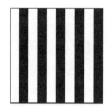

The way that the GIF algorithm compresses information explains the difference in file size. Large blocks of identical information that read from the top left and go across toward the right are well compressed. On the other hand, when information changes (for example, a color change), the GIF compression method starts to lose its power.

A GIF image in one solid color the same size as Figures 21.1 through 21.4 is 1,146 bytes—not much smaller than Figures 21.1 and 21.3. You can see the losses that happen, though, when you start breaking up the horizontal runs of a single color. Imagine how much room a vertical gradient would take up!

What all of this means to you as a Web graphic designer is that there are no hard-and-fast rules when it comes to image compression. Sometimes GIF will be the method of choice, and sometimes it won't. You'll really have to examine each image independently. For the most part, though, GIF works well with images that have a limited color palette.

There also are some cases when the only choice is to use GIF. One of these is when you want some of the image's information to be transparent.

Transparent GIFs

Transparent GIFs are handy when you have a background pattern on your Web pages. Without the Transparency option, you're limited to having a rectangle around your images, as in Figure 21.5.

Figure 21.5 shows a Web page with a GIF at the top. The GIF wasn't saved with the Transparency option activated. As a result, a dark rectangle appears around the word *Nontransparent*. Figure 21.6 shows the same Web page; in this example, however, the GIF was saved with the transparency option turned on.

Notice how the background pattern is visible around and even through the letters. This Transparency option is available in most of today's graphics programs.

FIGURE 21.5

Example of a non-transparent GIF.

FIGURE 21.6

An example of a transparent GIF.

Saving Transparent GIFs with Paint Shop Pro

Version 6 makes it easy to save a transparent GIF. To do so, follow these steps:

1. Open a new image (or an existing one if you'd like to remove its background).

2. Create the image you want. I'm using the stylized ampersand shown in Figure 21.7.

21

FIGURE 21.7

A stylized ampersand.

You might want to make sure that you've saved a copy of your file in the native Paint Shop Pro format before you reduce the colors and save the file as a GIF. That way, you'll have the original file with its layers and channels intact, should you need to make changes in the future.

3. Choose File, Export, Transparent GIF. Doing so will bring up the Transparent GIF Saver dialog box (see Figure 21.8).

FIGURE 21.8

The stylized ampersand being transformed into a transparent GIF.

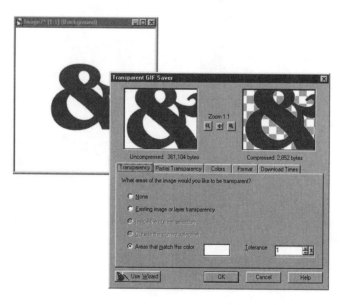

4. Place a check mark in the Areas That Match This Color option and move the mouse pointer over your image. The cursor will become a small dropper. Click over the color that you want to become transparent. You'll see that color disappear in the preview window in the Transparent GIF Saver dialog box.

5. Click OK to bring up the Save As dialog box, name your file, and save it. That's all there is to it!

You may have noticed the Wizard button in the Transparent GIF Saver dialog box. Clicking this button will bring up a wizard that can help you use some of the more esoteric options of creating a transparent GIF. These include choosing a background color that will closely match the background you intend to display your GIF image against. This can be important if there is a lot of antialiasing in your image. I encourage you to explore the wizard to see what it has to offer.

JPGs

JPGs or, more properly, JPEGs, for *Joint Photographic Experts Group* (pronounced "jay-pegs"), is a somewhat misunderstood compression method. Images compressed using the JPG algorithm often get a bad rap from users who view the resulting images with 256-color systems. Because JPGs are 24-bit images, they often dither badly on 8-bit systems. On a 16- or 24-bit system, however, a JPG saved with a high-quality setting can be a fairly high-quality image. In addition, the JPG image can often be much smaller than the same image saved with another compression method.

Did You Lose Something?

Another misunderstood aspect of JPG files is that the compression algorithm used is known as a *lossy compression method*. In other words, some information is discarded during compression. Losing information may seem like a problem but, in fact, it saves a lot of space while changing the quality very little. With an appropriate quality setting, the lost information is not readily visible to the human eye. The savings and the quality work against each other, though, as you can see from Figures 21.9 through 21.11. These figures were saved with Ulead's SmartSaver from within Paint Shop Pro 6.

 SmartSaver is an export plug-in available from Ulead. This plug-in enables you to export GIFs, JPGs, and PNGs from within Paint Shop Pro. SmartSaver offers real-time previews, varying levels of compression, color depth, and more. Visit Ulead on the Web at www.ulead.com, where you can download a demo version of this export plug-in.

Figure 21.9 was saved at 100 percent quality and is 82,098 bytes. It closely resembles the original scan, which is 449,974 bytes.

21

FIGURE 21.9

Scan of Marianne saved as 100 percent–quality JPG.

Figure 21.10 was saved in the same manner except that the setting was changed to 55 percent. I'm not sure what the final print will look like in the book, but on my screen it was very difficult to see any difference. This version, though, takes up only 9,443 bytes. Quite a large savings.

FIGURE 21.10

Scan of Marianne saved as 55 percent–quality JPG.

The final JPG (Figure 21.11) was saved with a setting of 10 percent quality. Although this image compressed the best, I think you'll agree that the last little saving in disk space (and download time) wasn't worth it. This file, which now takes up 3,593 bytes, isn't the best quality.

You can see, though, that the JPG format enables you to save a lot of space and bandwidth without compromising the quality of your Web graphics. Another problem that can occur because of the lossy compression method happens to images that are edited and resaved in the JPG format. Figure 21.12 is a 300 percent blowup of the GrafX Design logo. Figure 21.13 shows the same logo edited and resaved as a JPG five times.

FIGURE 21.11

Scan of Marianne saved as 10 percent quality JPG.

FIGURE 21.12

GrafX Design logo saved as a JPG.

FIGURE 21.13

GrafX Design logo edited and resaved as a JPG five times.

Notice the marks around the image in Figure 21.13. They're in Figure 21.12, as well, but they're not as noticeable. These marks are called *artifacts* and are a result of the way that the JPG compression algorithm works. Along with the added artifacts, resaving a JPG many times can actually add to the size of the final image.

21

The solution? Always save a copy of your images in a 24-bit *lossless format* such as BMP, PCX, or TIFF, as well as compressing them into JPGs.

> Lossless compression formats use a method of compression that assures that no information is lost. An image can be compressed and uncompressed many times with no changes to the image. Compared to lossless compression formats, lossy compression methods achieve much higher compression ratios, but they do so by discarding some of the information that makes up the image. Normally, the fact that these methods discard information is not a problem. The compression algorithms discard information in such a way that the changes are too subtle to be picked up by the human eye. The changes can become apparent, though, at very high compression rates or after successive compressions.

An even better approach is to save your work in the format of the image program you're using. For example, you should always save a copy of any important graphic being worked on in Paint Shop Pro as a PSP file. Keeping these extra copies enables you to save the program's extra features along with your images. Saving a PSP file in Paint Shop Pro, for example, keeps all the layer and channel information. Most of the larger imaging programs have their own formats. These programs normally have the option of saving both GIF and JPG Web-ready images, as well.

Why Use JPG?

After reading the last bit about JPGs and how this method discards some information, you may be wondering why you should use this format for your Web graphics. Take another look at Figures 21.9 and 21.10. Figure 21.9 is more than 82,000 bytes, and Figure 21.10 is just over 9,000 bytes! I doubt that you can really tell the difference between the two. I normally save with a much higher setting and was rather surprised myself at the quality of Figure 21.10.

Remember, too, that Figure 21.9 is a JPG that is already much smaller than the original 24-bit image. The bottom line is that if you have an image with a subtle blend of color, such as a portrait or a gradient, JPG is a good format.

GIF or JPG?

The debate over which format is better still rages every so often on Usenet. My opinion is that each format has its place, just as the native formats of the various image programs do. Under some circumstances, a JPG beats out a GIF file in terms of quality and size; at other times the best choice is GIF. Personally, I take the time to view my images in both formats using SmartSaver. I also take the time to play around with the number of colors when previewing my images as GIFs, as well as trying out the different palettes.

When I'm previewing a JPG, I try different quality settings. There really is no hard-and-fast answer. Even after creating more computer graphics than I can count, I still play around with each new image to get the best quality/size ratio that I can.

Adjusting Color Depth

Color depth is a way of describing how many colors your hardware and software are capable of displaying. The buzzwords most often used are 8-bit, 16-bit, and 24-bit. Of course, color depth is sometimes described by the actual number of colors being displayed, such as 256 colors or 16.7 million colors.

Hardware is the real determining factor. Your Web browser, for example, will display as many colors as your system can use. The next limiting factor is the type of image being displayed. GIFs are capable of displaying only 256 separate colors. However, these colors can be chosen from all 16.7 million available colors. JPGs can display up to 16.7 million colors, which makes the JPG format a popular choice for photographs and other real-world images.

8-Bit Color

Eight-bit or 256 colors is what many systems use, although they are often capable of displaying more. Sometimes referred to as Video Gate Array (VGA), 8-bit is somewhat limited. With your system set to 8-bit, you're at the mercy of your browser software, as you'll see later, in the section on palettes.

16-Bit Color

Sixteen-bit color, often referred to as "hi color," is a good choice if your system's video memory is limited. Using 16-bit color is a great compromise between speed and color. With 16-bit color, up to 64,000 colors are possible (65,536 actually). With 64,000 colors, your Web-viewing experience will be much more enriched. Using this color depth reduces the need for dithering.

Dithering, a process used to fool the eye into seeing more colors than are actually available, is discussed in depth a little later in this hour.

21

24-Bit Color

Twenty-four–bit is the best color depth to use when creating and viewing computer images. To use this color depth, though, your video card must have at least 1MB of memory. The reason is that for each pixel you must have 24 bits (or 3 bytes) of memory available. With a little simple arithmetic, you can see that a 640×480 screen, which has 307,200 pixels (640×480), requires 307,200×3 bytes per pixel, which equals 921,600 bytes. Now that you have a basic understanding of color depth, it's time to look at palettes.

Using Palettes

Traditionally, a palette was a surface where an artist mixed colors before applying them to the canvas. In computer graphics, a palette is somewhat similar. Most graphics programs have a window where you can pick your colors. In certain circumstances, your color choices are limited. Those limited sets of colors also are referred to as *palettes*.

Palettes are more important when working with GIF images. Because of their limited color depth, GIF images can use only a select palette. This palette, though, can contain a different selection of colors. Sometimes you have control over the selection of the colors and, unfortunately, sometimes you don't.

Problems with Limited Palettes

One problem associated with limited palettes is that, if you choose to work with a limited palette while creating your images, many of the features of your graphics programs will not be available to you. Options such as drop shadows and blurring need to have access to the full range of colors to do their magic. The alternative here is to create your image using higher color depth and then reduce the depth.

You should always keep a copy of the image with its color depth set at the higher resolution. This extra copy makes applying subsequent changes much easier. Saving your image as a BMP, a TIF, or a PCX, for example, is something you should always consider doing. These formats tend to take up a little more room, though, so you might also want to consider having some sort of backup system if you're going to be creating lots of images.

How to Build or Select a Palette

You can build a palette in a number of ways. You can load an indexed (or GIF) image into your graphics program. Having done so, the palette associated with that image will be available to you. Most software also allows you to build a palette color by color. You can open up the palette and add, edit, or remove colors from it. Figure 21.14 shows the Edit Palette dialog box from Paint Shop Pro.

FIGURE 21.14

The Edit Palette dialog box.

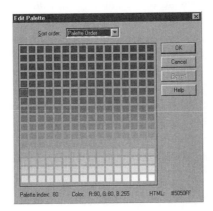

Double-clicking one of the colors in the Edit Palette dialog box brings up the Color dialog box (see Figure 21.15).

FIGURE 21.15

The Color dialog box.

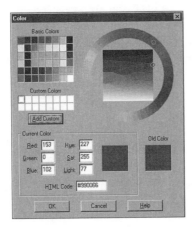

21

You can change the color you double-clicked to any one of 16.7 million other colors. In Paint Shop Pro, just enter the RGB values in the boxes in the lower-right corner of the dialog box. This new color is then available in the palette. Note that the HSL model is available in the Color dialog box, as well.

Exact Palette

The *exact palette* is built from the colors currently being used in an image. If the number of colors exceeds that for the palette you're building, you can change some of the colors to others that are similar or you can allow the program to dither the colors for you. Normally, this becomes an issue only when you need to convert the image to a lower color resolution mode before saving the image.

Adaptive Palette

Most Web browsers use an *adaptive palette* when loading an image that doesn't fit their own color palettes. There are a few gotchas involved here, though. You'll be okay if all the images share the same palette. If, on the other hand, you have a couple of images that use different palettes, you may find that your images have dithered terribly.

The problem is that while you're working on your images, you're probably working on them one at a time, right? So you create one image, save it, and go on to create the next one. You get this great idea for a different set of colors and create the second image with a completely new color scheme from the first. You then save the image after adjusting the mode appropriately. Still no problem.

You then sign on to the Internet and load your Web page. Oh-oh! The colors on both images look really bad. What happened? Well, what happened is that if the browser is running on an 8-bit setup, it can't show you 256 colors from one image and another 256 from the next. It can display only 256 different colors at one time. This limitation brings us to the dreaded Netscape or Web palette.

Web Palette

The Web palette is the scourge of Web graphics artists the world over. This palette consists of 216 colors that, if used when constructing your images, display your images the same way on every platform.

I say *scourge* because 216 colors is not very many, and the color choices are abysmal. For example, there are only 6 shades of gray.

 You can download the Web-safe palette from Jasc Software, Inc.'s site at http://www.jasc.com/netpal.zip or at GrafX Design's Web site at http://www.grafx-design.com/files/netpal.zip.

Why 216 colors and not 256? Because the operating system—Windows, for example—and the browser—Netscape, let's say—use 40 colors between them, which leaves 216 colors. This palette is sometimes called *the cube*, which refers to its being a 6×6×6 cube: six colors wide, six colors high, and six sides (6 times 6 times 6 equals 216).

Because of the popularity of Web graphics, many graphics programs now include a version of the Web palette. Although this feature makes the process of creating images that use this set of colors easier, it doesn't change the fact that you are limited to this particular color set.

So, what can you do? One answer is to use your own set of colors, being careful that all your images use the same restricted palette. The other option is to hope that many readers of your pages will be using machines capable of displaying more than 256 colors. I wouldn't bet on this for a while, though. Many Web surfers are still using older 386 machines.

Of course, you could build your graphics with these limitations in mind and take them into account when the images are really important for navigation around your site.

Previewing Your Images in SmartSaver

One product that can help if you're using a high-color resolution system and are worried about what your readers will see is Ulead's SmartSaver Pro software (see Figure 21.16).

FIGURE 21.16

Ulead's SmartSaver Pro.

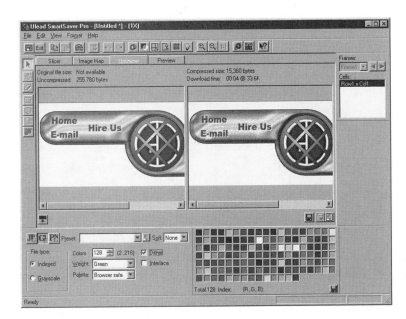

21

Although you are seeing the preview in black and white, you can probably tell that there's not much difference between the original on the left and the image on the right. The image on the right is what my GrafX Design logo would look like when displayed using the Netscape palette. Even though I eventually saved this image as a JPG to take advantage of the subtler gradient available when using a higher-color resolution, I was pretty sure that the readers who ventured onto my pages wouldn't be too disappointed by the quality of this image. To add some assurance, I created most of the subsequent images with a color palette that was close to the chrome-and-blue scheme I had used for the main logo.

SmartSaver Pro is valuable for more than its preview screen, though. This software also enables you to choose from a wider range of colors than would normally be available. Notice the Colors spin control near the bottom left of Figure 21.16. You can set any value between 2 and 256. Playing with the numbers means that you can shave some extra weight off your images while keeping the colors and quality at an acceptable level.

SmartSaver Pro works with both GIF and JPG images and lets you set a variable quality for JPGs, as well. SmartSaver Pro acts as a "File, Export" extension to Paint Shop Pro. You can also use SmartSaver Pro on a standalone basis. Either way, SmartSaver Pro is something to consider if you create a lot of Web graphics.

SmartSaver Pro is a shareware product available from Ulead. Registration is about $59. You can download a trial version from Ulead's Web site at `http://www.ulead.com`. Although SmartSaver Pro doesn't overcome the Web palette limitations, it reduces the frustration level.

Understanding Dithering

Dithering, which applies only to GIF images, is one of those big bugaboos that is constantly argued about on Usenet. *Dithering,* put simply, is a process of constructing one color from a combination of other colors. You may remember from school how blue and yellow, when mixed together, give you green. Color mixing is the principle behind dithering.

In practice, dithering is quite complex. There are several mathematical functions available when dithering images. One of these is known as *diffusion* (see Figure 21.19). Which dithering processes are available with your software depends on which program you're using. Just as you must decide which format to save your files in, you must also select which dithering process to use. I suggest experimenting with several images to see which method best suits a particular image. The dithering choice is usually made when you decrease the color depth of an image.

Image software, be it your graphics program or your browser, resorts to dithering when it cannot display the entire color palette of an image. The results can vary. Figure 21.17 is an image that hasn't had its colors reduced.

FIGURE 21.17

Twenty-four–bit image.

Figure 21.18 is the same image reduced to 16 colors (or 16 levels of gray, if you will). No dithering has been applied.

FIGURE 21.18

Sixteen-color image with no dithering.

Notice the distinct banding in Figure 21.18. Without the help of dithering, the process to reduce the number of colors must choose a nearest match. On the other hand, the diffusion method of dithering was applied to Figure 21.19 during color reduction.

FIGURE 21.19

Sixteen-color image reduced with diffusion dithering.

Some people may regard the speckling, which is a result of the dithering, as unacceptable. You'll have to decide how to handle this problem when it comes to designing your own Web graphics. If you're going to display 256-color images that were created as 24-bit images, you'll have to decide whether to dither. One option is to choose colors that closely match those available in the palette that the images will ultimately be displayed with.

21

Understanding Antialiasing

Before I explain what antialiasing is, I'll cover aliasing. Of course, these two subjects are closely related. People almost never discuss aliasing, though.

Aliasing

Aliasing is what happens when analog data is represented on a digital system. A curved line drawn on a grid is a good example of analog data on a digital system (see Figure 21.20).

FIGURE 21.20

A line of a grid representing analog data on a digital system.

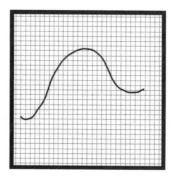

When the analog data is converted to digital, some problems arise. The digital system in this example is the grid. To convert the analog line to a digital line, each point in the grid may represent either a point in the line, by being filled in, or an area where the line does not exist, by remaining white. A square cannot be partly filled; it must be either filled in or not. That's all part of its being digital.

Okay, no problem, right? The line goes through the different squares, so you fill in each square that the line goes through. This requirement isn't a problem with some of the portions of the line, such as the portion circled in Figure 21.21.

FIGURE 21.21

A portion of the line that is easily converted to digital.

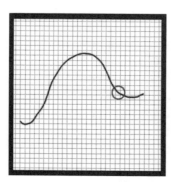

But what about sections like the one circled in Figure 21.22?

FIGURE 21.22

A portion of the line that is not easily converted to digital.

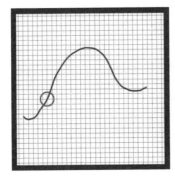

That portion cuts right across the intersection of four points. That's where aliasing comes in. An algorithm decides where all the portions fit in the digital system.

Figure 21.23 demonstrates what the resulting digital line might look like.

FIGURE 21.23

A digital version of the line.

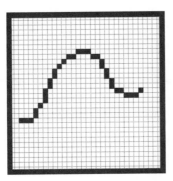

See how it looks choppy? The same thing will happen to any aliased text you display on your Web pages.

Antialiasing

Is there a solution? Yep! It comes in the form of—ta-da—*antialiasing*. What antialiasing attempts to do, using mathematics again, is to fill in some of the digital system with colors that are between the two adjoining colors. In this case, a medium gray would be between the black and the white. Some gray squares placed in the grid might help soften up the *jaggies* (see Figure 21.24).

21

FIGURE 21.24

Anti-aliased line.

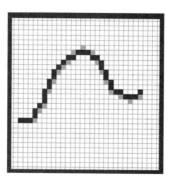

Keep in mind that this example was drawn by hand, and the resolution of the final printing in the book may not show an improvement. To give you a better idea of aliased versus antialiased, here are a couple of lines drawn with Paint Shop Pro. The first, seen in
Figure 21.25, is aliased.

FIGURE 21.25

An aliased line.

Figure 21.26 shows an antialiased line drawn in Paint Shop Pro.

FIGURE 21.26

Antialiased line.

So there'll be no mistaking the difference, Figures 21.27 and 21.28 are the aliased and
the antialiased lines, respectively, blown up 500 percent.

FIGURE 21.27

The aliased line at 500 percent.

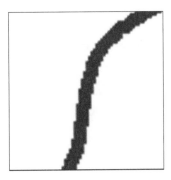

FIGURE 21.28

The antialiased line at 500 percent.

Notice the jagged appearance of the line in Figure 21.27, whereas the line in Figure 21.28 is smooth. Of course, at this resolution, the line in Figure 21.28 seems a little blurry. This factor is something else to consider when using the antialiasing option for your graphics. The fuzziness can be especially problematic with text. Text, as well as the rest of an image, is generally antialiased whenever it is resized, so you may want to add text only after you have decided on the final size of your image. This technique helps keep your text more readable.

Summary

Hour 21 was another fun hour. There was a lot of information here, though, and I covered a lot of theory. You are now well armed when it comes to creating Web graphics. Hour 22, "Buttons and Seamless Tiles," covers the creation of buttons, GIFs, and other images that you can use on your Web pages.

21

Workshop

The Workshop contains a question and answer section to help answer the most commonly asked questions and quiz questions to help you solidify your understanding of the material covered.

Q&A

Q What is an algorithm?

A An algorithm describes a set of steps designed to solve a particular problem. The algorithm can even start out as a mathematical expression that programmers convert into a programming language so that a computer can solve the problem.

Q How do you pronounce GIF?

A Believe it or not, this question appears on Usenet from time to time. When it does, it sparks a huge debate that often goes on for weeks at a time. It can be pronounced either with a soft *G,* as in *JIF,* or with a hard *G,* as in *GIFT.* I've held discussions with someone who uses the former, while I happily go on using the latter. Because we both understood what we were discussing, it didn't really matter. Of course, as evidenced by the heated Usenet debates, some people like to make an issue out of it. And so goes Usenet.

Q What is bandwidth?

A *Bandwidth* describes how much information can travel over a system such as the Internet. Although tons of data can travel very quickly over fiber-optic cables, few of us have this state-of-the-art cabling coming into our homes or offices. The bandwidth of the copper wiring that the phone system uses, which most of us connect to the Web with, is somewhat limited. Therefore, keeping file sizes down is important. Of course, you don't want to lose too much image quality, so there's a constant battle between bandwidth and image integrity.

Q Where does the number 65,536 colors come from in 16-bit color?

A The number 65,536 is the number you get if you raise 2 to the power of 16 (16-bits equals two possibilities—on and off or 0 and 1—and 16 bits). Likewise, 2 raised to the power of 8 yields 256—256 colors equal 8 bits. Finally, 24-bit equals 2 raised to the power of 24 (which equals 16.7 million colors).

Q What if I have an 8-bit system? What do I do about using 24-bit mode when creating my images?

A Although the program will be set internally to 24-bit, you'll still see only 8-bit images on your screen. As long as the software is set to high-color resolution, there should be no problem. Even though your hardware may be limited to 8-bit color, you'll have to set the software to the higher-color resolution to work with all the possible options.

Quiz

1. Which two file formats can you currently use for Web graphics, and why only those two?

2. What is a transparent GIF? What does it help you do?

3. What is dithering?

4. How does antialiasing improve the quality of your images?

Answers

1. You can currently use the GIF and JPG file formats when saving your images for the Web. These two formats are the only ones that today's Web browsers fully recognize without the help of plug-ins.

2. A transparent GIF is an image saved in the GIF format with one particular color tagged so that the software displaying the GIF image will not display that one tagged color. This allows whatever is behind that portion of the image to show through. This feature enables you to create images that have irregular edges, instead of being surrounded by a rectangle.

3. Dithering is a way of decreasing the color depth of an image. The decrease in color depth is performed in such a way that subtle changes in the original are "faked" through the use of patterns using fewer colors.

4. Antialiasing improves the look of an image by softening the edges. Antialiasing is accomplished by adding pixels using colors between the two colors that make up the edges.

21

HOUR 22

Buttons and Seamless Tiles

When it comes to creating or maintaining Web sites, you'll need to create several types of graphics. The most common types are buttons and seamless tiles. Fortunately, Paint Shop Pro excels at helping you create these types of graphics.

The following techniques related to buttons and tiles are covered in this hour:

- Creating ordinary buttons
- Creating 3D textured buttons
- Creating seamless tiles with Paint Shop Pro

Creating Buttons

Buttons are an important part of any Web page. They help your visitors navigate through your site and can even tell people a little about your style and the style of your site.

Buttons can range from the plain and ordinary, such as regular filled rectangles, to the more elaborate, such as 3D buttons, to the outrageous, such as wildly textured and weirdly shaped buttons.

Ordinary Buttons

You can create simple buttons with ease in Paint Shop Pro. Simply select the Preset Shapes tool (it resembles a blue rectangle with a red ellipse over it), set the foreground color to the color you want your buttons to be, and draw some shapes.

You'll want to add text, of course, or some type of icon (see Figure 22.1).

FIGURE 22.1

Some simple buttons created in Paint Shop Pro.

The buttons shown in Figure 22.1 were created with techniques from the early hours in this book. To create these images, I used tools such as the Preset Shapes tool, the Text tool, and the Draw tool.

Simple buttons are okay and, in some cases, are even better than something more elaborate. If you're selling a product, for example, that has nothing to do with graphics or imaging, you might not want the navigational elements on your site to get in the way of the product you're actually selling.

If, however, you want something a little flashier, you're in luck. Paint Shop Pro does that, too, with a little help from you, the digital artist.

More Elaborate Buttons

22

You can get more elaborate by simply adding shadows or some dimensionality to your buttons. To get the effect of depth, you'll need to make a few selections and use some gradients. Here's how you can add depth to a rectangular button that would ordinarily be, well... ordinary:

1. Open a new image at the size you want your button to be (or a little larger).

2. Select the Selection tool (it resembles a dashed-line rectangle) and, in the Tool Options window, set Selection Type to Rectangle.

3. Draw a rectangular selection that mostly fills the image.

4. Set the foreground color to a light shade of the color you want the button to be and set the background color to a dark shade of the color you want the button to be. I choose light blue and dark blue.

5. Select the Flood Fill tool (it resembles a tipped-over paint bucket) and, in the Tool Options window, set Fill Style to Linear Gradient.

6. Click the second tab in the Tool Options window and select Foreground-Background as the Gradient and set the direction to 135 degrees.

7. Click within the selection to fill the area with the gradient (see Figure 22.2).

FIGURE 22.2

The beginning of a 3D rectangular button.

8. Choose Selections, Modify, Contract and enter a number that will give you the size of border you want. Try 10 or so, depending on the size of your button.

9. Swap the foreground and background colors by clicking the small, bent, two-headed arrow below the foreground and background color swatches.

10. In the Tool Options window (click the first tab), set the match mode to None. This setting ensures that the complete selection is filled, even though it is currently filled with a gradient. Normally, you'll want the fill to stop when it "sees" a color change. Choosing None for the match mode makes the fill cover everything, regardless of what's currently occupying the space.

11. Click within the selected area to fill the inner rectangle with the opposite linear gradient (see Figure 22.3).

Hour 22

FIGURE 22.3

*A completed 3D rec-
tangular button.*

These buttons are easy to make, can be virtually any shape (try using circles or ellipses), and look great on a Web page. They are also easy to modify for any color scheme.

Complex 3D Textured Buttons

Paint Shop Pro also enables you to create textured 3D buttons. The next exercise shows you how to use layers and blending modes, along with selections, to create buttons that are more complex.

Open a new file and give it 200 as the width and 100 as the height. Also, make sure you use 16.7 million as the color depth. Set the background color of the image to white for now. Then follow these steps:

1. Create a new layer by clicking the Create Layer icon in the upper-left corner of the Layer palette.

2. Select the Selection tool and, under the Selection tab in the Tool Options window, set the selection type to Rectangle and set Feather to 0.

3. Draw a rectangular selection, as shown in Figure 22.4.

FIGURE 22.4

*A rectangular
selection.*

4. Select the Flood Fill tool and fill the selection with black. You can do so by setting the foreground color to black, selecting the Flood Fill tool, setting the fill style to Solid Color in the Tool Controls, and clicking within the rectangular selected area. You'll now have a black rectangle.

5. Select the Selection tool and set the style to Ellipse, set Feather to 0, and turn off the Antialias option.

6. Place the cursor's crosshairs in the middle of the left side of the black rectangle and draw down and to the left until you have an ellipse that covers part of the left side of the rectangle (see Figure 22.5).

FIGURE 22.5

An elliptical selection drawn on the left side of the rectangle.

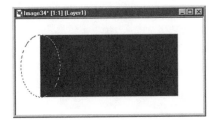

7. Set the Lock Transparency toggle to on (it's the last icon to the right in the Layer palette, and it resembles a small lock). The small lock next to the layer's name should be visible (it normally has a red X across it).

8. Set the foreground color to a shade of gray, select the Flood Fill tool, set Fill Style to Solid Color, and click in the selected area. Only that part of the area taken up by the button should turn gray (see Figure 22.6).

FIGURE 22.6

An elliptical selection partially filled with gray.

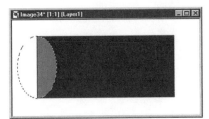

9. Select the Mover tool, right-click the elliptical selection, and drag it to the right side of the black rectangle. Select the Flood Fill tool and fill the right ellipse with the same gray color (see Figure 22.7).

FIGURE 22.7

Both ellipses filled with gray.

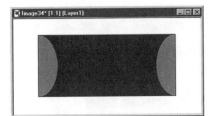

10. Choose Selections, Select None.

11. Select the Magic Wand tool and click the black area of the button to select it.

12. Select the Flood Fill tool and set Fill Style to Linear Gradient.

13. Click the second tab in the Tool Options window and set Gradient to Metallic.

14. Set Angle to 180.

15. Click anywhere in the black area within the selection.

    You should have something that resembles Figure 22.8.

FIGURE 22.8

A Metallic gradient fills the middle of the button.

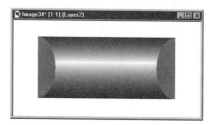

16. Choose Selections, Select None.

17. Select the Dropper tool and pick up a light color from the gradient. Get close to the highlight, but don't take the actual highlight color.

18. Select the Flood Fill tool, set the fill style to Solid Color, and click the left side of the button to fill it with a much lighter gray.

19. Select the Dropper tool and pick up a color from the shadowed area of the button. Use the Flood Fill tool to fill the right side of the button with the darker gray color.

20. Select the Magic Wand tool (it resembles a small magic wand) and click outside of the button. Choose Selections, Invert to invert the selection. This technique is a great way to select an area that has several colors.

21. Choose Image, Blur, Gaussian Blur and set the value to about 2.00.

You'll now have a great 3D button, as shown in Figure 22.9.

FIGURE 22.9

3D button created with selections, fills, and a Gaussian Blur.

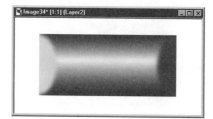

Let's see what else you can do using the Layers feature. Try these steps:

1. Open a textured file. You can find textured images all over the Web, or you can invent your own. This book shows you how to create a wood texture (Hour 9, "Creating Cool Text Effects") and a brushed-metal texture (Hour 16, "Special Effects").

2. To keep the same size selection, choose Edit, Copy with the first image (the button) current. Make the texture file current and choose Edit, Paste, As New Layer.

3. Choose the Mover tool and move the button around until it covers that area of the texture that you'd like to copy. Choose the Magic Wand tool and click somewhere outside the button. Choose Selections, Invert. Make the texture layer current and choose Edit, Copy.

4. Make the button image current. Choose Selections, None and choose Edit, Paste, As New Layer. If you need to move the texture around so that it covers the button, you can use the Mover tool.

5. With the texture in place, set the texture layer's mode to Overlay. (The Layer Blending mode can be set from the pull-down menu in the Layer palette; see Figure 22.10.)

FIGURE 22.10

Texture overlaid on a 3D button.

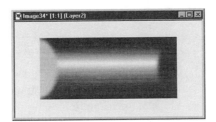

If you find, like I do, that the button is a little too bright or that there should be more texture showing, no problem. Obviously, you can't add to the opacity of the texture—it's at the max. However, you can reduce the opacity of the button layer. Try setting it to about 70 percent. Hmmm... that doesn't seem to have any effect. Try turning off the Background layer. Voilá!!! A more professional button would be hard to find (see Figure 22.11).

FIGURE 22.11

Final 3D, textured button.

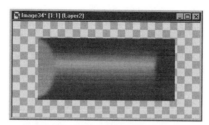

Creating Seamless Tiles

A *seamless tile* is an image that, when tiled or repeated, forms a seamless pattern. Therefore, you can use a relatively small image file that will tile itself on your Web page. Creating seamless tiles is something that is discussed constantly on Usenet.

Of course, the object is to get the sides to match up so that the smaller tile appears to be one large image when it's placed on your pages. Before showing you how to create a seamless tile, I'll explain the basic principles.

The Basics of Seamless Tiles

The object of a seamless tile, once again, is to get the edges of your image to match up so that when the image is tiled, it appears to be one big image. Demonstrating this is easier than trying to explain it.

Suppose you have an image that you want to tile, and suppose the image is square. (This technique works just as well if the image is a rectangle.) The goal is to swap the diagonal quarters of the image. (I *told* you this concept was hard to explain.) To get a better idea of what I'm talking about, take a look at the diagram in Figure 22.12.

FIGURE 22.12

Quartered image, showing the original placement of the quarters.

$$\begin{array}{|c|c|} \hline 1 & 2 \\ \hline 3 & 4 \\ \hline \end{array}$$

What you need to do is cut the image into quarters and swap the diagonal corners. This step allows your image to tile seamlessly. When you move the pieces, the image should resemble Figure 22.13.

FIGURE 22.13

Quartered image with the final placement of the quarters.

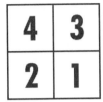

The reason this technique works is hard to see, but essentially you're cutting the image and rearranging it so that the edges formed by the cutting process are on the outside of the new image. Because the new edges were joined before you cut them, they match up when the image is tiled. Although this process is hard to visualize, it does work.

Figure 22.14 shows a textured image created with Kai's Power Tool Texture Explorer.

FIGURE 22.14

A textured image created with Kai's Power Tools.

Figure 22.15 shows the same image with the corners numbered as in Figure 22.12.

FIGURE 22.15

The textured image showing the numbered quarters.

Of course, you don't have to draw the numbers on the image. I've done so here to demonstrate the process more clearly. Figure 22.16 is the image after the quarters have been swapped. Note that the numbers are still in place.

FIGURE 22.16

The textured image showing the numbered quarters with corners swapped for tiling.

Figure 22.17 is the image with the quarters swapped and the numbers removed. This image will now tile seamlessly.

FIGURE 22.17

The textured image with quarters swapped for tiling.

You may notice, however, that although the edges now match up, the center of the image has a vertical seam and a horizontal seam running through it.

If you get rid of the vertical and horizontal seams, this image will be ready to tile. The way to get rid of the seam is to use the Clone tool. Although it's a little difficult to master, the tool is very effective, as you'll see in the next section.

Creating Seamless Tiles with Paint Shop Pro

Creating seamless tiles with Paint Shop Pro requires a little work; you must cut and paste the four quarters yourself. Follow these steps to create your own tiles:

1. Open a textured image and note its dimensions. This information is visible on the status bar at the bottom right of the screen.

2. Create a new file with the same dimensions as the textured image (see Figure 22.18).

FIGURE 22.18

The textured image and a new image in Paint Shop Pro.

As described earlier in this hour, you must swap the diagonally opposed quarters.

3. Select the Selection tool and set its selection type to Rectangle and Feather to 0.

4. Place the cursor in the middle of the textured image. Remember that computers start counting at zero, not one. Therefore, the middle of the sample 200×200 textured file will be 99,99—not 100,100. You can see where you are on the image by looking at the mouse coordinates displayed at the bottom-left of the Paint Shop Pro screen.

22

5. With the cursor in the middle of the image, click and drag the mouse to the upper-left corner of the image. Release the mouse and choose Edit, Copy.

6. Click somewhere in the new image to make it current and choose Edit, Paste, As New Selection.

7. Move the selection into the opposite corner of the new image from where it was in the textured image (see Figure 22.19).

FIGURE 22.19

The first corner moved to the new image.

8. Continue cutting and pasting until all quarters have been moved to the new file (see Figure 22.20).

FIGURE 22.20

All quarters moved to the new image.

9. Select the Clone Brush tool (it resembles two small brushes) and right-click to select a source area. Move the mouse around the seamed center area, drawing over the seams until you can no longer distinguish the seams.

You can also use the Paint Brushes tool to fine-tune the image. After using the Clone Brush and working with it a bit, I ended up with the image in Figure 22.21.

FIGURE 22.21

Final seamless tile in Paint Shop Pro.

To see what the final seamless background would look like, I created a new 600×600 image in Paint Shop Pro and, using the Paint Bucket tool, filled the new image with the seamless tile (see Figure 22.22).

FIGURE 22.22

A tiled example of the final seamless tile.

Summary

You can find tutorials and techniques for creating more types of Web graphics all over the Web. You might want to start at GrafX Design (`http://www.grafx-design.com/`) or at Jasc Software, Inc. (`http://www.jasc.com`).

That's pretty much it for the part of the book that covers Paint Shop Pro. The next two hours show you how to use Animation Shop to create animation.

Workshop

The Workshop contains a question and answer section to help answer the most commonly asked questions and quiz questions to help you solidify your understanding of the material covered.

Q&A

Q Why do gradients look 3D?

A A gradient can give the appearance of depth because we perceive lighter colors as being closer and darker colors as being further away.

Q Can you use any shape for buttons?

A Absolutely! Some people may argue that a button should look like a button, but this is not the case. As long as people can identify the image as a button, you should be able to use any shape.

Q Is it worthwhile to use buttons from Web libraries?

A It can be. Some libraries contain really good images. You may prefer to create your own, though, so that your Web pages look original.

Quiz

1. Which tools in Paint Shop Pro do you use most often to create basic buttons?

2. How can gradients help you create more-sophisticated buttons?

3. Why is tiling important when producing images for the Web?

4. Which tool is primarily used to create a tiling effect?

Answers

1. The Preset Shapes tool is a good starting point. You can use it to create the basic shapes you need for most buttons.

2. Gradients can give buttons a 3D quality.

3. When you create an image that can be tiled, only that small image is loaded. The browser takes care of tiling the image. Using a small image that tiles is preferable to using a large image, because of the time involved in downloading large images.

4. The Clone Brush is often needed to cover up seams that appear during the process of creating an image that can tile seamlessly.

HOUR 23

Animation

Animation is one of the hottest topics on the Web today. You can use Animation Shop alone or with Paint Shop Pro to create cool animations for your Web pages.

Jasc's Animation Shop 2, which ships with Paint Shop Pro 6, is powerful yet easy to use. In this hour, I explain the following concepts:

- What animation is and how it works
- When to use animation
- Creating your first animation, including animated GIFs for your Web pages
- Editing your first animation
- Using transitions
- Creating text effects

Animation Concepts

Whether it's an animated GIF for your Web page or the latest box office blockbuster, all animations are basically the same.

The concept involves rapidly displaying a series of images, or frames, so that the human eye is fooled into seeing one long, continuous moving picture.

In movies, for example, each frame is captured on film and is then displayed on a screen, using a movie projector. Each frame is displayed for a very short time, followed by the next frame, and so on.

In animated GIFs, a digital artist uses computer software to create each frame. The frames are then displayed, using other software such as a Web browser. Because each frame is rapidly displayed in succession, the person viewing the animation sees one continuous movie.

Why Use Animation?

I have to tell you, I was one of the last people to jump on the animated GIF bandwagon. At first, I found the animations cheesy and poorly done. As the animations got better and the software to create them more powerful, I changed my tune.

In the world of the Web, many different elements are competing for your reader's attention. Even a single Web page can offer dozens of images for your reader's eyes to wade through. This situation is the same on virtually every Web page. If you want to run a banner ad, how do you attract a reader's attention? How do you get his or her eyes to see through all the other flashy, attractive graphics on the same Web page?

One answer is animation. By animating an image, you make it stand out. You make it attract the reader's attention. Many of the ad banners you see at the top of Web pages these days are animated.

Animation Shop enables you to animate your ads and buttons, and other graphical elements, too.

Building an Animation

Recall that an animation is a series of images or frames. You can create these frames in Paint Shop Pro or, to some extent, in Animation Shop.

You should be able to start Animation Shop by clicking the Start button at the bottom of the Windows 95 screen and choosing Programs, Paint Shop 6, Animation Shop 2. Alternately, if you're running Paint Shop Pro, you can choose File, Run Animation Shop.

Animation Shop's interface is simple and quite similar to Paint Shop Pro's (see Figure 23.1).

FIGURE 23.1

Animation Shop's interface.

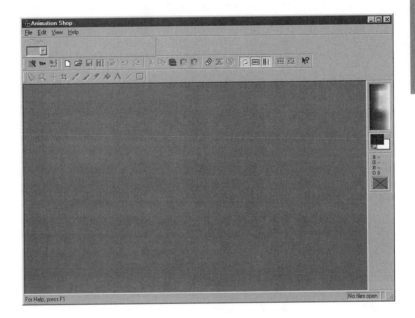

23

The tools are quite basic and of more use to touch up an animation than to create one. Creating an animation with both Paint Shop Pro and Animation Shop is quite easy, though, as the following exercise shows.

Creating Your First Animation

The best way to learn how to use Paint Shop Pro to create an animation is to dive right in. Try this exercise:

1. Start Paint Shop Pro.
2. Create a new 400×100, 72-pixel-per-inch image with the background color set to black and the image type set to 16.7 million colors.
3. Create a second image with the same settings.
4. Turn on the grid (View, Grid).

5. Select the Preset Shapes tool (it resembles a small blue rectangle with a red ellipse in front of it).

6. In the Tool Options window, set the shape to Circle and the style to Filled.

7. Set the foreground color to green and, in the first image, draw a circle near the left side. I used the grid, placed the mouse pointer at the center of the second vertical line (with the grid set to 50 pixels), and drew a 55-pixel circle.

   I repeated this process with red and drew a circle in the second image at the center of the second-to-last vertical line (see Figure 23.2).

FIGURE 23.2

Two images containing colorful circles.

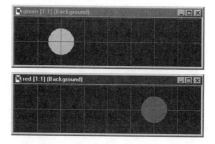

8. Save each image. I saved them both as PSP files in a temporary folder and called the first one green and the second one red (inventive, eh?).

9. With the images safely saved on your hard drive, run Animation Shop.

10. Choose File, Open and open the Green.psp image. You should see the image appear on the screen.

11. Choose Animation, Insert Frames, From File.

12. Browse to the folder where you stored the PSP files and choose the Red.psp file. You'll now have one image with two frames.

    You may see only one frame, but you can use the slider bar at the bottom of the image to scroll between both images (see Figure 23.3).

Now you have all that's necessary for an animation. It might be a simple one, granted, but it is indeed an animation. To see your new movie, choose View, Animation.

When the flashing circles start to drive you crazy, close the animation by clicking the small X in the upper-right corner of the window. That's it! You've created an animated GIF!

FIGURE 23.3

Two-frame animation in Animation Shop.

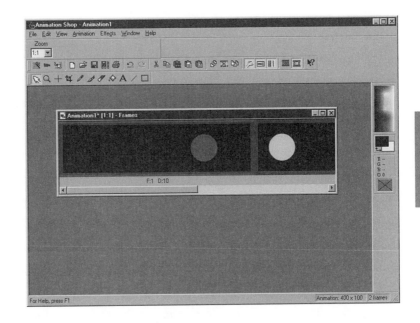

Of course, it was small, and it didn't do much. However, with a little tweaking, it could be pretty cool, as simple as it is. In fact, I have a similar animation running in the middle of an image on my Web page. You can view the animation by entering the following URL into your Web browser: `http://www.grafx-design.com/HireUs.html`.

On that page, you'll see a small interface with two blinking lights. The concept behind those lights is the same as the ones you've just created.

The lights I used are smaller (and a little less annoying). I also played around with adding frames with the lights turned off and both lights turned on, and I played with the inter-frame timing, as well.

Even as small as those lights are, they grab your attention. They're almost hypnotic (and that's the intent).

Editing Your First Animation

If you'd like to tweak the animation you just created, you can do so in Animation Shop. The first step is to create a blank, black rectangle to serve as a frame in which both lights are off. To do so, follow these steps:

1. From Animation Shop, choose Animation, Insert Frames, Empty.

2. For the moment, leave the defaults set in the Insert Empty Frames dialog box and click OK. You'll now have a new frame in your animation.

3. You can use the scrollbar at the bottom of the window to scroll to the frame. You'll see that it's empty—transparent, in fact.

4. You can fill it with black by setting the foreground color to black and using the Flood Fill tool to fill the entire frame with black.

5. You can view the new version of your animation by choosing View, Animation. Because of the speed with which your frames are being displayed, the extra frame is hard to see.

Now try this:

1. Stop the animation if it's still running.

2. Select the Arrow tool and use it to choose the all-black frame.

3. Choose Animation, Frame Properties.

4. Under the Display Time tab, enter **100** for the display time and click OK.

5. Run your animation again (View, Animation). Be sure to save this animation, as you will use it in the following sections.

Notice the difference? The lights flash, then there's a pause, followed by the lights flashing, another pause, and so on.

You can edit this animation further by adding other black frames (adding blank frames) or changing the amount of time that a frame is displayed.

Using Transitions

Animation Shop has some built-in effects—called *transitions*—that can be used with your animations. A transition is a way to move from one image to another. Transitions include effects such as fading from one image to another.

To see how transitions work, follow these steps in Animation Shop:

1. Select the middle black frame with the Arrow tool and choose Edit, Delete to delete that frame. You'll be left with the first two frames: the green light and the red light.

2. To run a transition effect on the animation, choose Effects, Insert Image Transition. Doing so brings up the Insert Image Transition dialog box (see Figure 23.4).

3. Transition effects add an effect between frames or from one frame to an effect.

   With the two frames of the current animation and the Blinds effect, the animation goes from one frame, the green light, to the other frame, the red light, giving the effect of blinds opening and closing.

FIGURE 23.4

The Insert Image Transition dialog box.

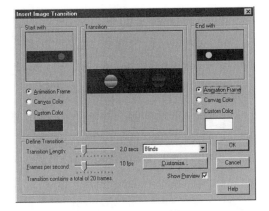

4. To see this effect, simply click OK and choose View, Animation. Note how the image goes through a transition from one frame to the other.

You can add different effects, as well. You can apply a long list of built-in effects to your animation.

Try the Fade effect with the two lights. This is better than the annoying flashing created in the first exercise.

Play around with some of the effects, and I'm sure you'll get some ideas of the types of frames that you'd like to create to use the effects. I think, for example, that the Spin effect would be a good way to treat some text.

Speaking of text, Animation Shop also enables you to create some text effects; they're discussed next.

Creating Text Effects

To create an animation using the built-in text effects, open a new file in Animation Shop (choose File, New) and choose Effects, Insert Text Effects. *Text effects, or text transitions,* are transformations involving text. For example, you can cause text to appear to wave in the wind.

In the Insert Text Effect dialog box (see Figure 23.5), you can add text and choose an effect.

Of course, you can create your own text animations, using Paint Shop Pro to create the text frames and then importing the frames into Animation Shop. You might want to play around with some of the built-in effects to see what's possible, though.

FIGURE 23.5

The Insert Text Effect dialog box.

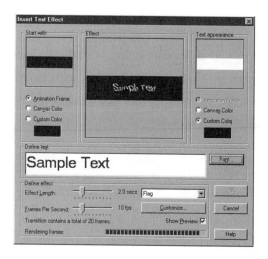

Certainly, if you want truly spectacular results, you'll want to create your frames in Paint Shop Pro. You can actually create a multilayered image in Paint Shop Pro and use the layers as frames for an animation. This technique enables you to create the best animations for your Web pages, as you'll see in the next hour.

Summary

This hour introduced GIF animation and Animation Shop. I showed you how to create a simple two-frame animation, how to insert a frame, and how to change the timing of the frames. I also showed you how to apply some of the built-in effects that come with Animation Shop.

In the next, and final, hour, I walk you through the process of using Paint Shop Pro and Animation Shop to create a more complex animation.

Workshop

The Workshop contains a question and answer section to help answer the most commonly asked questions and quiz questions to help you solidify your understanding of the material covered.

Q&A

Q How do I use layers as frames?

A That option is covered in the next hour.

Q Can I drag images directly from Paint Shop Pro to Animation Shop?

A No. You need to save your images from Paint Shop Pro and then open them in Animation Shop.

Q If I place a frame in the wrong place, can I move it quickly to the right location?

A Yes. You also can cut and paste frames or copy and paste them.

23

Quiz

1. What is an animation? How can an animation help make your Web page a better place to visit?

2. What is a transition? What program do you use to add transitions to your animations?

3. What is an animated GIF?

Answers

1. An animation is an image composed of a series of frames that, when repeated, gives the illusion of movement. Animations can add to the quality of a Web site in the same way that good images can.

2. A transition is a transformation that takes place between one image and another. These are usually effects such as fading. You can use Animation Shop's built-in transformations, or you can use various effects in Paint Shop Pro to create your own.

3. An animated GIF is a GIF file that contains several frames that can be played in an image viewer or Web browser. As these frames are displayed, they give the illusion of movement, much the same as motion pictures do.

HOUR 24

Advanced Animation

The best way to create an animation is to create a layered image in Paint Shop Pro and open the PSP file as a multiframed animation in Animation Shop. With the file saved as a PSP file, you can go back and make any changes, add new layers, rearrange the layers, and so on.

These two programs form a powerful combination for creating animated GIFs for your Web pages. I cover the following advanced animation topics in this hour:

- Using layered images and masks in animation
- Creating a spinning globe animation
- Understanding advanced animation techniques

Using Layers and Masks in Animation

Using Paint Shop Pro and Animation Shop together enables you to create amazingly complex animations.

You can create an image in Paint Shop Pro, using layers, masks, and any of the effects you'd like. Then you can import the resulting file into Animation Shop as a multiframed animation.

The following section shows you how to build a spinning globe animation.

Putting Your Own Spin on the World

You'll need to find an image of the world that has been flattened. Many clip art sites and CD-ROMs have maps of the world and globes, so you should be able to find one similar to the one I'm using.

If you're handy with the Paint Brushes tools, you might even create your own. Figure 24.1 shows the image I'm using.

FIGURE 24.1

The (pre-Columbus) world.

This map shows the world flattened out. Actually, the map shows two copies of the world so that you can wrap the entire image around a sphere and not miss any parts or have any unruly seams.

The image I'm using is 630×150. To leave some space around the edges of the new image that I'll create, I open a new 200×200 image. What I'll be doing is cutting and pasting 150×150 portions of the flattened globe into different layers of the new image. Follow these steps:

1. Open a new 200×200 image.

2. In the Background layer, create a centered, blue circle that's 150 pixels in radius (see Figure 24.2).

FIGURE 24.2

This circle will become the oceans.

3. Make copies of the blue circle for each layer that you will be pasting a portion of the globe onto.

   You can make the copy by clicking and dragging the Background layer onto the Create Layer icon each time you want to create a new layer.

4. Then copy and paste a portion of the globe to a new image, resize the canvas to 150×150, and apply the Circle Deformation filter (choose Image, Deformations, Circle) to the new image. This deformed portion of the globe will be copied again and pasted onto the new blue circle layer.

5. Repeat this process until you've copied the entire globe into new layers of the new file.

I'll walk through creating the first few layers:

1. I've opened the World image and created a new 200×200 image (see Figure 24.3).

24

FIGURE 24.3

The World and Ocean files in Paint Shop Pro.

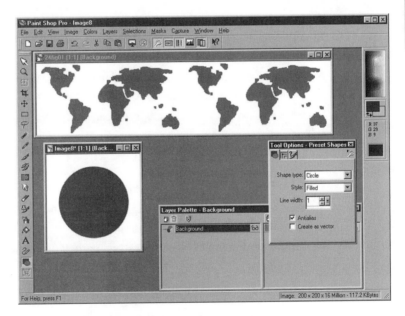

2. To start, select the Selection tool, set the selection type to Square and the Feather value to 0, and turn off antialiasing.

3. Place the mouse pointer at 0,0 in the World image and make a 150×150–pixel selection.

4. Choose Edit, Copy to copy the selection to the Clipboard.

5. Then choose Edit, Paste, As New Image.

6. Expand the image size with Image, Resize because only the portion of the image that has information gets pasted.

   Therefore, because of the transparent background, the image comes in smaller than 150×150.

7. To resize the new image, choose Image, Canvas Size and enter **150** for both New Width and New Height.

8. To make a sphere of the new area that you've copied from the flattened world, apply the Circle deformation with Image, Deformations, Circle.

   Doing so wraps the image around a sphere, giving it back its shape (remember that you are using a flattened image of Earth).

9. Choose Selections, Select All and Edit, Copy to copy this portion of the world to the Clipboard.

10. Add a layer to the Globe image (the one that you created and added a blue ball… er, oceans to) by clicking and dragging the Background layer onto the Add New Layer icon.

11. Name this layer World01 by double-clicking the layer in the Layer palette and giving the layer a name in the dialog box that appears.

12. Paste the portion of the world you just created directly onto this layer by choosing Edit, Paste, As New Selection.

That's how each layer is created.

To create the second layer, follow these steps:

1. Start the selection on the World image at 20,0 (for each new layer, move 20 pixels to the right) and copy and paste this selection.

2. Resize and deform it and then select it and paste it onto a new blue circle.

Create each new layer the same way until you have 15 World layers. You'll need all 15 to get the entire globe into the animation.

Saving and Optimizing Files in Animation Shop

To save the image so that it can be opened in Animation Shop, I turned on all the layers except the Background layer. (I turned off most of them as I created each layer to avoid confusion.)

Animation Shop adds each visible layer as a frame when it opens a PSP file.

With the file saved, it's time to open it in Animation Shop. Before doing so, though, you must change the preferences in Animation Shop. In Animation Shop, choose File, Preferences, General Program Preferences and click the Layered Files tab (see Figure 24.4).

FIGURE 24.4

Setting the Layered Files preferences in Animation Shop.

Place a check mark in the Keep Layers as Separate Frames check box. This feature causes Animation Shop to open a multilayered file and keep each layer as a separate frame. It's a very powerful feature.

With the preferences set up properly, it's time to open the image. Choose File, Open and browse to the file you saved in Paint Shop Pro. In my case, it's the Spin file (the final image I saved in Paint Shop Pro).

To view the animation, choose View, Animation. If the image checks out, you can save it as a Web-ready animated GIF.

Before saving the file, you should optimize it. To do so, choose File, Optimization Wizard. This step opens the Optimized Output dialog box (see Figure 24.5).

FIGURE 24.5

Animation Shop's Optimized Output dialog box.

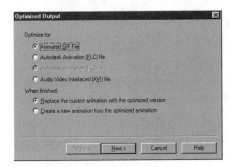

Place a check mark in the Animated GIF File and the Create a New Animation from the Optimized Animation check boxes. Click Next. Then choose the Optimization setting you want (see Figure 24.6).

FIGURE 24.6

*Animation Shop's
Animation Quality
Versus Output Size dia-
log box.*

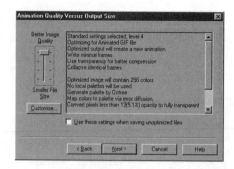

Most times, you'll want the maximum compression to keep your file sizes small for
the Web.

You'll have to judge how the settings affect the image quality, though. Sometimes making an image as small as possible is not the way to go. If you find that the quality of the
final image suffers, you might want to sacrifice a little size for some quality.

You'll see a dialog box with several progress charts, and then you'll see the final optimization dialog box that shows you the savings you get from the optimization (see
Figure 24.7).

FIGURE 24.7

*Animation Shop's
Optimization Results
dialog box.*

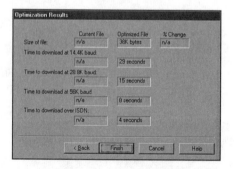

This final dialog box shows you how much space is saved, the optimized file size, and
the time it will take to download at various modem speeds. On my 56Kbps modem, the
spinning globe takes eight seconds to download.

The nice thing about working with Paint Shop Pro and Animation Shop together is that
if, for example, I find this file to be too large, I can simply resize the file in Paint Shop
Pro, resave it, and open it again in Animation Shop.

Spreading Your Wings

If you'd like to practice some of the techniques I've described in this hour, you can open the `bttrfly.psp` file that comes with Paint Shop Pro.

Open it in Paint Shop Pro and examine each layer; you can open the file in Animation Shop as well to see how the final animation turned out.

I suggest you create a few animations using images created in Paint Shop Pro. Start with a few layers and see how the process works; then attack a more ambitious project. Remember to have some fun and try different things as you work with both of these amazing programs.

Summary

24

In this hour, I showed you how to create a multiframe animation from a multilayered Paint Shop Pro file. I also introduced you to the optimization process. I encourage you to build a few animations and experiment with both Animation Shop and Paint Shop Pro.

I hope you enjoyed this book and that you have as much fun reading it as I did writing it. See you on the Web (virtually speaking, of course).

—T. Michael Clark

Workshop

The Workshop contains a question and answer section to help answer the most commonly asked questions and quiz questions to help you solidify your understanding of the material covered.

Q&A

Q Is there a limit to the number of layers you can have?

A Although I imagine there must be some sort of limit, I have not yet encountered it. I doubt that, in the course of creating images and animation frames, you'll ever come across a limit, either.

Q Can I animate JPEG images?

A Good question, and one I've seen and responded to before. Unfortunately, the answer is no. It's the properties of the GIF file that enable it to hold the various frames that make up an animation. I suppose you could, if you wanted to, write a Java program that would constantly replace JPEG images over each other.

Although this technique might work, it wouldn't really be practical. Animated GIFs are fairly compact, will run on virtually any browser, and require no programming.

Q Can I load JPEG images into Animation Shop?

A Although the final animation will be a GIF file, you certainly can build it from JPEG files.

Quiz

1. How do you properly save a Paint Shop Pro image with multiple layers into Animation Shop?

2. How are masks and layers imported into Animation Shop from Paint Shop Pro to make them animations?

3. What does Animation Shop do to each visible Paint Shop Pro layer in its own format?

4. Where do you set the Animation Shop preferences for importing and exporting files?

5. What is optimization? How does it help you?

Answers

1. You first have to turn on all the layers you want to import, because Animation Shop adds each visible layer as a frame. Then you simply save the image as a PSP file. The resulting file can then be opened as a multiframe file in Animation Shop.

2. Masks aren't imported, but the effect they have on a layer will still be evident in the animated image. Every layer is imported as a separate frame in the animation.

3. Each visible layer in a PSP file is converted into a frame in Animation Shop.

4. In the General Program Preferences dialog box, click the Layered Files tab and place a check mark in the Keep Each Layer as a Separate Frame option.

5. There are different types of optimization. Essentially, each type tries to minimize the final file size while maintaining the quality of the image.

PART VI

Appendixes

Hour

APPENDIX A

Installing Paint Shop Pro 6

As with many of today's programs, Paint Shop Pro comes with a built-in installation program that should run automatically upon insertion of the CD-ROM.

> Before you get started with the installation and periodically thereafter, you should stop by the Jasc Web site (http://www.jasc.com) to see if Jasc has made any point releases available. *Point releases* are bug fixes and updates to the program. These updates are available free of charge to registered users. You should be able to download the updater program and install it by following the instructions on the Web site.

Under most conditions, you should be able to choose the default settings for the installation.

If you're new to Paint Shop Pro or you want to see the new features, you can choose to take a tour. The guided tour on the CD-ROM does a great job of introducing version 6.

APPENDIX B

Paint Shop Pro Resources

For more information on Paint Shop Pro, you can try three basic areas: the Web, Usenet, and other published material.

Try these Paint Shop Pro tutorial Web sites:

- GrafX Design at `http://www.grafx-design.com`
- Jasc Software, Inc. at `http://www.jasc.com`
- i/us at `http://www.i-us.com`
- Cheap Tricks at `http://www.iland.net/~delevan`
- Sumrall Works at `http://www.sumrallworks.com`
- Wagoner Paint Shop Pro Tutorials Unlimited at `http://www.kconline.com/fwagoner/indexpsptu.htm`

Many of the preceding sites also contain links to other Paint Shop Pro tutorial Web sites, so if you don't find what you want right away, keep digging.

Try these Usenet sites:

- comp.graphics.apps.paint-shop-pro
- comp.graphics
- comp.graphics.misc
- alt.graphics
- comp.infosystems.webwww.authoring.images

Software companies on the Web include the following:

- Jasc Software at http://www.jasc.com
- Auto F/X at http://autofx.com
- Alien Skin at http://www.alienskin.com
- MetaCreations at http://www.metacreations.com
- Corel at http://www.corel.com
- Adobe at http://www.adobe.com
- RAYflect at http://www.rayflect.com
- Flaming Pear at http://www.flamingpear.com
- Xara at http://www.xara.com

Finally, you can read my other book, *Paint Shop Pro Web Techniques,* published in 1997 by New Riders (ISBN: 1-56205-756-1). It includes many more Web-specific techniques and examples and, although the book was written for version 4.0, most of the techniques also work in version 5.0 and version 6.0.

INDEX